Endorsements of *The Simple Path to Union with God*

"That creative minorities are the future of the church, Joseph Ratzinger [Pope Benedict XVI] has declared several times. But what kind of 'creativity'? Love Crucified is certainly a mi̶ community like others. But its 'creativity' ̶ efforts by several Christians. It is a 'cre apacity to 'receive' what the Lord Jesus towards union with the salvific love of ieve that Jesus, with His Cross and Resu us from sin but wants to transform us; for those to believe that Jesus not only heals our wounds but turns them into a fountain of light by uniting them to His; for those who dare to believe that Jesus not only wants us to know Him by faith but wants to welcome us in His heart, The Path will be a discovery tailored to their expectations. And even more."

FATHER GABRIEL ASCENCIO, LC, PH.D.
Professor of Philosophy

"This work offers a beautiful insight into reflections on becoming more united to the heart of Jesus Christ. The testimonies, the insights, and the prayerful reflections draw one closer to Christ. It is a tool for growing in the spiritual life and understanding the power and depth of spiritual motherhood."

DEB BAUER, PH.D.

"The Simple Path to Union with God is an extraordinary source of inspiration to me. It contains both a very profound theological content and a very insightful guide to the spiritual life. It has helped me tremendously as spiritual reading and in my life of prayer. I have found, through almost every one of its pages, material that I could interpret as if it were directed precisely to me in order for me to reflect and pray about how to improve my life journey and my relationship with Jesus Christ. Its emphasis and deeply wise and compassionate words on our communion with the different aspects of the love of God present in the Cross are of decisive importance for our personal need to surrender and convert to the truth of our faith which is contrary to many distortions of it. I highly recommend it to anyone interested in taking seriously the path for authentic happiness and peace."

DOCTOR ANTONIO LOPEZ, PH.D.
Professor of Philosophy and Theology

The Simple Path
to
Union with God

The Simple Path to Union with God

The Simple Path
to
Union with God

For those who choose to respond to Christ's thirst:
"Suffer all with Me, no longer two but ONE,
in My sacrifice of love."

The Simple Path to Union with God is the spiritual formation
manual of the
Love Crucified Community
www.LoveCrucified.com

This Path was consecrated to the Immaculate Conception
at the grotto of Our Lady of Lourdes, France.
16th of April, 2016.

By a Mother of the Cross with a Missionary of the Cross.

The Simple Path to Union with God

Bible references, except when otherwise noted, are from the Revised
Standard Version, Catholic Edition.

ISBN: 978-0-9972664-0-5

To purchase this book or for more information:
www.lovecrucified.com
Book and information in Spanish: www.amorcrucificado.com

Cover: Statue of the Pieta, gardens of the sanctuary of Our Lady of La
Leche, St. Augustine, Fl., USA. Photo by Fr. Jordi Rivero.

CONTENTS

PART II
ASPECTS OF LIVING THE PATH

Foreword

The work of the Holy Spirit in the faithful throughout the ages is well documented in mystical literature, but it is difficult for many to believe that the same Spirit is working marvels among us today. Our times are characterized by a godless mentality, yet the powerful presence of the Holy Spirit is evidenced in many ways: The Second Vatican Council, a string of great popes, Marian apparitions, movements, new communities, extraordinary modern saints…

God is also working among his favorite instruments, his little ordinary children. One of these is a wife and mother, whom in this work we will call a "Mother of the Cross" (MOC) since this is how we call the women of our community. In 2006, she began to confide in me the messages she was receiving from God the Father, Jesus and the Blessed Mother. They come to her without locutions or apparitions, yet they are distinct from her own thoughts. They come mostly during Eucharistic adoration.

She was coming to me for spiritual direction, but the Lord's words to her were also challenging me to enter with all my heart into His crucified love as a victim soul and to bring Him many victim souls. I was afraid and I struggled to respond but the Lord led me along His way. Soon others also responded and the Love Crucified Community was founded in March 11, 2008. I am forever grateful to the Lord and His instruments.

"The Simple Path to Union with God" is based on the grace of living the messages of the Lord our community. It has helped us to go deep into Scripture, the magisterium, the popes, and the saints. The result is a joyfully life in the Holy Spirit as victims of love, united to Jesus crucified. The Lord asked that it be published and shared with all. It is my prayer that you too are drawn to live this grace.

Fr. Jordi Rivero
Missionary of the Cross

Acknowledgments

The Simple Path to Union with God is the fruit of the love of God revealed in Jesus crucified and risen. It is a gift that we received in our daily Eucharistic encounters. Our Blessed Mother guided every step as we strived to put it in practice in our ordinary hidden life.

With deep gratitude, we acknowledge the beloved brothers and sisters of our Love Crucified Community. Some of their testimonies appear in this Path to show that it is not just ideas but truths that transform lives in Christ. We are also grateful to all who helped in editing the manuscript.

Regarding Private Revelations

The Catechism teaches regarding private revelations:

Throughout the ages, there have been so-called 'private' revelations, some of which have been recognized by the authority of the Church. They do not belong, however, to the deposit of faith. It is not their role to improve or complete Christ's definitive Revelation, but to help live more fully by it in a certain period of history. Guided by the Magisterium of the Church, the *sensus fidelium* (sense of the faithful) knows how to discern and welcome in these revelations whatever constitutes an authentic call of Christ or his saints to the Church.[1]

The purpose of *The Path to Union with God* is precisely this: "to help live more fully" the revelation of Christ in the heart of the Church in our times.

God continues to speak through humble men and women to awaken us to the love He Revealed at the Cross. The importance of these messages is greater in times like ours when those living the faith are subject to great trials.

St Paul teaches us to be open to the Spirit and, at the same time, to be careful not to be fooled, "Do not quench the Spirit, do not despise prophesying, but test everything; hold fast to what is good, abstain from every form of evil" (1Th 5:19-22).

---

[1] *Catechism of the Catholic Church*, n.67.

Introduction

The new life we received in baptism is like a tiny seed meant to grow into a full life in Christ. The purpose of our time on earth, then, is to pursue this growth along a path of continuous transformation. This is the path to Calvary where we partake in Christ's sacrifice of love to the Father and partake of the life of the Holy Trinity. St. Paul describes this path as a race in which we must give our all: "For his sake I have suffered the loss of all things, and count them as refuse" (Phil 3:8-12).

Speaking through a Mother of the Cross, Our Lord called us to ascend Calvary with Him and conquer darkness:

> *I am making all things new... Live in the power of My crucified love. The darkness will not prevail but the Light will conquer the darkness. Be My light in the world... The hidden force will conquer the darkness of Satan but My hidden force must be intensified and grow. God will do great things through His holy remnant of victim souls[2]. It is time for My messages to be published. You must be willing to be My voice and ascend Calvary as ONE with Me to be crucified. It is this obedience to My Will that will make all things new in the unity of the love of the Most Holy Trinity. Pray and respond as ONE. (8/9/12)*

The Lord's words, "Behold, I make all things new," applies to each one of us. They are fulfilled as we ascend to Calvary and unite

---

[2] "Victim soul" is explained in Ch. 6.

with Him at the Cross. This is the way of *The Simple Path to Union*. He needs each one of us, His hidden force, His holy remnant, to grow, pray and respond as *ONE*. This is the way to conquer Satan and make all things new.

It seems incredible that God could need us for anything, but it's true. From the beginning of time, God the Father willed that the perfect sacrifice of His Son be completed through Christ's body, the Church (including you). St. Paul tells us that the sacrifice of our life, united as ONE to the "Word of the Cross[3]," becomes the power of God.

"The power of God" might seem like something far beyond our reach. But remember, the purpose of our time on earth is to seek union with God, to be ONE with Christ's heart. Remember as well, we won't be traveling alone. All those who answer God's call to unite with Him at the Cross will be part of the holy remnant. The Holy Spirit and Our Blessed Mother will be with us, consoling and guiding us along the path to union, which is truly simple but narrow and difficult.

Once we make a conscious decision and say— "Yes, my Lord, I will love You and be Your victim, united to You, the Perfect Victim" —our new life in Christ is set ablaze. We can now begin to see the rebelliousness of our flesh, which was holding us in bondage to sin. We then submit our flesh to Jesus so that He can take full authority over us. By this act of submission, we "put on the armor of light ... put on the Lord Jesus Christ" (Rom 13:12-14), and the words of the Mass, "Through Him, with Him and in Him," become a reality in our daily lives.

This new life does not come free of pain and suffering. Our

---

[3] Cf. 1 Cor 1:18, The "Word of the Cross" is the revelation of the Cross: Jesus, who loved us unto death at the Cross. Jesus, Love Crucified, is the power of God to overcome all evil.

difficulties do not simply vanish. *The Simple Path to Union* is the narrow path of the Cross. **This is why we need to unite ourselves to Mary and, through our consecration, give our "yes" as one with hers.** She, who is the perfect model, brings us to the foot of the Cross to form us in true humility and repentance.

Once we surrender and truly become docile, the Holy Spirit leads us into Our Lord's pierced side. This passage leads us to the Sacred Heart of Jesus where we are consumed in the fire of the Holy Spirit, which is love. As we are transformed in Jesus crucified, our "Yes!" to the Father turns our suffering into grace for the world. This new life fills us with the joy and happiness all human hearts long to possess.

1. I Am the Way, Diary of a Mother of the Cross (MOC)

> Jesus: *If I am the way, that means the way has already been set for you. There is only one way that leads you into the embrace of the Father for all eternity. I came so that you may know the way. The way is simple but the path is obscure and hidden.*[4] *All those that desire to find this path will find it, but there are few, My daughter, that find it and even fewer who travel upon it.*[5] *This is a constant torture of My Heart and My Mother's, to see such few souls on this path that I opened for you and made smooth with My precious Blood.*
>
> *I am the way. Look at Me, follow Me. I am the innocent Lamb of the Father Who abandons Himself*

---

[4] Until we receive the light of the Spirit, the path of the Lord remains for us "obscure and hidden."

[5] Cf. Mt 7:14, "For the gate is narrow and the way is hard, that leads to life, and those who find it are few."

to be sacrificed so that you may have life. I am poor and humble, born of very simple holy parents. I am pure, the unblemished Lamb. I am perfectly obedient to the will of the Father. I am beauty because I live and remain in the Light of the Father with the Holy Spirit. I am Love, incarnated Love.

The Holy Spirit will lead you through My path to eternal life... My daughter, there is a SIMPLE PATH, for your God is simple and knows your weakness. You were on a path to Me, but a very difficult and complicated path, full of dangers because it is the path of your own will. When you gave Me your fiat in Medjugorje[6], you entered My way. You now know by experience the difference in these paths. My way is simple, safe, full of consolations, peaceful... It leads you to the interior transformation of your mind and heart. The deeper you enter My path the easier your travel becomes. (12/12/11)

---

[6] In 2006, when Jesus asked me to be His victim soul.

How to Read and Live
"The Simple Path to Union with God"

The Path is not the type of book that is read at once from cover to cover. We need to ponder it slowly, in small segments, and then go back to it over and over. Only in this way do we allow the Lord to take us deep into its message. The Path has been given to us by God to prepare us to be His witnesses, martyrs, and warriors for these "decisive times." The Lord for years has been telling us to "prepare" for the "fiercest battle at hand." Yet, He doesn't leave us on our own; He, as our loving Father, comes to prepare us Himself.

The Path is to be lived, not just read. Through the Path, Jesus is purifying, healing and dressing us with God's armor for the great battle we have entered. Through the Path, Jesus draws us to live His Word and enter His Heart. The Lord is making us His "living hosts" so that His light radiates through us to penetrate the darkness around us.

The Path is not linear in the sense of leaving behind previous stages as we advance. The Path is an organic whole, in which ALL of it, as the Holy Spirit possesses us, becomes our very life. Each of the teachings of Our Lord needs to become branded in our hearts. This is a grace that God will give each of us, but we have to be willing to work hard by meditating on the Path daily and persevere in living it.

Monsignor Ron Sciera wrote this message to his brother priests:

Brothers in Christ: *The Path to Union* is not a spiritual periodical, nor a theological reflection. What is it?

It is a "way," a "shortcut" to enter into the fire of The Sacred Heart of Jesus, where the Holy Spirit dwells. It is an answer to prayer if we want to be healed of the wounds that we have buried because it's too painful to go there or because we live in false pride and denial.

The Simple Path is a journey, a way of living our everyday life UNITED TO CHRIST. Many priests are already familiar with it and are AMAZED (I am one of them) at the healing it has brought to their lives and the ease with which they are delivered from selfishness, impurities, false pride, spirits of control, and all the demons that haunt us, that shame us, that confuse us, that play with our feelings and emotions.

These demons have one objective: To rob us of our freedom in Christ and the faith that with Him we can walk on water. Yes, brothers, that's the faith Christ calls us to have; but we prefer the comfort and security of cowering in the boat, excusing ourselves by our weaknesses, instead of grasping our Blessed Mother's hand, holding it tightly and learning to walk with her as Jesus did.

You have to "eat" *The Simple Path* like Ezekiel ate the scroll in the presence of God.[7]

---

[7] Cf. Rev 10:9; Ezek 3:1-3.

Part I

The Path to Union

Love Must Be a Passion

As we begin the Path, we need to know where we want to go: Jesus Christ. He is the Way, the Truth and the Life. We can be the lovers God created us to be only if we are one with Christ in His passion. His passion is divine love lived in human frailty to the last consequences of suffering and death. This love is the power and wisdom of God, which at the Cross, defeats Satan forever.

Without entering into His passion, we may pass as nice people but will never be fully alive. Passionate love holds nothing back from God and always wants to give more of itself. It expands the heart to a greater desire for God's love. Christ reveals Himself to such souls to depths beyond imagination. They become icons of Christ. Nothing can separate them from Love. The Cross is for them an opportunity to love more.

Few have the courage to live this love. Christ must be allowed to dismantle our fantasies about God, about religion and about ourselves. We must let Him show us our true selves, touch our wounds, and go deep within to uncover sins we have hidden under justifications and excuses. We must then abandon ourselves to Mary so that she can take us to the foot of the Cross and into His Heart. The few who persevere, we call "saints." To be among them is our Christian vocation.

Our Lady of Grace,
teach us how to become vulnerable

Chapter One

Journey with the Holy Spirit and Mary

1-A
New Life in the Holy Spirit

The Spirit changes those in whom He comes to dwell; He so transforms them that they begin to live a completely new kind of life ... cowards become men of great courage. — St. Cyril of Alexandria[8]

---

[8] "Commentary of the Gospel of John," Office of Readings, Thursday of the 7th week of Easter.

—The Holy Spirit Awakens My Soul —
by a Missionary of the Cross

When I was a college student my mother invited me to a prayer group. I was amazed at what I found there: people openly spoke with God, praising Him and expressing their love and gratitude. Someone would share a word from the Lord, another would confirm it with the Bible. For the first time in my life, I saw Christians praying for each other on the spot by laying hands. Those who came with burdens found peace and strength in the Lord. You could see in their faces the joy of having encountered Christ.

As I continued going to the prayer group, the experience of the Holy Spirit working in my life grew. I had already received Him as a child in Baptism and Confirmation, but just as St. Paul told Timothy to "stir into flame the gift of God that you have,"[9] I, too needed a stirring! The central grace I received was a deep awareness of the love, majesty, and power of Jesus Christ. Everything I had learned in the Church came to life: The Eucharist, the Bible, Our Blessed Mother... With this grace came the desire to respond to His love and to bring Him as many people as I could. Then one day, while they prayed for me, I knew the Lord was calling me to the priesthood.

Why had I never experienced God and community like that before? I had been raised in a practicing Catholic family and received a good formation in Catholic school. I was practicing my faith sincerely, yet something was missing. Until now, I had not known that God wanted to have an intimate relationship with me, deeper than any love affair. I knew from the Acts of the Apostles and the lives of the saints that the Holy Spirit worked wonders and acted in the lives of Christians in other times, but our culture,

---

[9] 2 Tim 1:6.

including my experience in Catholic circles, was telling me that such interaction with God was no longer possible.

Pope Benedict XVI addressed the importance of having a faith encounter with Christ:

> Being Christian is not the result of an ethical choice or a lofty idea, but the encounter with an event, a Person, which gives life a new horizon and a decisive direction. … Since God has first loved us,[10] love is now no longer a mere *command*; it is the response to the gift of love with which God draws near to us. … Christians are people who have been conquered by Christ's love. but this initiative, far from limiting our freedom and our responsibility, is actually what makes them authentic and directs them.[11]

When I told my pastor about my priestly vocation, he dismissed it along with my testimony of how the Spirit was working in my life. He said it was all based on emotions and would not last. Now, after over thirty-four years as a priest, I still find that most people do not know the Holy Spirit, nor expect Him to enter their lives in a deeply powerful way. I understand their skepticism because I too saw the danger of emotionalism and fascination with spiritual highs, but I could not ignore the true work of God on account of abuses. The question for me became, "Is this the work of the Holy Spirit, and if so, how do I respond to Him?"

---

[10] Cf. 1 Jn 4:10.
[11] Lenten message, 1 Feb., 2013, w2.vatican.va.

— The Spirit Speaks Through the Popes —

The popes, especially since the Second Vatican Council, have been telling us, that to live an authentic Christian life, we need to experience an intimate relationship with Christ and live in the power and direction of the Holy Spirit. God, in His infinite mercy, is breaking through the secularism of our time and is powerfully manifesting His presence, **first because He loves us and wants us to enter into an intimate union with Him, and secondly because only with His power can we draw others to Him.**

The popes urgently exhort us to respond! Pope St. John XXIII, in the document convening the Second Vatican Council, expressed his intention and hopes in this way:

> May there thus be repeated in the Christian family the spectacle of the Apostles gathered together in Jerusalem, after the Ascension of Jesus to heaven, when the newborn Church was completely united in communion of thought and of prayer with Peter and around Peter, the shepherd of the lambs and of the sheep. And may the divine Spirit deign to answer in a most comforting manner the prayer that everyday rises to him from every corner of the world: **"Renew your wonders in our time, as though in a new Pentecost, and grant that Holy Church, united in unanimous and intense prayer around Mary, the Mother of Jesus, and guided by Peter, may spread the Kingdom of the divine Savior, a Kingdom of truth, of justice, of love, and of peace. Amen."**[12]

The Second Vatican Council renewed our understanding of the

---

[12] Apostolic Constitution *Humanae salutis*, 25 Dec., 1961.

absolute need for the Holy Spirit in the life of the Church and of the faithful.[13] The post-conciliar popes insisted on this. Blessed Pope Paul VI, amid increasing dissidence and turmoil, reminded us that what we need most is to receive anew the fire of the Holy Spirit:

> **What do we feel is the first and last need of this blessed and beloved Church** of ours? We must say it, almost trembling and praying, because as you know well, this is the Church's mystery and life: The Spirit, the Holy Spirit. It is He who animates and sanctifies the Church, her divine breath, the wind of her sails, her unifying principle. …
>
> **The Church needs a perennial Pentecost**; she needs fire in her heart, words on her lips, prophecy in her outlook…She needs to be temple of the Holy Spirit, total cleansing and interior life … needs to feel again … the praying voice of the Spirit that, as St. Paul teaches, takes our place and prays in us and through us "with unutterable groans" and interprets the words that by ourselves we would not know how to direct to God (cf. Rm 8:26-27). Do not you listen? The Church needs the Holy Spirit. The Holy Spirit in us, in each one of us, in all of us together, in us who are the Church. So, let all of us ever say to Him, "Come."[14]

> We would like today, not only to possess the Holy Spirit immediately but also **to experience the sensible effects and wonders of this marvelous presence of the Holy Spirit within us.**[15]

---

[13] Cf. *Lumen Gentium*, n12.

[14] General audience, 29 Nov., 1972, w2.vatican.va.

[15] Homily, Solemnity of Pentecost, 18 May, 1975.

Pope St. John Paul II spoke often about the powerful renewal taking place in the Church and its transforming effect on the faithful:

With the Second Vatican Council, the Comforter recently gave the Church … a renewed Pentecost, instilling a new and unforeseen dynamism. Whenever the Spirit intervenes, he leaves people astonished. He brings about events of amazing newness; **he radically changes persons and history**. … It is not only through the sacraments and the ministrations of the Church that the Holy Spirit makes holy the people, leads them and enriches them with his virtues. … He also distributes special graces among the faithful of every rank.

The institutional and charismatic aspects are co-essential as it were to the Church's constitution. They contribute, although differently, to the life, renewal, and sanctification of God's People.[16]

Pope Benedict XVI

"God's love has been poured into our hearts through the Holy Spirit which has been given to us" (Rom 5:5). Nevertheless, **it is not enough to know the Spirit; we must welcome Him as the guide of our souls,** as the "Teacher of the interior life" who introduces us to the Mystery of the Trinity, because He alone can open us up to faith and allow us to live it each day to the full.[17]

---

[16] Pentecost vigil, 30 May 1998. The pope based his teaching on *Lumen Gentium*, n.12 (II Vat. Council), w2.vatican.va.

[17] Message to the young people, XXXIII World Youth Day, 2008, w2.vatican.va.

Pope Francis

Trust in the Holy Spirit, for it is He who "helps us in our weakness" (Rom 8:26). But this generous trust has to be nourished, and so we need to invoke the Spirit constantly. … It is true that this trust in the unseen can cause us to feel disoriented: it is like being plunged into the deep and not knowing what we will find. I myself have frequently experienced this. Yet there is no greater freedom than that of allowing oneself to be guided by the Holy Spirit, renouncing the attempt to plan and control everything to the last detail, and instead, letting him enlighten, guide and direct us, leading us wherever he wills. The Holy Spirit knows well what is needed in every time and place.[18]

— A Renewed Mind in the Holy Spirit —
Divine Wisdom Enlightens Human Logic

God endowed us with a mind so that, as His beloved sons and daughters, we could respond to His love and wisdom. Then our minds would have authority over our will, faculties, and body. But, by sinning, we rejected God's authority over us and our minds came instead under the authority of our selfish will and the desires of the flesh. St. Paul writes about sinful men: "They became futile in their thinking and their senseless minds were darkened. Claiming to be wise, they became fools."[19] Lacking the light of God, we do not know why we exist and live on the surface. We are driven by the need to look good, to measure up, to succeed in the world. Underlying this is the fear of losing control and of failure.

We all need to be redeemed by Christ so that the Holy Spirit

---

[18] *Evangelii Gaudium*, n.280. w2.vatican.va.
[19] Rom 1:21-22.

restores our minds under God's love, wisdom, and authority. This involves a profound transformation. Our part is to surrender to the Lord, die to our old self and begin to think with the mind of Christ. We are tempted to resist this grace from God and must enter into battle for our minds by rebuking the lies of the devil, the illusions and deception of the world which contradicts the truth that the Lord has given to us. As we do this, our minds will come under the authority of God and He will give us authority over our own lives, over our thoughts and feelings.

— Testimony —
Christ Renewed My Mind

I want to continue sharing my experience in the hope that it will help you recognize the same patterns in your life and your need to give God authority over it.

After my encounter with the Holy Spirit, I began to see the ways in which I was still in control and was hoping to find happiness in many things. I prided myself in being an engineering student because I thought it made me important and would enable me to achieve my dreams. To get what I wanted, I would make deals with God. For example, I thought my happiness would consist of having a beautiful wife and living "well." So, when I sensed that God was calling me to the priesthood, I promised Him that if I became an engineer and got married, I would donate lots of money to support seminarians in India. Then, instead of only one priest, God would have many! My logic was not God's will, but I could not see it because the things I wanted were in and of themselves good. Yet my motives were selfish. Pride, lust and other capital sins impaired my discernment.

Without the Holy Spirit, my logic was at the service of my

selfishness. I could perform tasks and solve problems, but I was not able to know fundamental realities: who is God, who are we in relation to God and others, what is the purpose of my life, what is marriage… In regards to my relationship with God the Father, I was like the older brother in the parable of the prodigal son: dutiful, respectful, obedient, "good" but incapable of understanding the heart of the Father. My logic needed to be enlightened and submitted to **God's wisdom**.

When I came closer to God, the enemy's battle to control my mind intensified. He knows that our salvation depends on our response to God, so he was desperate to hold on to me, mostly by planting doubts and fear about what God was doing. At this point, I could understand why many give up.

I wanted to open my heart to the Holy Spirit, but I was afraid to let go of my attachments and control. **My will was weak because I relied on my human strength instead of trusting in the power of God**. This means that I assessed what I could do based on my human strength. In light of this, I felt it would be impossible to be a priest because I was too shy to speak in public. In addition, the idea of celibacy for life seemed too hard to bear.

Having only my logic and strength to rely on, I was tormented by many anxieties and I feared many things that I could not control: fear that I was not attractive, that I would not succeed, that I would be rejected if people really knew me. The Holy Spirit brought to light those fears and showed me God's love. I still had to work hard, but now I could trust in the Lord to be with me. I had been like the blind man of the Gospel; but when the Spirit opened my mind, I was able to see the world in a new way and act accordingly.

We could think we love the Lord and yet continue to ignore the promptings of the Spirit. That is why St. Paul addressed the following words to Christians: "You should put away the old self of your former way of life, corrupted through deceitful desires, and be renewed in the spirit of your minds, and put on the new self, created in God's way."[20]

A sign that our minds are being set free by the Holy Spirit is that we recognize in ourselves the "deceitful desires" described by St. Paul and resolve to enter the path of the Cross to be renewed. The Lord did not die on the Cross so that we would be content merely with being nice people. He gave His life so that we could be transformed and become ONE with Him.

The Holy Spirit leads the saints to venture beyond human logic. In the parable of the talents, the Lord teaches us to be **audacious.** Instead of burying our talents by opting for a secure life, He wants us to have the faith to risk it all. This is what the Blessed Mother did when she visited Elizabeth instead of staying home to protect her own pregnancy and reputation, and what St. Joseph did when he embraced his role as spouse of Mary. I encourage you to examine the life of your favorite saints to discover their audacious trust in the Holy Spirit.

---

[20] Eph 4:22-24, NABre.

Old man	New man in Christ
Mind limited to human logic	Our logic enlightened by God's wisdom
Mind self-absorbed: desires, problems	Mind open to divine wisdom, attentive to God
Relies on human strength	Relies on the power of God
No expectation that God will act	Trusts in God's commitment to us
Word of God is reduced to norms and ideas that adjust to our logic	Word of God reveals the mystery of God; new divine life – thinks as one with Christ
False perception of reality relations based on the ego, e.g., Marriage seen as fantasy	A true vision of reality and relations based on divine wisdom.
Thoughts and feelings controlled by ego	Thoughts and feelings respond to God's love
Life is to seek pleasure, be #1	Life's purpose: love without counting cost

If we live in the Spirit, we are attentive to God and submit to Him everything we do. We ask of Him in every situation, "Lord what do you want of me?" "Am I trusting in your power or in my human strength to carry this out?" Likewise, we submit to Him our thoughts. We ask Him: "Is this thought coming from Your wisdom or from my human logic?"

—My Spiritual Awakening Was Only the Beginning—

My spiritual awakening at the prayer group was only the beginning of my journey to union with God. I realized that the Lord had much more work to do on me and that what I had experienced was more like Mt. Tabor than Pentecost. The Apostles were not to stay on the mountain, even though that is what they wanted. The Lord revealed to them His glory in order to give them the courage to go with Him to the Cross. I too need courage to go with Jesus to the Cross. There is no Pentecost without the Cross.

After twenty-five years of priesthood, the Lord showed me through a sister that the battle for the salvation of His people required not just good Christians but transformed Christians willing to walk together the path of the Cross. This led to the foundation of the Love Crucified Community. This was another turning point in my life which is summarized in the following message given by the Blessed Mother to a MOC:

2. Proclaim the Cross Everywhere to Everyone to Prepare for a New Pentecost, Diary of a MOC

You are called to proclaim the Cross everywhere you go, to everyone. My people desire to be holy without the Cross; even My priests desire comfort and an easy life more than sacrifice and suffering. This is their detriment. No one can be sanctified by the Holy Spirit without the Cross.

Before there can be a new Pentecost, My people must come back to the Cross to receive the Holy Spirit and be sanctified. This is your mission.

Jesus said: *Tell them (priests) to gaze at My love crucified and to allow My Mother to bring them to the foot of the Cross with those that love Me* (I felt St. John, Mary Magdalene…). *My priests must be My fortified wall of bronze to sustain My Church. They will be called to bring My flock to the foot of the Cross and receive the power of the Holy Spirit. These souls filled with My Holy Spirit and*

> *transformed by My crucified love will cry out, "Abba, Father, save us!" and through this corporate cry, united to My Mother of Sorrows, the Church will receive its New Pentecost.* (7/7/08)

The Cross, embraced with love and trust, leads to the happiness that the world does not know. This is the path of all the saints. St. Veronica Giuliani wrote: "I found myself in the arms of the Crucified One. What I felt at that point I cannot describe: I should have liked to remain forever in His most holy side."[21]

Many want the gifts of the Holy Spirit but few love enough to go to the Cross. St. John of the Cross writes:

We must then dig deeply in Christ. … In him are hidden all the treasures of the wisdom and knowledge of God. … The soul cannot enter into these treasures, nor attain them, unless it first crosses into and enters the thicket of suffering enduring interior and exterior labors. … The gate that gives entry into these riches of His wisdom is the cross; because it is a narrow gate, while many seek the joys that can be gained through it, it is given to few to desire to pass through it.[22]

The Simple Path to Union with God that you are entering is meant to help you if you are resolved to persevere in the path of the Cross in order to be part of the faithful remnant of our Lady in these decisive times.

---

[21] http://www.lovecrucified.com/saints/veronica_giuliani.html.

[22] *Spiritual Canticle*, cited in the Office of Readings on the feast of St. John of the Cross, 14 Dec.

1–B
Mary is the Gate

3. Give Your All to Mary So You Can Enter the Narrow Path,
Diary of a MOC

> *Jesus: Mary is the secure entrance into My path. Satan has created many paths to deceive My children. But none of them have Mary at the entrance. When you consecrate yourself to the Mother of God, you give her your all. The perfect consecration to My Mother is giving her your life, your all, your will. Then she can lead you by the hand to the foot of My Cross where My way begins.*
>
> *Many consecrate themselves to Mary as a pious prayer but have no intention of entering My path. These souls are then quickly deceived by the paths of Satan with many allurements, and they render My Mother helpless to help them. This creates many piercings in the Heart of Mary. But those that give their complete abandonment to My Mother enter through her the narrow path of the Cross, which is My way.[23] (12/12/11)*

On the day of our Baptism, we were consecrated—made sacred—by becoming sons and daughters of God. From here, our life in God needs to grow through the path of the Cross to reach its fullness in Christ. He said: "If any man would come after me, let him deny himself and take up his cross and follow me" (Mt 16:24).

---

[23] Cf. St. Luis G. de Montfort.

We cannot walk this path alone. God gave us a family, the Church, and the powerful intercession of our Blessed Mother. The purpose of consecration to Mary is to live with her our baptismal consecration, to unite our "yes" to Mary's "yes" in total abandonment to God.

We did not choose Mary. God did. He entrusted His Beloved Son to her. Pope Benedict XVI wrote:

> Mary is 'blessed' because — totally, in body and soul and forever — she became the Lord's dwelling place. If this is true, Mary does not merely invite our admiration and veneration, but she guides us, shows us the way of life, shows us how we can become blessed, how to find the path of happiness.[24]

The Father's choice of Mary was confirmed by Jesus on the Cross. It is significant that He waited until the day of His sacrifice, in which Mary fully participated, to say to her, "Woman, behold your son!", and then to the disciple, "Behold your mother!" With these words, He commissioned her to do for us what she had done for Him: to prepare us, to accompany us, to help us unite our crosses to His as one sacrifice offered to the Father for the salvation of the world. She brings us to the docility of Jesus on the Cross, a docility of total trust and obedience. Blessed Mother Teresa of Calcutta wrote: "[Mary's] role is to bring you face to face, as John and Mary Magdalene, with the love in the Heart of Jesus crucified."[25]

Our part is to respond like St. John: "And from that hour the disciple took her to his own home" (Jn 19: 26-27). We too need to

---

[24] Homily, Solemnity of the Assumption, 15 Aug., 2006, w2.vatican.va.
[25] Blessed Mother Teresa of Calcutta, "Letter to Missionaries of Charity," 25 Mar., 1993.

take Mary to our homes as our mother and live intimately united to her, seeking her guidance and submitting our daily life to her in complete confidence.

Consecration is not only the initial commitment; it is a way of life that we ratify daily. We run the risk of romanticizing our consecration by wrapping it with superficial piety and offering to God many things that make us feel holy. We need to ask Mary to give us the courage to expose and to face our hidden sins. We need to walk with Mary to the Cross. Saint Alphonsus Liguori wrote: "She offered Him not aromatic spices, nor calves, nor gold, but her entire self, consecrating herself as a perpetual victim in His honor."[26]

4. My Martyrs Consecrated to the Holy Spirit Through Mary, Will Usher a New Pentecost and the Reign of Mary,
Diary of a MOC

> *My daughter, the mission of the Love Crucified Community is to bring souls, through consecration to Mary, to the feet of Jesus crucified. They will enter the Cross through the gate of Mary. You will teach them the way to union with God. You will proclaim consecration to the Holy Spirit through the Spouse of the Holy Spirit, Mary Most Sorrowful. I desire for this time to be the time of My greatest martyrs. It is the blood of My martyrs united to the blood of Jesus Christ that will usher in the new Pentecost with the reign of the Queen of Heaven and Earth. I desire countless hidden martyrs like My*

---

[26] St. Alphonsus Liguori, *Glories of Mary,* www.marys-touch.com/Glories/DiscIII.htm.

> *spouse[27], the Queen of Martyrs. Here lies the POWER OF GOD and the full power of the Holy Spirit, which will be poured out through the POWER OF THE CROSS. (9/15/10)*

Mary teaches us by her example the most important reason to go to the Cross: Love. We want to go to the Cross because Our Lord is suffering there for us. Love calls upon love. He loved us first and we want to respond. Mary's love is the gate to the love of the Most Holy Trinity.

5. Open Your Heart to Mary and You Will Know the Trinity, Diary of a MOC

> As I began to pray to my Lord this morning in the Blessed Sacrament, I was ONE with Him on the Cross. I asked, "My Lord what is Your desire this morning?" I could feel His grace flowing into my heart. He said,
>
> *I desire to fill you with all the treasures of heaven.*
>
> I then saw a treasure chest filled with oysters containing precious pearls. I picked one oyster and opened it and saw one beautiful blue-gray pearl. Then Jesus said:
>
> *Receive the pearl of Mary in your heart. Mary is your Queen Mother. She is perfect purity and holiness. She is ONE in the life of the Trinity above all the angels and saints. She is the perfect human being perfected in the image and likeness of God.*

---

[27] The Church is the spouse of Christ. Mary and the martyrs are exemplars of the Church.

> *She possesses the Holy Spirit fully; therefore, she possesses in perfect UNITY the Father and the Son. She is the pure vessel of My Precious Blood; therefore, all graces flow from her as the vessel of the wellspring in the Most Holy Trinity. She is your Mother and advocate before Me and our Father. Every son and daughter who opens his heart to her to receive her spiritual milk will come to know the Father, Son, and Holy Spirit, who live in her. Come every day of Advent to your Mother's feet to receive from her pure milk, and you will come to know and love My Spirit. (11/28/11)*

We need to ask ourselves, "Am I willing to allow Mary to take me to Jesus Crucified?"

6. The Holy Spirit Released at the Cross, Diary of a MOC

> *The Holy Spirit formed My human heart in all its perfection. He, the Holy Spirit, lives in Me as I live in the Father and the Father in Me. The Holy Spirit is released with all His power from the fire of My Sacred Heart when souls approach Me with humility at the foot of My Cross. The Holy Spirit flows from the fire of My crucified love. Only love can wage war against the darkness of Satan and win. It is purified love that I need for the decisive battle at hand. Therefore, My little one, bring Me victim souls.* **The Holy Spirit is received as a seed in baptism but He is fully stirred into flame in My Cross.** *It is united as one to My Mother at the foot of the Cross that the Holy Spirit begins to possess your*

mind, heart, and soul. (7/11/11)

*To continue this Path, prepare for Marian consecration. We suggest the book *33 Days to Morning Glory* by Fr. Michael Gaitley[28]. It combines the methods of preparation to consecration of St. Louis de Montfort, St. Maximilian Kolbe, St John Paul II, and St. Teresa of Calcutta.

1-C
Why Should We Want to Go to the Cross?

The Cross is not part of God's creation. It was men who invented it to subjugate others through torture and fear. The Cross represents all the sufferings of humanity caused by Satan and our sins.

Satan came against Jesus with all his fury, threatening Him with suffering and death to stop Him from fulfilling His mission. But Jesus' love for the Father and us is stronger than fear. He defeated Satan by choosing to embrace the suffering of the Cross to the end.

To impose crosses on others is evil, but to choose to persevere in love when faced with the cross is the power of the love of Christ. Pope Benedict wrote, "God, who became a lamb, tells us that the world is saved by the Crucified One, not by those who crucified him. The world is redeemed by the patience of God. It is destroyed by the impatience of man."[29] The Lamb conquered the Cross and

---

[28] Download the book here: http://www.holytrinityptc.org/33-days-to-morning-glory.html.

[29] Pope Benedict XVI, homily at the beginning of the Petrine ministry, 24 Apr., 2005, w2.vatican.va.

turned it into the glorious sign of His love, the only power that defeats Satan and offers salvation to all.

Christ has defeated Satan; but for a time, the battle continues against His Body, the Church. We can defeat him only if we are one with the Lamb, conducting ourselves as He did.[30] The Cross, therefore, is not a type of spirituality among many; it is the only way to become one with Christ. Pope Benedict XVI taught that "The way of the cross is, in fact, the only way that leads to the victory of love over hate, of sharing over egoism, of peace over violence."[31] "Whoever omits the cross, omits the essence of Christianity."[32]

In the first homily of his pontificate, Pope Francis confirmed this:

> When we journey without the Cross, when we build without the Cross, when we profess Christ without the Cross, we are not disciples of the Lord, we are worldly: we may be bishops, priests, cardinals, popes, but not disciples of the Lord. My wish is that all of us …will have the courage, yes, the courage, to walk in the presence of the Lord, with the Lord's Cross; to build the Church on the Lord's blood which was poured out on the Cross, and to profess the one glory: Christ crucified. And in this way, the Church will go

---

[30] 1 Jn 2:5-6: "The way we can be sure we are in union with him is for the man who claims to abide in him to conduct himself just as he did."

[31] Angelus, 10 Feb., 2008, w2.vatican.va.

[32] Joseph Cardinal Ratzinger, "The New Evangelization," Address to Catechists and Religion Teachers Jubilee of Catechists, 12 Dec., 2000, www.ewtn.com/new_evangelization/Ratzinger.htm. Cf. 1 Cor 2:2.

forward.[33]

— Why Speak About the Cross if Jesus is Risen? —

We must proclaim the Cross of Christ because it is one seamless mystery with His death and resurrection. St. Paul had encountered the risen Lord, and yet he wrote, "I decided to know nothing among you except Jesus Christ and Him crucified."[34] He exalts the Cross because it is there that Christ revealed the unconditional love of God for us. To exalt the Cross also means to believe in the power of living our crosses with Jesus with the assurance of the resurrection. We say with St. Paul, "I have been crucified with Christ; it is no longer I who live, but Christ who lives in me."[35] With his eyes fixed on Jesus crucified, St. Paul entered Christ's love and had the power to crucify the rebellion of his flesh and persevere in trials.

St. Paul tells us that when "the world did not know God through wisdom," Christ came to save us through the "folly of the Cross."[36] He came to suffer with us in our trials. But **in our pride, we still reject the Cross and try to save ourselves according to our human wisdom.**

Mercy is not an idea or a thing that God sends to help us resolve our problems. God sent His Son. **Jesus IS Mercy, and its full manifestation is His love crucified. To reject the Cross is to reject mercy.**

The love of the Cross is foolishness to the world because it does not believe that the Cross has the power to defeat evil. On Good

---

[33] Homily to cardinals, 14 Mar., 2013, w2.vatican.va.
[34] 1 Cor 2:2.
[35] Gal 2:19-20.
[36] 1 Cor 1:21,24.

Friday Jesus was seen, even by His disciples, as a defeated man, a total failure. When we see good people suffering and evil acting with impunity, we ask, "Where is the power of love?" It appears as foolishness. However, when we choose to continue loving in adversity, we begin to discover the power of the love of God, "the word of the Cross … the power of God,"[37] of which St. Paul writes based on his own experience.

If we do not embrace the Cross with Jesus when love requires it, we will never know true love, and the inevitable sufferings would be rendered a meaningless waste that makes us bitter.

Pope Benedict XVI observed that, "In the face of the horror of Auschwitz there is no other response than the Cross of Christ: Love descended to the very depths of the abyss of evil to save man in his core, where human freedom can rebel against God."[38]

Satan knows our fear of suffering and uses it as a threat to keep us from loving when faced with difficult decisions. Jesus also experienced the human aversion to suffering and asked the Father to spare Him. He prayed: "My Father, if it be possible, let this cup pass from me." Yet, He did not abandon the will of the Father. He said, "not as I will, but as thou wilt."[39]

With Jesus, we can overcome all fear and be set free. St. John Paul II taught us that "The Crucified Christ reveals the authentic meaning of freedom; he lives it fully in the total gift of himself and calls his disciples to share in His freedom."[40]

---

[37] 1 Cor 1:18.
[38] Audience, 31 May, 2006, w2.vatican.va.
[39] Mat 26:39.
[40] *Veritatis Splendor*, n.85, w2.vatican.va.

— The Cross Changes Suffering
into a Declaration of Love —

We can't give explanations as to why God permits suffering. Yes, we could say that suffering is the consequence of the abuse of freedom; we could say that God does not take away our freedom because, without it, we could not love. But when we experience the reality of suffering, no explanation suffices. We must go beyond explanations and follow Christ to Calvary so that our hearts may be pierced with His.

St. John Paul II

Christ does not explain in the abstract the reasons for suffering, but before all else, He says: "**Follow me! Come! Take part through your suffering in this work of saving the world; a salvation achieved through my suffering! Through my Cross**." Gradually, as the individual takes up his cross, spiritually uniting himself to the Cross of Christ, the salvific meaning of suffering is revealed before him. He does not discover this meaning at his own human level, but at the level of the suffering of Christ. At the same time, however, from this level of Christ, the salvific meaning of suffering descends to man's level and becomes, in a sense, the individual's personal response. It is then that man finds in his suffering interior peace and even spiritual joy.[41]

When we experience trials, such as the loss of loved ones, illness, financial crisis, or injustice, we are not called to endure them like the Stoics, who trained themselves to bear all things without feelings. Instead, we suffer with Christ allowing Him to

---

[41] *Salvifici Doloris*, n.26, w2.vatican.va.

work in us to bring all things to a good end.

Pope Benedict XVI

This is the "folly" of the cross: a folly capable of changing our sufferings into a declaration of love for God and mercy for our neighbor; a folly capable of transforming those who suffer because of their faith and identity into vessels of clay ready to be filled to overflowing by divine gifts more precious than gold.[42]

The Cross is, first of all, a declaration of God's love for us, a love that is not satisfied until we respond and our hearts are inflamed with love for Him. Then, the fire of His love becomes the power that moves everything in us. We no longer just bear the crosses in our lives; we embrace them with gratitude as an opportunity to love Him, and to radiate this love to all.

Pope Benedict XVI

The more we imitate Jesus and remain united to him, the more we enter into the mystery of His divine holiness. We discover that He loves us infinitely, and this prompts us in turn to love our brethren. Loving always entails an act of self-denial, "losing ourselves," and it is precisely this that makes us happy.[43]

St. John Paul II, *Salvifici Doloris*

Down through the centuries and generations, it has been seen that **in suffering there is concealed a particular power that draws a person interiorly close to Christ, a**

---

[42] Speech, 14 Sept., 2012, <u>w2.vatican.va</u>; cf. 2 Cor 4:7-18.
[43] Homily, Solemnity of All Saints, 1 Nov., 2006, <u>w2.vatican.va.</u>

special grace. To this grace, many saints, such as Saint Francis of Assisi, Saint Ignatius of Loyola and others, owe their profound conversion. A result of such a conversion is not only that the individual discovers the salvific meaning of suffering, but above all, that he becomes a completely new person. He discovers a new dimension, as it were, of his entire life and vocation. This discovery is a particular confirmation of the spiritual greatness, which, in man, surpasses the body in a way that is completely beyond compare. When this body is gravely ill, totally incapacitated, and the person is almost incapable of living and acting, all the more do interior maturity, and spiritual greatness becomes evident, constituting a touching lesson to those who are healthy and normal.[44]

Our suffering, by itself, is useless; but God, from the beginning of time, willed that the perfect sacrifice of His Son be completed in His Body, the Church, which is each one of us. That is why the Lord told us in our community of Love Crucified: "Suffer all with Me, we are no longer two but one in My sacrifice of love."

— The Cross Is a Treasured Pearl —

The Cross, when accepted with love, is the treasured pearl of Matthew 13; happy are those who, upon finding it, rush off to give up all they have to possess it. Too often we have allowed Satan to interfere with our search for this precious pearl. St. Ignatius of Antioch, a second century Father of the Church, asked:

---

[44] 2 Nov, 1984, w2.vatican.va.

Why is it that we are not all wise when we have received the knowledge of God, which is Jesus Christ? Why do we perish in our stupidity, not knowing the gift the Lord has truly sent us? My spirit is given over to the humble service of the cross, which is a stumbling block to unbelievers, but to us salvation and eternal life.[45]

St. James reminds us that the love of the Cross—the precious pearl—is wisdom that we need to ask for in faith and seek to acquire at any price because, without it, all suffering, pain, and the Cross itself, are utter foolishness and a stumbling block.

> My brothers, count it pure joy when you are involved in every sort of trial. Realize that when your faith is tested, it makes for endurance. Let endurance come to its perfection so that you may mature in everything. If any of you is without wisdom, let him ask for it from God who gives generously and ungrudgingly to all, and it will be given him.[46]

---

[45] St. Ignatius of Antioch, "Letter to the Ephesians," II Century.
[46] Jas 1:2–6.

Chapter Two

At the Foot of the Cross

2-A
Come to the Feet of Jesus

The love of Christ has drawn the saints of all ages to the foot of the Cross. St. Alphonsus wrote:

> You are the King but the King of love! With humility, then, and tenderness do I draw near to kiss Thy sacred feet, transfixed for love of me; I clasp in my arms this cross, on which You, being made a Victim of love, willed to offer Thyself in sacrifice for me.[47]

Mary longs to take us with her to the Cross, to the most tender and intimate union with Jesus in love and suffering.

---

[47] St. Alphonsus Liguori, *The Passion and the Death of Jesus Christ* (Benziger Brothers, 1887), 113.

7. At the Cross We Begin to See, Diary of a MOC

> *Mary immediately turns your gaze to My crucified Love, but many cannot see Me because their eyes are covered by the darkness of sin. Mary, your advocate, and Spouse of the Holy Spirit, immediately calls upon My Spirit to come to the aid of your soul. The planks of pride, self-love, vanity, and sins of all kinds are revealed to you by the Holy Spirit. It is here at My feet, through the gift of repentance, that you begin to see. Grace builds upon grace, but also, each grace removes a veil that keeps the eyes of your soul from seeing the glory of God before you and the darkness that keeps you from hearing the whisper of God within you. (12/12/11)*

We kneel next to Mary at the foot of the Cross and in the depth of our hearts we:

- Humbly kiss and adore the feet of our Lord asking for the gift of knowledge, which is twofold: Knowledge of GOD and Knowledge of SELF.
- Seek true sorrow for our sins, the Gold of Precious Repentance.

Jesus taught Venerable Concepcion Cabrera (Conchita)[48] what takes place when we go to His feet:

When you arrive at My feet, humbled and pure, self-denied

---

[48] Mexican mystic Ven. Concepcion Cabrera de Armida (Conchita), wife and mother of 9 children, foundress of the Works of the Cross. Her writings have been a great influence to our community. Cf. http://lovecrucified.com/saints/conchita/[conchita.html

and recollected, you will understand many truths of self-knowledge, illuminated by the very light of God; you will touch the depth of your misery, you will cry for your failures, you will understand My predilection for you and you will experience the fortitude and the peace of the Holy Spirit. …

When I see you approaching Me, to find breath and life, here at My feet, I will pour out My graces. I abound in tenderness, and I wish to bring you nearer and nearer to Him who is your life, by means of perfect virtues, of constant humility and voluntary self-denial.[49]

Jesus's words to Conchita bring to mind **the woman of the Gospel who bathed Jesus' feet with her tears,** dried them with her hair. She continued kissing them as she anointed them with costly ointment.[50] We are so afraid of making ourselves vulnerable to love in this way. How much more if we have a reputation as sinners! She must have known that she was going to be judged and was likely to suffer their wrath, yet her love was greater than all her fears.

One day I realized that, if I had been at that banquet, I would have judged this woman as Simon the Pharisee did. But Jesus exalts her intimate expressions of love as an example to be proclaimed everywhere the Gospel is preached. Jesus led me to realize that I had to repent and allow the Lord to teach me to love as she did. Jesus wants us to have her humility and vulnerability so that we can passionately and openly lavish our love on Him and one another without fear. This is the pure love for which He thirsts.

At the Last Supper Jesus washed the feet of His Disciples.

---

[49] Id., *Holy Hours*, (Alba House, 2006), 217- 218.
[50] Cf., Lk 7:36-50.

His gesture was more than an exhortation for them to be humble servants. Jesus was teaching them to love to a depth of intimacy they had never known. Like the woman at the banquet, He showed them a love that is vulnerable and intimate, even knowing that in a few hours they would betray Him.

To touch the feet of another is a very personal experience. We do not feel comfortable touching feet nor having ours touched. Most of us, especially men, can understand the reaction of Peter when he refused to have Jesus wash his feet.

Our feet represent our hearts. Just as we may keep our feet covered because they may be ugly or dirty, we also try to keep our hearts covered and do not expose them even to Jesus. But He insists that we allow Him to touch us because He wants to bring us out of our isolation and draw us close to Himself.

Pope Benedict XVI explains how the Lord, washing the feet of the Apostles, reveals Himself as the love of the Father:

"Having loved His own who were in the world, He loved them to the end" (Jn 13:1). God loves His creature, man; He even loves him in his fall and does not leave him to himself. … He kneels before us and carries out for us the service of a slave: He washes our dirty feet so that we might be admitted to the banquet and be made worthy to take our place at His table.

In this, the entire mystery of Jesus Christ is expressed. … The basin in which he washes us is his love, ready to face death. Only love has that purifying power which washes the grime from us and elevates us to God's heights. … The basin that purifies us is God himself, who gives Himself to us without reserve to the very depths of His suffering and His death. … **The Lord's love knows no bounds, but man can**

put a limit on it.[51]

At the Cross, Jesus' feet were nailed. Who was there to kiss Him? It is difficult for us to approach Him, to kneel before Him, to kiss His feet. We know that He loves us, and we feel that we love Him too, but our hearts remain distant. We find it easier to do things for Him, to be busy solving problems, than to show our love by kissing Him. Men, including priests, feel more comfortable relating in a practical way or at the intellectual level, but in order for them to love as they were created to love, in the image and likeness of God, they too, must make themselves VULNERABLE at the feet of Jesus crucified and expose the depths of their hearts. Jesus desires for us to love Him as He has loved us. This is why kissing His feet is necessary for the healing of both the masculine and feminine hearts.

8. Kiss My Wounded Feet, Diary of a MOC

> *My daughter, it is My Mother who first approached Me and kissed My pierced feet. This act of humility and love was to show mankind how to approach Me at the foot of the Cross. It is the blood from My precious feet that has the power to anoint your lips with the power of My Word. They are few, My daughter, who approach Me at the foot of the Cross to kiss My wounded feet. Blessed are they who follow My Mother in humility. (6/11/10)*

At the foot of the Cross, as we kiss the feet of Jesus, we need to ask for the gift of knowledge, to know God and to know

---

[51] Homily, Holy Thursday, 13 Apr., 2006, w2.vatican.va.

ourselves, so that we can repent. It is then that the planks of pride and self-love are removed from our eyes.

— Testimony —
A Mother Comes to Self-Knowledge
by Making Herself Vulnerable at the Cross

As adoration requires complete vulnerability, I thought I was completely open, but my community was telling me that I wasn't.

One deep wound which I received years ago, occurred with a vicious rape. I write about it in my book, *Warrior for Justice: The George Eames Story*, so I don't mind talking about it here. I can't begin to imagine how many women, like me, have struggled all their lives to figure out how to deal with the same or similar wounds. Many never deal with them. Many never realize that our wounds should be submitted to the light of Christ on our spiritual journey. Consequently, if I can help anyone understand this a little better, I'm determined to do so.

Though I honestly could not see where this wound occurring from my rape was a problem in my life after all these years, I promised myself recently to do the inner work needed to work through it completely. I journaled several pages, trying to see my way through it. Then during adoration, I was given this one sentence: I AM STRIPPED OF MY GARMENTS.

My deepest wound: I am stripped of my garments. This happened to me during the rape; every covering was taken away from me. I was denuded. For hours. I see immediately Jesus being stripped of his garments, stripped at crucifixion.

Suddenly I understand. This is the wound which gives me entrance into Jesus' wound. Stripped of power, stripped of control, exposed, and completely vulnerable. My response for years—I covered myself with the lies: I have to be in control. I can't be vulnerable. I have to be self-sufficient. I don't want anyone to see me this way. I can't bear to be touched in an intimate way.

I covered myself, and now Jesus wants to strip all away in order for me to enter His vulnerability. I cannot be crucified with Jesus until I am stripped of my garments.

I understand His vulnerability for the first time. I literally feel my pain again, and in that pain, I feel His in a remarkable, sharp way. This wound of Christ is hidden from us because it does not appear as an actual wound, but it was a deep wound to his soul, to his spirit as a man, to his psyche. As it was to mine.

This is our greatest fear and discomfort—to uncover our inner selves, to expose what is sacred, what is inviolable to all who pass by. To expose ourselves. There is no greater vulnerability. Yet God asks it of us. All women, all men. This is where our crucifixion begins. It is in our vulnerability that we become truly accessible, to God and to one another.

The Ethiopian eunuch mentioned in the Acts of the Apostles was reading Isaiah 53:7-8 and could not understand, so he asked St. Philip to explain to him:

> Like a sheep, he was led to the slaughter,
> and as a lamb before its shearer,
> so he opened not his mouth.
> In his humiliation, justice was denied him.

The lamb—sheared, denuded, stripped, then sacrificed—the Lamb of God. Jesus on the cross is the epitome of vulnerability: stripped, exposed, violated, powerless.

I revisit George, my husband, in his final months, days, the same image of one utterly exposed, vulnerable, powerless. How powerfully I saw in him Jesus, crucified and suffering; and I embraced him, his body, his vulnerability. That kind of intimacy is available only when we allow ourselves to be truly vulnerable to another.

I see now how through all my wounds, I enter the wounds of Jesus, stripped, exposed, rejected, abandoned, alone. Now I am one with Jesus crucified. The only access to the Resurrection is through the Passion.

9. As You Kiss My Feet, How Far Are You Willing to Walk with Me? Diary of a MOC

My daughter, My Cross without Me is nothing but agony; My Cross with Me is new life. I came, My little one, to bring you new life. Your life without the saving grace of My Precious Blood is death and darkness. I came to restore you to your original state of grace as a daughter of the Father, a daughter who is pure and holy as God is pure and holy, a daughter created for Love and to be love, a daughter to reflect and radiate the beauty of God Himself.

The Cross is your sole wealth and happiness on earth because it is your path to new life. It is the place of encounter between a creature and the Trinity. Yes, My daughter, that place of encounter with the Father, the Son, and the Holy Spirit. You enter the Cross through the gate of My Mother. She accompanies you to the foot of the Cross to kiss My pierced and wounded feet. This first encounter is the awakening of your soul. It is through this act of humble love, in imitation of My Mother, in which you receive the gift of knowledge, therefore, receiving the gold of precious repentance.

My feet represent My desire to bring My Gospel to the ends of the world. On earth, they were continuously walking, moving forward in love of my Father's mission, which was My mission because We are One with the Holy Spirit.

As you kiss My feet ask: How far are you willing to go to proclaim My mission that I have placed in your heart? Will your feet reach the summit of Golgotha? Will you continue to love and be faithful to My mission when you are persecuted and misunderstood, many times by those closest to you?

How far are you willing to walk for Me? Are you willing to remain at My feet and wash them with the perfume of your tears and sacrifices as Mary Magdalene did? (2/24/11)

2-B
Knowledge of God and Self

Sin has blinded us to our sinfulness. Jesus told St. Faustina, "the soul does not even know her own self."[52] The result is that we minimize our sinfulness and fail to see the damage it causes. But St. John tells us that, "if we say we have no sin, we deceive ourselves, and the truth is not in us" (1 Jn 1:8). We need to be set free from this state of deception by begging the Holy Spirit for the gift of self-knowledge. This can happen only through our encounter with Jesus at the Cross.

We lack self-knowledge because we are afraid to see the truth, what requires a change in us. Instead of facing our wounds, fears and wrong-doing, we try to make deals with God, offering Him good works to appease our consciences. At the same time, we use many masks to hide our sins. We should not be satisfied having some superficial self-knowledge; we should seek to live wrapped in the gift of self-knowledge by humbly acknowledging our sins, our nothingness and our inability to do anything without the grace of God. St. Peter tells us: "Wrap yourselves in humility" (1 Pet 5:5). Jesus will then give us self-knowledge in surprising ways through people, situations, and Scripture.

Following is a testimony of a husband who received self-knowledge through a painful experience.

---

[52] St. Maria Faustina Kowalska, *Diary: Divine Mercy in My Soul* (Stockbridge, Ma. USA: Marian Press, 2003), n.1528.

— Testimony —
Receiving Self-Knowledge Through a Painful Experience

Last night, as I went to bed, I turned to kiss my wife good night. Suddenly, I felt a very painful pinch on my lower back. She quickly got me a heating pad and some medication. The next morning, I was still in pain and my left leg was numb. I feared that my back might give out. I was frustrated, annoyed, and just wanted to lay down and apply heat to my back so that I could find some relief.

It was then that I realized the gift I had taken for granted for way too long: the gift of my wife's love. I saw that the pain I was suffering was much less than what she had been suffering for more than six months. The Lord opened my eyes to my selfishness. It was like a revelation. My nuisance/pain had me upset; yet, my wife wakes up early every morning, gets the children ready, takes them to school, goes to work, runs errands all over town, picks up the children, takes them to CCD or baseball practice or dance or whatever school event is scheduled for the day, and then cooks for all. She does all this and her back pain is worse than mine.

The Lord gave me the opportunity to appreciate my wife's suffering and to share her pain so that I may gain a deep appreciation for her spousal love. Her dedication to me in my pain made me realize that I must share in her pains and joys so that our relationship may be forged into the solid bond that the Lord intends it to be.

Sharing sufferings and joys with her strengthened our relationship with each other and with Christ. Then I began to see the suffering of our Lord for me. In the same way that my eyes were opened to my selfishness with my wife, I saw my selfishness towards God.

Before having the experience above, this husband had started going to the Cross to ponder Christ's love. He allowed Jesus' gaze to penetrate his hardened heart and begged the Holy Spirit for the gift of knowledge. It was then that the Spirit revealed to him his lack of sensitivity towards his wife's suffering. Lack of self-knowledge was a plank that blinded him.

Luke 6:42

How can you say to your brother, "Brother, let me take the speck out of your eye," when you yourself fail to see the plank in your own eye? You hypocrite, first take the plank out of your eye, and then you will see clearly to remove the speck from your brother's eye.

10. Seeing Our Misery, Abandonment, and Perseverance: Key to Progress, Diary of a MOC

It is My souls that willingly see their misery revealed to them by My Spirit [and who respond] with cries and tears of sorrow that touch the Heart of Abba, Father, and He quickly comes to embrace them with His forgiveness through My crucified love. Souls advance from this part of My Path (My feet), depending on their docility to the lights of the Holy Spirit on their many patterns of sin. It is here that My path is most strenuous and difficult because each soul must abandon its will to Me. Letting go of human ways and control is difficult for every soul, but, with each response of genuine effort, God pours forth His mercy upon that soul.

The soul that lives wrapped in the gift of

knowledge grows in true humility and is then able to advance in My path on the wings of the Holy Spirit. At times, you fall and have setbacks; but do not get discouraged, for these falls are meant to help keep you wrapped in the gift of knowledge, the gift of knowing that you can do nothing without the grace of God. Satan will try to use the tactic of discouragement, making you believe that you cannot continue on this narrow path; it is then that you must beg the Holy Spirit and My Mother to come to your aid, and they will help strengthen you.

It is here, at My feet, that you must persevere with great discipline of spirit, because your spirit is weak because the appetite of your flesh is so strong. As your spirit is strengthened, the appetite of your flesh is weakened. Love is the greatest means to strengthen your spirit. As you come to know Me and experience My love, your spirit is strengthened.

Many never advance from this beginning stage because of lack of perseverance and eventually enter a different path that is more pleasing to their flesh. This is a deep suffering of My Heart and Mary's Heart. (12/12/11)

— From Hardness of Heart to Purity —

It may happen that, when we go to the feet of Jesus, we are unable to see His gaze and we remain unmoved, simply sitting there, feeling nothing. This usually happens because our hearts are hardened, and we are caught up in ourselves. The plank of sin covers the eyes of our soul, preventing us from seeing, knowing and coming into direct contact with God's love. But we should not despair. Recognizing our illness is already an important gift of self-knowledge and the first step towards healing.

Pope Benedict

How can it be that man does not even want to "taste" God? When man is entirely caught up in his own world, with material things, with what he can do, with all that is feasible and brings him success, with all that he can produce or understand by himself, then his capacity to perceive God weakens, the organ sensitive to God deteriorates, it becomes unable to perceive and sense. … It can happen that … man, as St Gregory says, no longer perceives God's gaze, to be looked at by Him, the fact that His precious gaze touches me![53]

---

[53] Homily, Switzerland Bishop's Conference, 7 Nov., 2006, LoveCrucified.com/articles_formation/benedict16/wedding_feast.html.

— Why Do Some Recognize Jesus While Others Don't? —

Because John the Baptist's heart was pure, his eyes were not veiled. He immediately saw the glory of God in Jesus as He approached him and was able to fulfill his mission by proclaiming, "Behold, the Lamb of God, who takes away the sin of the world." But throughout the Gospels, Jesus exposed the hardness of heart of many. He confronted the Scribes who were "questioning in their hearts" the healing of the paralytic. Jesus went directly to the root of the problem and asked them, "Why do you question thus in your hearts?"[54] On another occasion, after healing the man with the withered hand on the Sabbath, Jesus looked at the Pharisees with "anger, grieved at their hardness of heart."[55]

Hardness of heart is not the exclusive domain of Christ's enemies; it is also found in those closest to Jesus, the disciples, who had left everything to follow Him. The gospel tells us that they did not recognize Him when he walked on water because "they had not understood the incident of the loaves. On the contrary, **their hearts were hardened.**"[56] They were amazed at the miracle but failed to grasp its meaning: Jesus has divine authority over creation. It is the same with us; our hardness of heart blocks us from understanding fully who Jesus is and what He is doing in our lives. Like the apostles, we all need to live the process of purification and allow God to take us beyond our expectations.

Why was it that John the Baptist, Simeon and Anna knew Jesus at a deeper level than others? The answer lies in hearts that seek with faith. A hardened heart is set in its ways. It reduces the work

---

[54] Mk 2:5-8.
[55] Mk 3:5.
[56] Mk 6:52, NABre.

of God to make it fit in its natural logic and experience. It is not open to see beyond what it controls. A pure heart, on the other hand, believes that for God nothing is impossible. It is docile and malleable, willing to be pierced, pruned and made new by God.

The soul which receives the gift of self-knowledge and sees the hardness of its own heart arrives at a moment of decision: It either accepts the gift or remains in darkness. Receiving the gift of self-knowledge hurts; it feels like a sting. The soul needs courage to admit its sins and the wounds caused by them and to go to the root of both. This is why most people pull back into the old self and do not enter the healing process. But if the soul perseveres, it receives the balm of Jesus' mercy; the planks fall away, and the light of truth enters. The fruit of this process is joy and peace.

Hebrews 4:12-13
> For the word of God is living and active, sharper than any two-edged sword, piercing to the division of soul and spirit, of joints and marrow, and discerning the thoughts and intentions of the heart. And before Him no creature is hidden, but all are open and laid bare to the eyes of Him with whom we have to do.

Psalm 51 is a powerful prayer of repentance for this stage of the Path. In this prayer, we beg the Lord to have mercy upon us and to cleanse us from all our sins. We cry out to God to create a clean heart in us, making it whiter than snow.

Important daily practice: Have a crucifix next to your bed. As you get out of bed, gaze on Jesus crucified and tenderly kiss His feet. Allow this to be a sacred moment of encounter, ask for the two-fold gift of knowledge and repentance and remain in this union throughout your day.

2-C

Sins Are Like Weeds

Sins are like weeds: we may cut the leaves, but **as long as the roots remain, more leaves will soon come up.** We must dig deep and pull out the entire root system—the hidden part, which thrives beneath the surface. Many times, in confession, we give the Lord only the visible sins (the leaves of the weeds), while we keep the roots underground. In a short time, we find ourselves repeating the same sins. To end this cycle of sin, we must be willing to look deep into our hearts with the light of the Holy Spirit to see the deep roots so we can pull them out.

For example, we confess that we yelled at our children. That is a leaf of the weed. It is fairly easy to see when it sprouts from our heart. But if we dig into our heart, we reach the roots that nourish that leaf: anger and impatience. These roots are attached to our wounds from the past. If those roots remain underground, they will soon sprout new leaves.

When we pull out the entire weed with its roots, a hole is created. The same thing occurs when the root system of sin is pulled out of our hearts. This uprooting is something we fear because the hole exposes wounds we would rather not confront.

For example, a man suffers and laments the behavior of his alcoholic father but does not realize how the bad relationship has deeply wounded his own heart. He continues with disordered behaviors after the father is no longer present. He is aware of some of his bad actions (the leaves) and wants to get rid of them.

However, he continues acting the same way because he is unable to go to the roots of his sin. Those sins are attached to the wound received from his father. This wound generates a lie that makes him think he is not lovable, that he has no worth.

We all have weeds in the garden of our heart; we all need to go to the root system, to our core wounds. These wounds are caused mostly by trauma (abuse or abandonment) or by unmet needs of the heart (to be loved, to be affirmed, etc.). We must dig deeply so that the Holy Spirit may illumine the darkness within us. This process begins when we go to the foot of the Cross. In time, it will bring forth our transformation into new men and women.

— Testimony —
Digging Deep into Her Heart,
She Came to Self-Knowledge and Healing

One morning I woke up and immediately heard the Lord clearly tell me, "Dear child of My Heart, today I want you to enter into the deepest recesses of your soul." I wondered what He meant. So, I went to the dictionary and learned five meanings for the word *recess*. The first is to step back, to recollect, and to find silence. The second refers to a hidden, secret or secluded place—to enter that deepest part of my soul. The third describes an area where light does not shine. This must be an area of sin, where the light of Jesus does not shine. The fourth meaning refers to thoughts or feelings that we are not aware of. These feelings or thoughts come from wounds inflicted to my soul. This is important to understand. The fifth is rest or relaxation, which means to rest in Jesus!

Several months later, I remember going to bed after having listened, for the second or third time, to a teaching from our community about self-knowledge. I asked our Mother to please show me if there was anything in me that needed to come to light. That night I had a disturbing dream with my uncle. I dreamt that we were without clothes and he said, "Let's go." I said "No" without fear or concern. When I woke up, I asked our Lady what it meant. Our Mother immediately took me to my childhood and showed me the many times that my uncle and father joked about my behind. They would make comments about my size. They would also touch me. As our Mother showed me all this, I felt that I had been violated… I felt naked. Then I understood the dream. From that morning on, Jesus and Mary began to reveal to me many similar occurrences throughout my life, violations of my person that may seem insignificant to society but not to me. There were the many times at school and parties when boys would tap me on the rear. There was the time when I was waiting for the bus, and a man exposed himself. Another time, a neighbor sat me on his lap and began to play "horsey." The most disturbing time was when an older man, also a neighbor, took me into his bedroom and started to touch my chest and look down my shorts. I have been disrespected. I have been violated. I have been molested.

These violations created in me insecurities, anxieties, fears, low self-esteem and many other disorders. Thus the Lord began to remove veils from my eyes, and I began to see my wounds. Until now, I had not known how to deal with these wounds, except to suppress them in the "deepest recesses of my soul." The anxieties, fears, etc. would not allow me to live in peace. They paralyzed me, and I would fall into sin. I could not grow and mature into an emotionally healthy person. I created walls and defense mechanisms to find some sort of peace and order.

Once the Lord Jesus brought these memories into my

conscience, I was able to suffer them united with Him. I was able to name the memories for what they truly are (abuse, mockery…) and to give them to our Lord on the Altar, as an offering to the Father, for the priesthood and the salvation of all. Soon the Lord lifted this weight from me. I can now breathe.

A friend called me months later to share a dream she had in which I was dancing, carefree and happy. It was a confirmation of what God had done. That is exactly how I feel—delivered! The most amazing thing is that this healing was also for my brothers and sisters. I can now see the wounds of others and help them.

When we root out sin, we should not fear being left empty. Jesus comes to fill our life. He said: "The thief comes only to steal and kill and destroy; I came that they may have life, and have it abundantly" (Jn 10:10).

11. Eyes Have Not Seen Nor Ears Heard,[57] Diary of a MOC

> *Eyes have not seen, nor ears heard what your God has prepared for you. I invite you to come and see. I will remove the veil that covers the eyes of your soul so that you can see what few are able to see. You will see the new Jerusalem in all her glory. She, more precious than gold or diamonds, will be yours to possess.*
>
> *Allow Me to remove the plank from your eyes that keeps you from contemplating the glory of God before you. Come, My daughter, and bring many to the foot of the Cross.*
>
> *Prostrate yourselves before the foot of My Cross and kiss holy ground. Rise and embrace My precious feet, and kiss My wounded feet. It is here, through this gesture of humility and love that the plank of pride and self-love is removed from blinding your sight. Touch My feet, bless My feet with your kisses and cleanse them with your tears. The Holy Spirit drew Mary Magdalene to this act of love in preparation for My crucifixion, and it is My Mother who completed this act of love and reparation at My crucifixion. It is here at My precious feet that you receive the gold of precious repentance. I desire for you to bring My sons to the foot of My Cross. (11/16/10)*

---

[57] Cf. 1 Cor 2:9.

2-*D*
The Gaze of Jesus

When we go deep to receive self-knowledge, to repent and to give Christ control of our lives, He unites our hearts with His to a depth beyond the blessedness of seeing Him with our eyes. Jesus says, "Blessed are those who have not seen and yet have come to believe."[58] They are blessed because they receive the gift of spiritual sight. Even those who see miracles, like the shepherd children of Fatima, need to go beyond human sight to be able to receive the gaze of God and learn to look with the same gaze. Pope Benedict XVI tells us that they encountered Mary in the depth of their hearts and that we can also encounter Jesus and Mary if we are attentive:

God, who is more deeply present to me than I am to myself,[59] has the power to come to us, particularly through our inner senses, so that the soul can receive the gentle touch of a reality which is beyond the senses and which enables us to reach what is not accessible or visible to the senses. For this to happen, **we must cultivate an interior watchfulness of the heart,** which, for most of the time, we do not possess because of the powerful pressure exerted by outside realities and by the images and concerns which fill our soul. Yes! **God can come to us and show Himself to the eyes of our heart.**[60]

---

[58] Jn 20:29.
[59] Cf. Saint Augustine, *Confessions*, III, 6, 11.
[60] Homily, Fatima, 13 May, 2010, w2.vatican.va.

St. Paul

That the God of our Lord Jesus Christ, the Father of glory, may give you a spirit of wisdom and revelation resulting in knowledge of Him. **May the eyes of your hearts be enlightened,** that you may know what is the hope to which he has called you, what are the riches of his glorious inheritance in the saints.[61]

— Jesus Gazes Upon the Rich Man —

The Gospels tell us that the gaze of Jesus has the power to reveal His love and to draw us to Himself. When the rich man came to Jesus, He "gazed at him and loved him, and said, 'there is one thing you lack. Go and sell everything you own and give the money to the poor, and you will have treasure in heaven; then come, follow me.'"[62]

What was the man's response? Pope Benedict XVI tells us: "The rich youth is not able to take this step. Notwithstanding that he has been the object of the loving gaze of Jesus, his heart is not able to detach itself from the many goods that he possessed."[63]

We, too, go to Jesus hoping He will help us find happiness, but based on our terms and expectations. Jesus also gazes at us, hoping to draw us to His Heart. Why do so few respond? Because **we are afraid of a love that calls for total surrender.** So we cling to our ways and then try to justify ourselves, as the rich young man did, by offering God our observance of the law.

_____

[61] Eph 1:17-18, cf. 1 Cor 2:9-10.
[62] Mk 10:21.
[63] Homily, 15 Oct., 2006, w2.vatican.va.

If we fail to enter the gaze of Jesus, we remain in our blindness, attached to our ways and distant from the love of God. We may believe that we have surrendered completely, but we have only fooled ourselves. The gaze is the encounter of love. When we are in love, the *other* is constantly in our hearts. When we are separated, we long for the presence of the other—for that precious togetherness when we can again enjoy the intimacy of gazing into our beloved's eyes. This gaze of lovers softens our hearts and allows us to put aside all else for the sake of our beloved.

After the rich man walked away sad because—as Pope Benedict XVI said—"his heart was unable to detach itself from his many possessions," Jesus looked at His disciples and said, "Truly I say to you, there is no one who has left house or brothers or sisters or mother or father or children or lands, for My sake and for the gospel, who will not receive a hundredfold now in this time … and in the age to come eternal life."[64]

By keeping our gaze fixed on Jesus, we allow Him to conquer our hearts; we avoid the sorrow of the rich young man and find true happiness in this life and the next.

12. The Gaze of My Crucified Eyes, Diary of a MOC

My children, climb the steps of My feet, My side, My Heart to reach the gaze of My crucified eyes.

•It is My gaze that will pierce your hearts and heal all pride, self-love, and vanity.

•It is My gaze that will awaken your hearts to love Love itself.

•It is through My crucified gaze that you will find the courage to continue on the path of life.

•It is through My crucified gaze that you will receive

---

[64] Mk 10: 29, 30.

> *the revelations of the mystery of suffering, which is the mystery of love.*
> *•It is through My crucified gaze that you will desire to be One with The Victim of Love; you will desire solely the Cross; you will desire the salvation of all your brothers and sisters and forget yourself; you will receive the power of the Holy Spirit to lay down your life as My sacrifice of love for the salvation of many.* (3/1/11)

Pope Francis, commented about St. Francis' relationship with Jesus:

Where did Francis's journey to Christ begin? It began with the gaze of the crucified Jesus. With letting Jesus look at us at the very moment that he gives his life for us and draws us to Himself. Francis experienced this in a special way in the Church of San Damiano, as he prayed before the cross which I too will have an opportunity to venerate. On that cross, Jesus is depicted not as dead, but alive! Blood is flowing from His wounded hands, feet, and side, but that blood speaks of life. Jesus' eyes are not closed but open, wide open: he looks at us in a way that touches our hearts. The cross does not speak to us about defeat and failure; paradoxically, it speaks to us about a death which is life, a death which gives life, for it speaks to us of love, the love of God incarnate, a love which does not die, but triumphs over evil and death. When we let the crucified Jesus gaze upon us, we are re-created, we become *a new creation.* Everything else starts with this: the experience of transforming grace, the experience of being loved for no merits of our own, in spite of our being sinners. That is why Saint Francis could say with Saint Paul: "Far be it for me to glory except in the cross of our Lord Jesus Christ" (Gal 6:14).[65]

St. Faustina wrote, "In difficult moments, I will fix my gaze upon the silent Heart of Jesus stretched on the Cross, and from the exploding flames of His merciful Heart, will flow down upon me power and strength to keep fighting."[66]

The gaze of Love is the path of intimacy that leads to the Sacred Heart. This is not only for women. While it is true that they are often more receptive, men, as Pope Francis reminds us, need to learn from them:

Women, in the Church and in the journey of faith, have had and now have a particular role in opening the doors to the Lord, in following him and communicating His face, because the gaze of faith always needs the simple and profound gaze of love. The Apostles and disciples find it harder to believe in the risen Christ. The women don't. Peter runs to the tomb, but stops at the empty tomb; Thomas must touch with His hands the wounds of the body of Jesus. Also in our faith journey, it is important to know and feel that God loves us; don't be afraid to love Him: faith is professed with the mouth and the heart, with words and with love.[67]

---

[65] Pastoral visit to Assisi, 4 Oct., 2013, w2.vatican.va.
[66] St. Faustina Kowalska, *Diary, Divine Mercy in My Soul*, n. 906.
[67] General audience, 3 Apr., 2013, w2.vatican.va.

13. You Are Insecure Because You Are Not Abandoned to Me, Diary of a MOC

My little one, I see how nervous and insecure you are because you are relying on yourself. Abandon yourself into My crucified embrace. Look in the depth of My eyes and contemplate the sorrow of your Beloved. Will you too, My little one, forsake Me? Do you not see how few souls I have that are completely abandoned in My Divine Will? I seek daughters and sons to be My instruments, to be My voice in the world, but I find very few willing to leave all to follow Me. (1/17/11)

14. I Wish to Heal your Blindness,[68] Diary of a MOC

Do you see the darkness that has consumed the hearts and minds of My people, the darkness that is consuming My Sanctuary? Do your eyes see the light of God that WILL consume this darkness or have you too become blinded by the darkness of the world? I wish to heal you of your blindness so that you can see the Son of Man in all His glory before you. To see is to believe. To see is to hope. To see is to become the beauty of what is revealed to you which is LOVE... (11/14/11)

The gaze of Jesus is the fire that moves us to love beyond our weakness. If we persevere with patience, the veils covering the eyes of our soul are removed, one-by-one, and we begin to see the gaze of Jesus—Love Crucified. This is this gaze that inflames our

---

[68] Cf. Lk 18:35-43, the blind man of Jericho.

hearts to love as He has loved us, by laying down our lives for Love and with Love. Saint Gemma writes:

> It would suffice for anyone to have just one of His glances. What force, what vigor he would feel! I feel that I would do anything for Him, to see Him content. The greatest torment would seem to me easy to bear supported by Him… **Oh, it is not possible to bear the sight of Him longing; and yet, how few are those who suffer with Him.** Very few, and Jesus finds Himself almost alone. It is so sad to see Jesus in the midst of sorrows! But how can one see Him in that state and not aid Him?[69]

The more we gaze upon the gaze of Jesus, the more we will see with His eyes and understand with His mind. It will also take us into a deeper union of suffering with Him. Through Him, with Him and in Him, we are now able to perceive the wounds of our brothers and sisters. We learn to gaze into their eyes and see into their hearts. By seeing only the exterior, we are deceived, and our perception of a person is easily distorted, leading us to judge. But **when we gaze into their hearts and see the wounds and the pain in the hearts of our brothers and sisters, we enter their pain and are moved to compassion.**

By suffering the pain of others with Jesus, we participate in His agony of love, and thus, begin to live the passion of His interior crucifixion. The removal of veils, therefore, brings our love for Jesus and our brothers and sisters to a deeper level than we've previously known.

This is exemplified by our Blessed Mother. She gazes upon us with the same gaze of her Son; therefore, as she tells us in a message

---

[69] Letter to Venerable Father Germano Ruoppolo, 9 Aug., 1900.

at Medjugorje, she looks into our hearts and sees our pain:

Dear children! As with motherly concern I look in your hearts, in them I see pain and suffering; I see a wounded past and an incessant search; I see my children who desire to be happy but do not know how. Open yourselves to the Father. That is the way to happiness, the way by which I desire to lead you. God the Father never leaves His children alone, especially not in pain and despair.[70]

—Keep Your Gaze Fixed on Jesus through Prayer—

Pope Benedict XVI taught the way "to be able to interpret the events of history and of our own life":

By raising our gaze to God's heaven in a constant relationship with Christ, by opening our hearts and our minds to Him in personal and communal prayer, we learn to see things in a new way and to grasp their truest meaning. Prayer is like an open window that allows us to keep our gaze turned toward God, not only for the purpose of reminding us of the goal toward which we are directed, but also to allow the will of God to illumine our earthly journey and to help us to live it with intensity and commitment.[71]

According to Ven. Fr. Felix Rougier, the gaze of the Father is love and tenderness; as we live in it, we are transformed in love:

---

[70] 2 Jan., 2012.
[71] General audience, 12 Sept., 2012, w2.vatican.va.

Loving attention consists of gazing on God, our Father. But when we look at Him, He also looks at us … that gaze fills me with joy, fortitude, and confidence; it gives me strength and sustains me. It tells me: "Love! Come! Climb to where I am and talk to me because you are my beloved son!" …

And if I yield to small temptations, that gaze pricks me like a thorn and purifies and cleanses me, because it is LOVE. And my soul remains closer than before to the heart of God, who wants it all for Himself. Oh, gaze of the Father, gaze of love, do not turn from me and my brothers! Make us pure, loving, happy and saintly![72]

After the Last Supper, Jesus took His disciples to Gethsemane so that they could be witnesses to the immensity of His love, "so that the world can see how much I love my Father."[73] In prayer, the Father and Jesus gazed at each other as they always do. This gaze strengthened Jesus to be faithful unto the Cross. But the disciples fell asleep. They thought they were prepared to give their lives for Jesus. Peter had said: "Though all become deserters because of you, I will never desert you."[74] But he had not learned to live in the gaze of the Father.

When we discipline ourselves to keep our gaze on Jesus' crucified love, our faith is perfected, and we can follow Him in our daily struggles all the way to the Cross.

---

[72] As cited by Ricardo Zimbro Levy in *Risking the Future*, 134-135. (Felix Rougier co-founded the Works of the Cross with Ven. Conchita).

[73] Jn 14:31.

[74] Mt 26:33.

15. My Gaze is Upon You, Diary of a MOC

I Am the Lord of Hosts. I Am your Redeemer and Savior who comes forth into the world from the love of our Father… I Am the Son of the living God. I came from heaven to earth because from the beginning of time I have known you… I have loved you as one with the Father and the Holy Spirit. ***I came upon the world to touch you, to gaze upon you and to suffer for you in My human nature, so that, through Me, you could come to know, touch and see the love of Abba for you.*** (12/12/12)

16. My Gaze Penetrates All Darkness, Diary of a MOC

My gaze is upon each of you. I see your struggles; I know your trials; I feel and suffer your sorrows; I collect your tears; I suffer with each of you.

Have perfect faith in the God that loves you… Believe in the power of your hidden ordinary lives lived through Me, with Me and in Me, ONE with Me, no longer two. Believe in My crucified love, in the power of My crucified gaze to penetrate all darkness. My gaze is upon you; allow Me to heal your wounds and purify all darkness.

My desire for you, My thirst for each of you, is to make you My living icons. My little ones, suffer all with Me, gazing upon My crucified love so that your suffering can perfect your faith and you can become My living chalices poured upon the world, redeeming, restoring and purifying with Me. Learn to wait upon the Lord, for that proves your love and perfects your trust. Be one in Me, with Mary as your

Mother. (8/11/12)

2-E

Temptations

—◦❖◦—

Temptations are not just bad thoughts; they are the weapons of a powerful invading force, of an enemy determined to destroy us. He attacks with **acedia** (spiritual sloth), which takes away our desire for all things related to the spiritual life; he attacks with **cravings** that overpower us, such as lust and greed; he attacks with an intense **turbulence** that confuses us during trials so that we lose perspective of reality and desire to run away from our commitments and relationships. Along with temptations, the enemy uses **fear of suffering.** He makes us think that if we surrender to temptation, our suffering will end and our struggles cease, but that if we resist, suffering will become unbearable. Then he enslaves us to sin and makes the path of the Lord appear too demanding. If our decisions are based on being comfortable and avoiding suffering, we will be defeated. We must believe that it is worth suffering for the sake of our union with Christ and trust that He is committed to us.

17. Be strong in Me, Diary of a MOC

> ***Be strong in Me.*** *Do not fall into the trap of believing that you are fighting this battle alone, for you are the hidden force united as one to My Mother, the angels and saints and each other. This knowledge will bring you strength.* (3/22/11)

According to St. Ignatius of Loyola, the devil acts like a military strategist. Before attacking a fortified city, he studies its defenses, looking for the weakest point. We need, therefore, to know our weaknesses and be resolved and disciplined to strengthen them under the Lord's authority. We need to be attentive to His orders and fight united with the brothers and sisters He gives us.

In times of trial, we are vulnerable to temptations that promise to resolve our problems. Like the Israelites in the desert, we are tempted to return to Egypt. It seemed better for them to be slaves than to persevere in the adverse conditions of the desert. To go forward, the Israelites needed to trust in God and to remain united as a people, no matter how difficult the way.

St. Ignatius also teaches that while we are under a storm we are being purified by fire and the Lord does not speak. Instead He gives us the grace to remain faithful to what He had told us previously. **Therefore, during the storm do not make changes in your life. Hold firm until calm returns**.

1 Cor 10:13

God is faithful, and he will not let you be tested beyond your strength, but with the testing he will also provide the way out so that you may be able to endure it.

Sir 2:1-6

My child, when you come to serve the Lord, prepare yourself for trials.

Be sincere of heart and steadfast, and do not be impetuous in time of adversity.

Cling to him, do not leave him, that you may prosper in your last days.

Accept whatever happens to you; in periods of humiliation be patient.

For in fire gold is tested, and the chosen, in the crucible of humiliation.

Trust in God, and he will help you; make your ways straight and hope in him

God permits temptations to perfect us in love and virtue. That is why we are tempted with what is most difficult for us, to be strengthened in the virtues we lack. For example, if we are impatient, we are tempted with situations that require the virtue of patience.

The Lord teaches us by example to endure trials. Temptations are our cross. When we carry it with Christ for the sake of love, He prepares us to be His witnesses. Saint Catherine of Siena writes about the trials of Jesus: "He practiced first what He afterward taught. … He fortified the minds of the disciples to confess the truth and to announce **this road, that is, the doctrine of Christ Crucified**." The Father told her: "(I give) the virtue of fortitude to whoever follows this road."[75]

God tells St Catherine that **He permits temptations so that we come to know Him and to know ourselves**:

---

[75] St. Catherine of Siena, *The Dialogue*, trans. Algar Thorold (London: Baronius Press Ltd. 2006), books.google.com.

One does not arrive at virtue except through knowledge of self, and knowledge of Me, which knowledge is more perfectly acquired in the time of temptation, because then man knows himself to be nothing, being unable to lift off himself the pains and vexations which he would flee; and he knows Me in his will, which is fortified by My goodness, so that it does not yield to these thoughts.

And he sees that My love permits these temptations, for the devil is weak, and by himself can do nothing unless I allow him. And I let him tempt because of love for you, and not through hatred,[76] **that you may conquer, and not that you may be conquered, and that you may come to a perfect knowledge of yourself, and of Me, and that virtue may be proved, for it is not proved except by its contrary.**[77]

The above teaching is supported by Judith 8:25-27[78]:

> Let us give thanks to the Lord our God who, as He tested our ancestors, is now testing us. Remember how He treated Abraham, all the ordeals of Isaac and all that happened to Jacob. … For as these ordeals were intended by Him to search their hearts, so now this is not vengeance that God exacts against us, but a warning inflicted by the Lord on those who are near His heart.

---

[76] God allows temptations because He loves us, to strengthen us and know Him and self.

[77] Id. *The Dialogue*, n.70.

[78] Cf. Hebrews 12:5-7,11-13.

2-F
Humility

—◆—

Just like each of you reading this Path, I desired to be humble, yet the Lord showed me that what I thought was humility, was actually false humility. He put these words in my heart:

18. Don't Hide Behind False Humility, Diary of a MOC

> *My little one, you must know who you are... It is I who am sending you and My Father who has chosen you... You are My witness, the light amidst the darkness...*
>
> *My daughter and pure vessel of the Father, you... must know the truth of who you are as the chosen vessel of the Father to lead this mission of evangelization. **Do not hide behind the mirror of false humility**. Proclaim... the truth and plan given to you.* (10/14/11)

My first reaction was to doubt this message. Is the Lord really telling me that I am chosen to be His witness, light amidst darkness, a pure vessel? Would I not fall into pride by believing this? Then, as I pondered the last words, *"Proclaim the truth and plan given to you,"* I saw them as a difficult challenge. I wanted to be humble and, for me, that meant to be quiet, to be in the background, definitely not to go out and proclaim!

The turning point came when I realized that I was not responding to God because I had an image of myself based on false humility. I could not believe that He would use me beyond what I was comfortable with. I was hiding *"behind the mirror of false humility."* Now God was telling me two essential things that I needed to know in order to have true humility and fulfill His mission:

    1) **"You must know who you are."**

    2) **"It is I who am sending you."**

We are all called to be Christ's witnesses, light in the darkness, pure vessels; we all need to identify the mirror of false humility behind which we are hiding.

We learn humility from God Himself. Yes, God is humble! Christ lived as one of us—little, vulnerable and obedient to the Father in everything. But He knew who He was and boldly faced all obstacles to fulfilling His mission. He did not shy away from speaking the truth for fear of reprisals or rejection. Through His humility, He allowed the Father to work wonders.

The gaze of the Father is upon the humble and contrite who have the audacity to believe and to carry out His will. He sees with delight His Son in them.[79]

19. Empty Self so that you can Be Filled, Diary of a MOC

> *You need to empty yourselves, being the nothing that you are, pure and empty, so that you can be filled with My living grace… "And from His fullness have we all received, grace upon grace"* (Jn 1:16). (3/9/09)

---

[79] Cf. Isa 66:2.

— Qualities of a Truly Humble Person —

a) A Humble Person Has Knowledge of God and Self.

When the Love Crucified Community began walking this Path, the Lord inspired us to go daily to kiss His crucified feet and to beg for the gift of knowledge. This was our focus as a community for an entire year before we could proceed with the Path. Knowledge of Jesus crucified made it possible for us to know ourselves with our miseries, weaknesses, wounds, disorders, fears and sins. At the same time, we grew in knowledge of who we truly are before God and the mission He has given us. Knowing our nothingness and knowing God's love for us are the foundations of the virtue of humility.

In the *Magnificat* prayer, Mary speaks of her lowliness: "He has looked with favor on his lowly servant," but she also proclaims the marvelous graces that God has bestowed upon her, "the Almighty has done great things for me." Mary's humility does not lead her to think negatively about herself. **She is humble because she knows God intimately and gives Him all the glory for who she is.**

20. Mary, in Her Humility, Proclaims the Greatness of the Lord, Diary of a MOC

> *"My soul proclaims the greatness of the Lord." My little one, these are the words from the mouth of My Mother as she enters the home of Elizabeth. Ponder these words with Me. My Mother lived her life in praise of the Father. She lived in the constant awareness of who the Father is. Her soul was in a constant state of awe.*
>
> *At the moment of the Incarnation, My human and divine Heart was fused as ONE with My*

Mother's and was consumed in the fire of love of the Holy Spirit. Together we proclaim the greatness of the Father.

In the knowledge of the greatness and majesty of God, Mary also had perfect knowledge of herself; therefore, she states that she is the handmaid of the Lord.

*My daughter, I desire that you **live more profoundly and perfectly in the knowledge of the grandeur, majesty and goodness of Abba,** our Father. In this way, you will live more perfectly as My handmaid. The perfect and holy handmaid of the Lord, Mary Most Holy, is moved by the Holy Spirit to serve her cousin, Elizabeth.*

*Do you understand, My little one, the direct correlation with the Mothers of the Cross? The Spirit of God moves the pure and humble of heart to serve as handmaids their brothers and sisters, sons and daughters, in the awareness of who God is, in order to become the handmaids of God. **The true knowledge of God will always move a soul to serve in pure humility.** You are the handmaids of the Lord; serve one another in the awareness of the immensity of God's love.* (09/18/11)

b) The Humble Person Speaks the Truth and Lives in the Truth.

Jesus reveals who He is: "I am the light of the world; he who follows me will not walk in darkness" (Jn 8:12). The Pharisees condemned Him for speaking the truth: "You are bearing witness to yourself; your testimony is not true" (Jn 8:13). Jesus insists on the truth: "Even if I do bear witness to myself, my testimony is true, for I know where I have come from and where I am going" (Jn 8:14). Jesus does not hide in false humility. He shows us true humility by speaking openly about who He is and why He came into the world. We also need to live our authentic identity in Christ knowing where we came from, who we are and our mission. Then it will be God who speaks and moves through us. Humble people do not have their own agenda; they are committed to their God-given mission.

The Lord wants us to have the humble boldness to speak the truth as He did. In humility there is no fear, there is confidence—not in self, but in God. He said to our community, *do not fear to speak the truth of the sin in the hearts of My people with courage and love and call them to repentance at My crucified feet.* Therefore, we need to know our fears and their root system so that they do not become a barrier that prevents us from living and speaking the truth:

- Fear rooted in shame, guilt. Adam and Eve hid from God after eating from the tree (cf. Gen 3:8).
- Fear rooted in low self-esteem, feeling incapable of fulfilling God's will for our lives. In the Parable of the talents, the servant hid his talent in the ground (cf. Mt 25:25).
- Fear rooted in self-love, lack of trust. Peter follows Jesus at a distance unable to defend him (cf. Mt 26:58).

Saints are often stereotyped as persons who, due to humility, shrink from telling the truth that needs to be told in difficult situations. No wonder St. Therese said that if the saints came back to Earth, most of them would not recognize themselves when reading what we have written about them. She confronted situations that everyone else tiptoed around, and she was willing to bear the consequences. Her sister Celine observed that "She was not soft or easygoing, but people turned to her out of a natural need for the truth." Therese loved enough to challenge souls to face the truth. This is her advice:

> We should never allow kindness to degenerate into weakness. When we have scolded someone with just reason, we must leave the matter there, without allowing ourselves to be touched to the point of tormenting ourselves for having caused pain or at seeing one suffer and cry. To run after the afflicted one to console her does more harm than good. Leaving her to herself forces her to have recourse to God in order to see her faults and humble herself. Otherwise, accustomed to receiving consolation after a merited reprimand, she will always act, in the same circumstances, like a spoiled child, screaming and kicking until her mother comes to wipe away the tears.[80]

Therese could be truthful to others because she first sought the truth about herself. She said, "I would prefer a thousand times to receive reproofs than to give them to others."[81] It is this humility that steers correction towards the healing truth of Christ.

---

[80] Therese of Lisieux, as quoted in Christopher O'Mahony, ed. and trans., *St. Therese of Lisieux: By Those Who Knew Her* (Dublin: Veritas Publications, 1975), 51.

[81] *Story of a Soul: The Autobiography of Saint Thérèse of Lisieux*, 239, https://books.google.com

c) A Humble Person Lives to Please God Above All.

St. Paul knew that we learn to be human by being one with Jesus, so he exhorts us:

> Have this mind among yourselves, which was in Christ Jesus, who, though He was in the form of God, did not count equality with God a thing to be grasped, but emptied himself, taking the form of a servant, being born in the likeness of men. And being found in human form he humbled himself and became obedient unto death, even death on a cross. Therefore, God has highly exalted him.[82]

St. Paul links Christ's humility to His obedience "unto death on a cross" because He lives solely to please the Father. We may think that we are obedient, but if we are not obedient unto the cross, we remain wimpy, mediocre, people pleasers and enablers. This is not true obedience nor is it humility; it's spiritual adolescence. Jesus "emptied himself" to teach us the way. As we have learned in this chapter, we must be willing to pull out the entire root system of our sins, fears, and disordered tendencies to come to know who we are and live to please God. This is what the Path is meant to do.

---

[82] Phil 2:5-9.

21. Allow Your Disorders to Come to the Light, Diary of a MOC

> *Trust; and with patient endurance,* ***allow all your*** ***disorders to come to the Light****. It is only in this way that you can be made pure in the furnace of God's love.* (8/6/13)

— Beyond "Being Nice" —

Jesus did not empty himself to be a "nice person" but to fulfill the mission of the Father. In fact, the word "nice" is not found in the Bible.

Most of us want to be "nice people," not realizing that it means to live in bondage to what others may think of us. We go through life seeking acceptance and in fear of being rejected or ignored. As a result, we seldom speak the truth. Dr. Raymond Richmond writes about humility in his excellent site, ChastitySF.com:

The virtue of humility frequently gets confused with "being nice." The truth is, Christ was humble but He wasn't "nice." He loved us—He spoke the truth—He was the truth—but He wasn't *nice*. To be nice is to accept anything, even sin itself. Why? Well, the deep unconscious motive for being nice is fear, the fear that, if you speak the truth you will offend someone who will then reject you and abandon you. To love is to speak the truth and, with non-judgmental bluntness, to call a sin a sin. …

To live in humility is to live always in total confidence of God's love, protection, and guidance and therefore to have no concern for yourself when others insult you—or praise you. Secure in God's love, you don't have to base your identity on whether or not others acknowledge you.[83]

Our self-image cannot depend on what others think of us. As St. Francis said, "What I am before God, I am." Our Blessed Mother was able to glorify God and proclaim who she is because she wasn't concerned that Elizabeth might think she was conceited. Her heart was centered in God, and her desire was to please Him.

— Not a Doormat —

Jesus commands us to take our Cross and follow Him, but that does not mean that we condone abusive behavior. To allow others to use us as "doormats," or to be unable to stand up for ourselves is to live in bondage and not in humility. Jesus came to set us free from disorders, fears, wounds and dysfunctions. If we remain in them, we cannot grow in humility.

> Luke 4:18
> The Spirit of the Lord is upon me, because he has anointed me to preach good news to the poor. He has sent me to proclaim release to the captives and recovering of sight to the blind, to set at liberty those who are oppressed.

---

[83] http://www.chastitysf.com/4humility.htm.

d) A Humble Person Is Able to Exercise Power and Authority.

Contrary to popular belief, **humility is compatible with the exercise of power and authority.** In truth, one who is humble operates with greater power and authority, that of the Holy Spirit. St Paul, writing to the Colossians, prays that they are "strengthened with all power" (Col 1: 11). That is why the humble do not cling to earthly powers, but if God calls them to a position of authority they exercise it with humility for His glory.

Through His humility, Jesus manifested the power and authority of God. The Gospel of Luke says, "They were astonished at His teaching, for His word was with authority.[84]" and, "with authority and power He commands the unclean spirits, and they come out" (Lk 4:36).

Jesus wants to give us His power; but to use it well, we need His humility. He said, "You will receive power when the Holy Spirit comes upon you." Jesus expects His followers to use this power not for themselves, but for His mission: "you shall be My witnesses" (Acts 1:8). This is humility.

The Scriptures are full of humble men and women acting in the power and authority of the Holy Spirit. In the Acts of the Apostles we see countless examples: "And with great power, the apostles were giving testimony to the resurrection of the Lord Jesus" (Acts 4:33). We see men performing miracles, "Stephen, full of grace and power, was performing great wonders and signs among the people" (Acts 6:8). We too need power and humility—It takes more of both to be His witnesses in our ordinary hidden lives than to perform miracles.

---

[84] Lk 4:32.

22. In St. Joseph's Humility God Manifests His Power,
Diary of MOC

> *St. Joseph centered his life in prayer and silence. He meditated on the Word of God daily in humility, seeking no places of honor for himself. Hidden, he remained content. Through the humility and purity of his heart, he was able to see the purity and holiness of Mary. When he learned that Mary was with Child, through his humility, he entered the hiddenness of his heart and sought to know the Will of God. This is what makes a great man: to seek the Will of God in all things.* **My power and strength were manifested in his docility and tenderness of heart.** *When men let go of their human tendency to control and rely completely on Me, they will begin to possess the true power of God. St. Joseph embraced Mary as the Mother of God and believed in humility. He embraced the mission of God revealed and contained in Mary Most Humble.* (3/19/11)

23. Humility Allows Us to Become Christ's Sacrifice of Love,
Diary of a MOC

> *You will desire the salvation of all your brothers and sisters and forget yourself; you will receive the power of the Holy Spirit to lay down your life as My sacrifice of love for the salvation of many.* (3/1/11)

24. Be Steadfast, Diary of a MOC

> ***Be steadfast… suffering all with Me*** *in My sacrifice of love and you will witness the power of Love… You will grow in great power and strength, not in the ways of the world, but in the ways of God.* (3/30/12)

e) A Humble Person Has Courage and Zeal for the House of the Lord.

Jesus told Peter, "Put out into the deep and let down your nets for a catch" (Lk 5:4). Jesus is calling each of us into the deep. It takes courage to leave the safety of the shore and live in the depth of faith, hope, and love, where we no longer are in control. Peter had the humility to let go of his plans, his securities, even of his expertise as a fisherman, and swim against the current of the world in obedience to the Lord.

Don Mauro Giuseppe wrote about the saints:

They had imperfections but they were filled with courage. They were humble in that they lived radically the call to love and gave themselves completely.[85]

Humility opens the way for courage. A humble person has renounced his ego for the Lord and can do what is most difficult. He can listen and respond. Such a person flies on the wings of the Holy Spirit to union with God.

---

[85] "Dom Mauro Giuseppe Lepori," *Magnificat,* Sept., 2013.

f) A Humble Person Has Childlike Innocence.

As a child trusts in his daddy, we live in complete dependence on God because we know His love and are able to trust Him.

> Isaiah 66:12-13
> For thus says the Lord: … and you shall suck, you shall be carried upon her hip, and dandled upon her knees. As one whom his mother comforts, so I will comfort you.

As a mother, I could relate to this Scripture because we carry our children on our hips and we place them on our knees to comfort and play with them. Have we come to know the love of our Abba like this? Do we believe that He carries us on His hips, that He delights in us and comforts us? As His sons and daughters, do we live in the security of knowing that we are in the palms of His hands? Only a person with childlike innocence knows the Father in this intimate way. This moved Jesus to exclaim: "I thank thee, Father, Lord of heaven and earth, that thou hast hidden these things from the wise and understanding and revealed them to babes."[86] Jesus teaches that our salvation hinges not only on having the humility of a child but also on welcoming and protecting it in others.

> Matthew 18:3-6
> Truly, I say to you, unless you turn and become like children, you will never enter the kingdom of heaven. **Whoever humbles himself like this child**, he is the greatest in the kingdom of heaven.

---

[86] Mt 11:25.

Whoever receives one such child in my name receives me; but **whoever causes one of these little ones who believe in me to sin**, it would be better for him to have a great millstone fastened round his neck and to be drowned in the depth of the sea.

Having the innocence of a child also means that we are so immersed in trust of God that we advance in His will without giving room to fear or to human considerations. This is exemplified by David when he stepped forward to fight Goliath confident that he could defeat the Philistine with a sling and five stones "in the name of the Lord of hosts."[87]

25. David Trusted in God with the Innocence of a Child, Diary of a MOC

*The Holy Spirit brought to my mind David and Goliath. How could it be that the little one, who could not wear the armor of the mighty warriors, defeated the giant? The ways of God are never the ways of the world. He was wearing the armor of God, and he possessed the power of God. He trusted in God with the innocence of a child. God defeated the enemy through His humble vessel so that all glory would be given to God, not man. **The enemy will be conquered and all things will be made new but never in the ways of the world.** God has chosen to give the sword of righteousness to His little mustard seed.*

You must remain little, insignificant and

---

[87] Cf. 1 Sam 17:45.

innocent, drinking the pure milk of the words I bring to you (cf. 1Pet 2). ...Live with the innocence of a child the mission given to you. Be little, pure and humble, be nothing, and it is I Who will do the impossible. Trust with the innocence of a child. ...for you are nothing, but I am God, and I will use My little ones to confound the mighty ones of the world. Believe in the power of My Cross and the power of My Precious Blood, for it is only through the Triumph of My Cross that all darkness will be conquered. Live, love and suffer as ONE with Me; and you will become the sword that will pierce this darkness. (11/12/11)

A humble person does not try to prop-up his identity bragging about titles, achievements or whom they know... Jesus said, *"Do not presume to say to yourselves, 'We have Abraham as our ancestor'; for I tell you, God is able from these stones to raise up children to Abraham."*[88]

g) A Humble Person Is Transparent.

A humble person is transparent, without masks, not pretending to be who he is not nor an image of what others want him to be. Dom Mauro Giuseppe Lepori writes about St. Peter:

He always leads us to Jesus. He unites us to Jesus because he never permitted his own fragility to separate his heart from Christ, even when he denied Him. Peter's

---

[88] Mt 3:9.

transparency is part of the Gospel of the good news of the redemption of Christ.

The story of the miraculous catch reveals the heart of Peter. Jesus tells him to go back into the deep to catch fish. Peter at first resists, because, being an experienced fisherman, he knows it is not the time to fish. Yet he obeys saying, "Master, we toiled all night and took nothing! But at your word I will let down the nets." When the miracle confronts him with his lack of trust in the Messiah and his attachment to his ways, he repents and "falls down at Jesus' knees." Imagine this big fisherman, this macho tough man, falling at the feet of Jesus to ask for forgiveness. He says, "Depart from me, for I am a sinful man, O Lord" (Lk 5:8). This is transparency; and Jesus makes this imperfect but humble man, the first Pope!

No one is humble and transparent from the beginning of this journey. We grow in these virtues as we submit to the Spirit and live the Path in our daily trials and situations. These are opportunities to discover Jesus, as Peter did, and to harmonize our thoughts, words, and actions with His in a constant intimate relationship.

26. Blossoms of Humility, Diary of a MOC

One day, when I entered the courtyard of my home, I noticed that our gardenia plant had new blossoms. I immediately went near to smell the flowers and was filled with joy by its fragrance. Later, as I prayed in my room, Jesus taught me:

My daughter, a plant grows in beauty when the flower begins to blossom. The gardenia is a lovely plant in your garden, but the day you walked in your garden and saw her flowers, you took greater attention of her and were filled with joy. She called you, through the lovely flower, to stoop down and smell her. This is an analogy of the human soul when she begins to blossom in true humility. She brings great joy to the Father; and He stoops down to smell her fragrance of humility, thus filling the Heart of God with joy.

My Lord how does a soul grow in the beauty of humility?

In order for a plant to blossom, she must be watered, nurtured and live under the rays of the sun. A soul, too, must be nurtured in daily prayer, given the food of the Eucharist, pruned in the Sacrament of Penance and live in the light of the Holy Spirit. But in order for humility to kill the deep roots of self-love, pride and vanity in a soul, she must come to My Cross for her heart to be plowed with My thorns and wounds. (3/11)

27. The Red Rose of Humility, Diary of a MOC

Mary: *Humility is the rose of pure fragrance that delights the Heart of the Father. Its petals open and expand revealing the beauty of its interior life. Humility in its perfection is red; that is why I reveal to you a red rose.* **Humility is clothed in the Precious Blood of my Son.**
–Its pure fragrance is love in suffering.
–Its beauty is Love crucified.
–Its petals are obedience, poverty, faith, silence, recollection, honesty, truth, innocence, boldness, zeal for the house of the Lord, tenderness, kindness, perseverance...

All its petals have blossomed from the purity of the Sacred Heart of Jesus. The radiance and beauty of each petal is the purity of God. Be the roses of humility at the foot of the throne of the Father. (8/22/12)

Pray the *Litany of Humility,* see prayers at the end of this book.

I looked for compassion, but there was none,
for comforters, but found none.
Ps.69:21

Chapter Three

Passage Through the Pierced Side of Jesus

"The side of Christ is the door that leads to His Heart"
Saint Bernard of Clairvaux

At our Lord's feet, we began to awaken to His love and to self-knowledge. This was a necessary preparation, but the Lord does not want us to stay at His feet. He wants to bring us into His Heart to become one with Him.

We reach the Lord's Heart through the passage created by the sword. This passage is a journey—a necessary process—that transforms our hearts from being like rocky soil, hard and infertile, into docile and tender hearts. This process is painful because our hearts must be pierced like those of Jesus and Mary. As we are made ready to enter His Sacred Heart, the healing of our wounds enters a deeper level; and we are tempted to find excuses to turn back and to follow Him at a comfortable distance. We need to persevere united with our Blessed Mother.

28. My Mother's Pierced Heart Was Fused to Mine, Diary of a MOC

> *The piercing with the lance created your passage into My Heart. My Heart was opened for all to enter with the piercing of the lance. My mother received this same piercing in her heart and suffered the pain and sorrow I could no longer suffer. This piercing fused our hearts together as ONE for all eternity. This is why Mary is the gate to enter My Love Crucified and My Heart. The Holy Spirit lifts you from My feet into the passage in My side. It is in this passage created by the spear that you are perfected in My virtues.*
>
> *Your soul needs to be clothed in the virtues of true humility and purity before entering the furnace of My Heart. It is the work of the Holy Spirit, with My mother, that forms these virtues in your heart and soul.*
>
> *Humility is acquired through constant knowledge of your misery and My mercy and love. You received the gift of knowledge at My feet, and*

you must always maintain yourself wrapped in this gift.

Purity of mind, heart, soul, and body is attained as you come in contact with Me, Who am all pure and holy. My mother is all purity, and it is she who will dress you in the white gown of purity.

She will cleanse you, little by little, of all the mud that remains on you after I pulled you out of the quicksand of your misery with the wood of My Cross. Through humility and purity, you will quickly attain perfection in all the other virtues if you persevere in prayer. (03/04/11)

3-A
Suffer with Him

— We Need to Touch His Wounds —

As we enter the passage to the Heart of Jesus, our own hearts are purified by direct contact with His wounds. Saint Bernard writes:

The secret of his heart is laid bare in the wounds of his body; we see revealed the great mystery of our God's infinite goodness; … the merciful tenderness of our God[89]

---

[89]. St Bernard of Clairvaux, Sermon LXI, *On the Song of Songs*, 41, http://www.apostleshipofprayer.net.

However, unless we touch His wounds, love remains an idea in our minds with no power to heal our hearts. **By touching His wounds, we touch His love**, the love by which He laid down His life for us. This is illustrated in the story of St. Thomas' unbelief. Because he had not touched the wounds of the Lord, he was unable to believe: "Unless I see in His hands the print of the nails, and place my finger in the mark of the nails, and place my hand in His side, I will not believe."[90] Thomas' cynicism reveals his hardness of heart. Then Jesus appears to him and invites him to touch His wounds. With this touch, Thomas receives a profound healing. By touching Jesus' wounds, he touches His incomprehensible love for him, a love that suffers all and continues loving even when Thomas had abandoned Him and then refused to believe in Him. When Thomas' wounded heart comes to know Jesus' love directly through His wounds, he exclaims: "My Lord and my God!" From that time on, the resurrection is no longer for him a story told by others.

Like St. Thomas, we are unable to be healed and transformed until we touch Christ's wounds that reveal His love for us. But we should not wait for an apparition. He tells us, "Blessed are those who have not seen and yet believe." He wants us to touch His wounds in our "ordinary" life.

---

[90] Jn 20:24-29.

— How Do We Touch His Wounds? —

We touch Christ's wounds **by uniting our sufferings with His**. This is the necessary process to union with God. St Paul tells us that there is a condition for us to be "children of God" and "fellow heirs with Christ": **"provided we suffer with Him."**[91] This condition exists because only through our own sufferings are we able to come personally to touch the sufferings of Christ. You might ask, "Why do I need to know personally the sufferings of Christ?" Because **when we touch Jesus' sufferings, we touch Love itself.**

For example, if we never suffer the pain of rejection, we can never come to know and experience the rejection that Jesus suffered. Therefore, only through our sufferings can we experience the sufferings of our Lord. Because this experience is the key to understanding the value of suffering, the Lord told us, **"Receive the treasured pearl of suffering."**

29. Love on Earth Must Be United to Suffering,
Diary of a MOC

> *My daughter, the purest love on earth must be united to suffering. I came from heaven to earth to suffer in expiation for the sins of the world. This is love.*
>
> *Pure love gives itself solely because of love. The love of the Trinity is pure love; therefore, the Father gives His life by giving to the world His only begotten Son. The Holy Spirit—this most pure love—flows, igniting the hearts to suffer with Me, so that they can enter in Love.*
>
> *The Cross, without My Sacred Heart, is useless*

---

[91] Rom 8:12-17.

> *suffering brought about by sin. But suffering united to My Cross is new life; it is participation in the work of redemption, which is participation in the life of the Trinity.*
>
> *These mysteries can be grasped only by a humble heart... Suffer all with perfect faith in My crucified love.* (1/13/11)

The saints are witnesses to the power of suffering with Christ for the sake of His love. St. Therese of Lisieux writes, "Suffering itself becomes the greatest of joys when we seek it as a precious treasure."[92] Jesus told St. Faustina: "There is but one price at which souls are bought, and that is suffering united to My suffering on the Cross. Pure love understands these words; carnal love will never understand them."[93]

Saint Louis Grignion de Montfort

God does not take account of what you suffer but of how you suffer. To suffer much but badly is to suffer like the condemned. To suffer much with valor, but for a bad cause is to suffer as martyrs of the devil; to suffer little or much for God, is to suffer like the saints.[94]

Later we will examine how to heal our wounds from the past by suffering them with Jesus. For now, we will focus on how to suffer our daily trials with Him.

What does it mean to suffer with someone? The Holy Spirit brought my memory back to a few years ago when my sister was

---

[92] *Story of a Soul*, Ch. 9, books.google.com.
[93] Saint Faustina Kowalska, *Diary, Divine Mercy in My Soul,* n.324.
[94] *Friends of the Cross* (Montfort Publications, 1995).

diagnosed with breast cancer. Her suffering pierced my heart to the point that I seemed to suffer more than she did, but my focus was not on my pain, but on hers. My heart was bleeding and crying when I accompanied my sister to her doctor visits and to Cleveland for her surgery. Her suffering and mine were one!

This taught me much about suffering. **To suffer with someone is very different than to suffer alone. When we suffer with someone, our focus is not on ourselves but on the other.** This is also true when we suffer with Christ. Therefore, if I want my life to be centered on Him, I need to unite my suffering to His and enter His suffering. His suffering will reveal His personal love for me. This union of suffering is the key to embracing my suffering as a treasured pearl.

Christ suffers all that we suffer because He loves us. Once we know this, we can respond by entering His Heart, receiving His tears and allowing Him to touch us with His wounds. Union with Christ in suffering and love teaches us that, if we, or someone we love, is suffering, we don't just "offer it up"; we actually enter into the suffering with him or her. This type of suffering is born of love and brings about intimacy.

3-A-1
— *Difference Between*
"Offer Up" and "Suffer With" —

Many of us were taught as children to "offer up" our hardships to the Lord. Although a good practice, sometimes we "offered up" to God in frustration, not knowing what else to do, hoping that God would use our suffering for some good. However, Jesus does not just "offer up"; He enters our suffering and intimately suffers with us because He loves us. Likewise, St. Paul did not tell us just to offer up our suffering to Christ but to "suffer with Him."[95] Yes, we need to offer up and to suffer patiently, but **to suffer with Him draws us into intimacy with Christ.** Pope Benedict XVI explains it in this way:

> To accept the other who suffers means that I take up his suffering in such a way that it becomes mine also. Because it has now become a shared suffering, though, in which another person is present, this suffering is penetrated by the light of love. The Latin word *con-solatio*, "consolation," expresses this beautifully. It suggests being with the other in his solitude, so that it ceases to be solitude."[96]

To illustrate how we can unite our suffering with Christ's, I share two life examples which touched my own heart. The first one is the devastating experience of a woman who suffered the rejection of her husband. The second is the experience of a Mother of the Cross, a woman from our community, who suffered the ordinary difficulty of trying to feed a son who refused to eat. Separately, the

---

[95] Rom 8:12-17.
[96] Encyclical *Spe Salvi* (In Hope We are Saved, 2007), n.38.

two examples are so different that they may appear to have nothing in common; but when viewed together, they show how ALL suffering—even the most ordinary trials of motherhood—can be united to our Lord's suffering and, therefore, become a source of immense grace.

— Her Husband's Rejection Takes Her to Jesus —

The first example involves a beautiful woman whose husband had told her, "I don't love you anymore. I want to leave." As I looked at her, I saw her love and the immense suffering of abandonment and rejection in her heart. I thought to myself, "My Lord, what can I possibly say to this woman?" All I had to share is what the Lord had taught me about suffering and how I do my best to live this knowledge in my own life. Praying to be able to help her transform her deep hurt into love, I said to her, "Let's walk together into the life of Jesus through the Gospels to come into contact with His suffering of rejection and abandonment."

First, we encountered the sorrows of Jesus when He returned to His hometown. His family and friends, angered by His teaching, rejected Him. "They rose up and put Him out of the city, and led Him to the brow of the hill on which their city was built, that they might throw Him down headlong." [97] As a result, He could not perform many miracles there. Can you imagine the pain of rejection in Jesus' Heart as His hometown kicked him out and even tried to kill Him?

We also pondered how Judas, one of Jesus' closest friends and a disciple, betrayed Him with a kiss. I asked her, "Have you ever taken the time to ponder the sorrow of our Lord's Heart as He

---

[97] Lk 4:29.

received the kiss of betrayal? Can you see His tears and feel His sorrow through your own pain?"

We then went to the foot of the Cross. I encouraged her to imagine Jesus looking down and seeing how few had followed Him to the end. "Can you see the gaze in Jesus' eyes as He sees only His Mother, one apostle, and a few women? After He had loved, healed, performed so many miracles and completely given Himself to so many, in the end, there were only a few standing by Him." Then I asked her, "As you suffer the pain of being abandoned by your husband, can you enter Jesus' pierced Heart and feel His suffering from abandonment?" I said, "Jesus knows personally the pain of rejection, and He is now suffering your pain with you. Will you suffer with Him by uniting your sorrows to His in order to obtain graces for your husband?"

We then discussed Our Lord's discourse in John 6, when, nearing the end of His life, He taught the people that He is the "Bread of Life." "As a result of this many of His disciples withdrew and were not walking with Him anymore" (Jn 6:66). We contemplated and entered the Suffering Heart of Jesus as He watched those He loved abandon Him. I explained that Jesus continues to suffer the pain of our rejection. "How many times do we reject His love, especially in the Eucharist? How many consecrated souls have left Him? How many Catholics have left the Church?"

She took all this into her heart; and, as a warrior of love, she fully accepted the power of her suffering of abandonment and united it completely to the sufferings of Jesus' Heart. She was now determined to suffer with Jesus for her husband. Month-after-month she continued to love him in spite of his rejection of her. She had a core group of friends praying with her and for her and her husband during this difficult time. These sisters gave her the strength to persevere through her suffering until they had the joy of seeing the husband come home. Their relationship was healed, and to this day they enjoy a happy marriage.

— We All Suffer Rejection at Some Point —

Our relationships will not always be healed as we would hope. We all know someone whose marriage was not restored even after years of suffering all with Christ. But in all instances, God permits our wounds for something much greater. For example, I have a good friend, married for over thirty years, whose husband left her and has not returned. I said to her: "Your marriage was not a mistake. God chose him as your husband from the beginning of time. But now his soul is in danger. You were chosen by God to be His vessel to help save his soul. By suffering and uniting with Jesus your wound of abandonment, you will obtain for your husband the graces of salvation."

30. I Was Abandoned, Diary of a MOC

> *I was abandoned by My beloved three apostles in the Garden of Gethsemane; but Abba came to console Me through the angel, and I saw each of you, My disciples of consolation and reparation. Abandon yourself simply and daily into My crucified embrace and you will never experience abandonment because you will possess ALL. I suffered abandonment so that you could enter into the fullness of life in the Blessed Trinity, living in the loving embrace of the Father, Son, and Holy Spirit. I call you, My family of LC, to suffer all with Me so*

> *that you can serve as My balm to alleviate My pangs of seeing so many of My children, especially My consecrated souls, abandon Me. At the same time, as My disciples of reparation, your suffering as one with Me saves many from the fires of Gehenna.* (3-9-11)

We need to beware of our tendency to become absorbed in our sufferings because that is the way Satan enters our wounds to fill them with resentment, division, and even hatred. We need to appeal to the power of the Cross so that the Holy Spirit moves us out of our self-absorption and directs our attention to our Lord's suffering. We must be careful not to withdraw our gaze from Him and into ourselves. When we are suffering, we need to remind ourselves to LOOK AT JESUS. We need to ask ourselves, "How did He suffer this pain? How does He continue to suffer this pain?"

Our pride wants to hold onto our wounds so that we can continue to resent and hate those that have hurt us. Satan uses this tendency to keep us in bondage. But when we watch Jesus suffer our pain and we meet His gaze, He lifts us out of the pit of our wound, heals us, and draws us to Himself. Let us remember that Jesus, too, was abandoned even in death; but that He will never abandon us. Lived this way our wounds become a passage into His Sacred Heart.

Let us then give thanks to the Lord for our wounds, for all that He is doing and permitting through them. By embracing our vocation even in trials and suffering, we allow the Lord to transform us into new men and women.

— Her Child's Unwillingness to Eat —

The second example is the experience of a young Mother of the Cross from our Love Crucified community. Her experience illustrates how our Lord wants us to suffer everything with Him so that even the smallest trials of everyday life can change us and impact the world.

One day, while trying to feed her son, the young woman became very frustrated. The child would spit the food out or throw it on the floor. Then she remembered the teaching on the value of suffering ALL with Jesus and began praying to the Holy Spirit for help to overcome her anger with love. In a moment of grace, the frustrated mother was filled with an incredible understanding. She made the correlation between her son rejecting the food she was giving him and the many Catholics who reject Jesus in the Eucharist. Through her suffering, she was able to turn her attention to Jesus and suffer with Him. The most ordinary task of feeding a child was transformed for this mother into a moment of immense grace.

This is the power of suffering even the smallest trials with the Lord. The young mother was able to enter intimacy with Jesus and receive the patience she needed with her son.

31. I Desire and Need for You to Suffer with Me,
Diary of a MOC

> ***Why do I desire and need for you to suffer with Me?*** *It is through My suffering that you come to know Love. Love is purified in suffering, but My suffering is pure love; therefore, when you suffer with Me, your love is purified in Me. This suffering with Me and loving with Me brings new life, a new creation.*
>
> ***By allowing all suffering to draw you into My sufferings and sorrows, you will come to know Love.*** *My Sacred Heart is pure love. You were created for Love; but how few, My little one, come to know Love and enter the joy of living in Love.* (8/27/11)

Suffering is very difficult for us, so we want to reject it. But the Lord teaches us that He permits suffering to bring us to union with His love.

32. Acceptance of Suffering, Diary of a MOC

> *This is most pleasing to Me.* ***Trust, for there isn't a suffering I permit that will not bring you into the union of love I desire.*** *Trust in the power of suffering all as ONE with Me. It is this power that will set the world on fire with My Spirit.* (7/9/12)

— Jesus Continues to Suffer with Us —

Jesus continues to suffer with us because He continues to love. St. Augustine writes:

> Christ is now exalted above the heavens, but he still suffers on earth all the pain that we, the members of his body, have to bear. He showed this when he cried out from above: "Saul, Saul, why do you persecute me? and when he said: I was hungry and you gave me food."[98]

When we unite our suffering with Jesus, we quench His thirst for pure love. He then deepens His union with us and heals our self-centeredness. Pope Benedict XVI writes:

> "Christ loved me and gave himself for me" (Gal 2:20). In the face of such disinterested love, we find ourselves asking, filled with wonder and gratitude: What can we do for him? What response shall we give him? Saint John puts it succinctly: "By this we know love, that he laid down his life for us; and we ought to lay down our lives for the brethren" (1 Jn 3:16**). Christ's passion urges us to take upon our own shoulders the sufferings of the world**, in the certainty that God is not distant or far removed from man and his troubles. On the contrary, He became one of us in order to suffer with man in an utterly real way —in flesh and blood. … hence in all human suffering, we are joined by One who

---

[98] *Sermons of St. Augustine,* as cited in the Office of readings of the Solemnity of the Ascension.

experiences and carries that suffering with us.[99]

In the encyclical *Spe Salvi,* the same Pope wrote:

To suffer with the other and for others; to suffer for the sake of truth and justice; to suffer out of love and in order to become a person who truly loves—these are fundamental elements of humanity, and to abandon them would destroy man himself. Yet once again the question arises: are we capable of this? Is the other important enough to warrant my becoming, on his account, a person who suffers? Does truth matter to me enough to make suffering worthwhile? Is the promise of love so great that it justifies the gift of myself? In the history of humanity, it was the Christian faith that had the particular merit of bringing forth within man a new and deeper capacity for these kinds of suffering that are decisive for his humanity. The Christian faith has shown us that truth, justice, and love are not simply ideals, but enormously weighty realities. It has shown us that God—Truth and Love in person—desired to suffer for us and with us. St. Bernard of Clairvaux coined the marvelous expression: ***God cannot suffer, but he can suffer with. Man is worth so much to God that He Himself became man in order to suffer with man*** in an utterly real way—in flesh and blood—as is revealed to us in the account of Jesus' Passion. Since in all human suffering we are joined by One who experiences and carries that suffering with us, *consolatio* is present in all suffering, the consolation of God's compassionate love—and so the star of hope rises. ... But

---

[99] Address to youth after Stations of the Cross, Madrid, Spain, 19 Aug., 2011, w2.vatican.va.

in truly great trials, where I must make a definitive decision to place the truth before my own welfare, career, and possessions, I need the certitude of that true, great hope of which we have spoken here. For this, too, we need witnesses—martyrs—who have given themselves totally in order to show us the way—day after day.[100]

33. Will You Suffer with Me to Save Souls?
Diary of a MOC

> *Will you suffer with Me? Will you unite with My suffering to purchase the redemption of many? You see, My suffering and resurrection have purchased the salvation of the world; but My Father, from the beginning of time, willed for the fulfillment of salvation to come through My Body, the Church. Therefore,* **the salvation of many souls is dependent on your response to suffer with Me.** (11/10/10)

We must ponder the mystery of the words above. The Lord tells us that the salvation of many souls is dependent on our response to suffer with Him. Do we realize the significance of this truth in our lives? Our sufferings united with Jesus' are the means to help save the souls that God has entrusted to us. We truly are His body, extending His love and salvation to them. God needs us to save souls! Venerable Conchita lived this truth so deeply that she clamored, "Jesus, Savior of mankind, save them, save them!"

---

[100] Pope Benedict XVI, *Spe Salvi*, n.39-40. w2.vatican.va

3-A-2
— *Redemptive Suffering* —

"A great price was paid to ransom you"
(1 Cor 6:20)

Why did Jesus pay such a great price for us? Because He loves us! His passionate love culminated in His Passion at Calvary. He did not come to show us an easy way to live in this world but rather to enable us to become ONE with Him in love and therefore also in suffering.

— Co-Redeemers and Martyrs with Christ —

To be one with Christ is to be both co-redeemers and martyrs. It is to suffer for others. St. Paul felt "great sorrow and constant anguish"[101] for the Jews who were separated from Christ. He had become one with Christ loving and saving. Pope Francis reminds us that the Christian mission is to heal "the open and painful wounds of humanity, which are also Christ's wounds."[102]

In the Acts of the Apostles, we see Christians acting as co-redeemers and martyrs, bringing salvation to the world. We see the price they paid. Like Christ, they suffered persecution, beatings, and martyrdom. Nothing could stop them.

Pope Francis reminds us that, while not all of us will obtain the glory of shedding blood for Christ, we are all called to lay down our lives daily as martyrs:

A Christian who does not take the dimension of

---

[101] Rom 9:2.
[102] Message to participants of Conference on human trafficking, 30 Oct., 2015, vatican.va.

martyrdom seriously in life does not understand the road that Jesus has indicated: a road that invites us to bear witness every day … with small everyday martyrdoms, or with a great martyrdom, according to God's will.[103]

This is the way of St. Therese of Lisieux, but few want to accept it. Many feel attracted to her famous saying, "My vocation is love!" Yes, we all want love. However, do we understand love in the way she did? Have we resolved to follow the way of love that made her a saint, a Doctor of the Church, and Patroness of the Missions?

She desired to be a martyr, and she succeeded, but not in the way she thought at first. She did not shed blood for Christ, but she united herself to Jesus as co-redeemer and martyr of love for all, especially for missionaries. She not only offered her sufferings for them but also accompanied them from her cloister with such profound love that she also suffered their sufferings and struggles and exhorted them to live the same radical love she lived. In a letter to a "brother missionary" she wrote:

It is His [Jesus] wish you should begin your mission even now, and save souls through the Cross. Was it not by suffering and death that He ransomed the world? I know that you aspire to the happiness of laying down your life for Him, but the martyrdom of the heart is not less fruitful than the shedding of blood, and this martyrdom is already yours.[104]

Another Carmelite who testifies to the value of suffering with

---

[103] Pope Francis, homily, 11 May, 2015, www.news.va.

[104] St. Therese, *Letters to her brother missionaries,* 1895, www.ecatholic2000.com/therese/sos23.shtml.

Jesus to cooperate with His work of Redemption is Saint Edith Stein, a respected Jewish philosopher who, after her conversion, entered the convent as Teresa Benedicta of the Cross and died a martyr at Auschwitz. She wrote:

> Unlike sciences learned in the university, the science of the Cross can be gained only when one comes to feel the Cross radically. Doctrine and life simply must be joined for the student who wishes to become learned in the mystery of the Cross.

She pondered why St. John of the Cross desired to suffer and concluded that he was motivated not merely by a desire to remember or resemble the suffering Christ, but also by the desire to suffer with Christ for the sake of the world, thus participating actively in its redemption. Edith Stein concluded that **suffering with Christ is both the path to intimacy with Him and the way to continue His saving mission.** Our suffering unites others to Jesus crucified:

> Do you want to be totally united to the Crucified? If you are serious about this, you will be present, by the power of the Cross, at every front, at every place of sorrow, bringing to those who suffer comfort, healing, and salvation.[105]

When we embrace our sufferings with the Cross of Christ, we receive "the power of God and the wisdom of God" (1 *Cor* 1:24). This powerful suffering puts us in the forefront of the spiritual battle to heal and to save many souls in ways that only God knows.

---

[105] As cited by Sister Joan Gormley in *Edith Stein and The Contemplative Vocation*, www.wf-f.org/03-2-EdithStein.html.

Fr. Kosicki wrote:

> **Nor is redemptive suffering a rejection of healing**; rather, it is a way of bringing total healing, that is, salvation to ourselves and others. One effect of healing is that it removes the obstacles within us that prevent us from recognizing the Cross and embracing the Cross and embracing it with joy.[106]

All our sufferings are opportunities to grow in intimacy with Jesus, to allow Him to draw us into His Sacred Heart and reveal to us the depth, height, breadth, and length of His love for us and for those for whom we suffer.

For example, if you suffer the distancing and lack of intimacy of a loved one, turn your attention to the Lord and let Him reveal to you the sorrows of His Sacred Heart: the sorrow for so many who distance themselves from Him, who don't even know what intimacy with God means. Then you can console the Lord in His sorrow and come to know His heart. This intimacy in suffering personally with Christ is love, and only love has the power to bless and transform our hearts.

Having accompanied Jesus in His sorrows, ask Him to accompany you in your sorrows: for your spouse, marriage, child, parents, friends… He will show you that those sorrows are already in His heart. Now that you are aware that Jesus cares, suffers, loves you, and is with you in your sorrows, **He gives you the strength to love those who have hurt you and to pray to obtain many graces for them** and many others.

The Lord will ask you to be attentive to the pain, fears, and wounds in the hearts of the people near you. Through them, you

---

[106] George W. Kosicki, Gerald J. Farrell, *The Spirit and the Bride Say, "Come!"* (Emi Press, 1991), 74.

enter the pain of God for all of humanity. You become poor, you mourn, you are meek, you thirst for righteousness, you are merciful, you are a peacemaker, you are persecuted... You live the Beatitudes! If you persevere living this way, your ordinary life will bear extraordinary fruits beyond your limits of time and space.

34. How to Live as His Companions of Love, Diary of a MOC

> I asked Jesus how to live as His companion of love. It is easy when I am in prayer, and He allows me to feel His presence and to see His gaze, but during the day there are so many distractions. Jesus said:
>
> ***Be attentive to each person you encounter in your life.*** *I live in them. I suffer for them and with them. This is My Body (Mt 35:31-41). My little one, have the docility of heart to receive the brokenness of all people into your heart as ONE with Me. This is participation in the love of the Trinity: to receive the wounds of your brothers and sisters and to give the sacrifice of your life, as ONE with Me, for their salvation and sanctification. This is Love.* (2/18/13)

3-A-3

— *"By His Wounds You Have Been Healed"*[107] —

In Chapter Two—*At the Foot of the Cross*—we learned the importance of digging deep within us to pull out our entire root system of sin. Now we learn that, buried with our sins, there is also a root system of **disordered tendencies**, anxieties, and fears that

---

[107]1 Pt 2:24.

are **infecting our wounds**. The devil has exploited those wounds to separate us from God and to prevent us from receiving love and giving love. When our wounds are healed, the devil is no longer able to exploit us as he did before.

— How Our Wounds Are Healed —

Only Jesus' wounds heal

We have already learned that we are healed by touching the wounds of Jesus. Only His wounds can heal because, unlike us, He willingly suffered them with pure love and forgiveness; therefore, Satan could not infect them with hate or any other poison. This means that Christ's wounds, instead of defeat, reveal and transmit the victory of His love. Isaiah writes, "He was wounded for our transgressions, He was bruised for our iniquities; upon Him was the chastisement that made us whole, and with His stripes we are healed."[108]

We acknowledge that we are wounded and seek to know our wounds

In order to allow Jesus to touch and heal our wounds, we need to acknowledge that we have them. At the foot of the Cross, we ask the Lord for the gift of self-knowledge. We ask specifically to be able to know our wounds, all of them, as real and deep as they are.

We have repressed our wounds and placed them in our dark room.

Because they are painful, we have repressed them and placed them in the dark room of our subconscious, where they remain

---

[108] Isa 53:5.

locked and out of sight. How do we repress our wounds? By trying to forget, keeping busy and entertained, wearing masks to create a new image for ourselves and by building walls of isolation against anything that may remind us of those wounds. But our wounds continue hurting us deeply and affecting our lives.

We must enter the dark room where those wounds lie, but it is difficult because we are afraid of facing them. We must resolve to enter battle using the spiritual weapons that God gives us (such as faith, courage, humility) to undo the masks, the busyness, and the walls. We need to allow the Holy Spirit authority over our life. Allow Him to unlock the dark room and **bring our wounds to the light of our conscience.** God the Father taught St. Catherine of Siena that we must work hard to bring to the "throne of conscience" what is hidden in us.

Before reaching the wounds, we must discover our disorders.

Acquiring knowledge of our wounds is a process. As we dig within ourselves, before reaching the wounds, we discover layers of **disordered tendencies that are affecting our behavior. A disorder is any behavior that is not virtuous, including bad attitudes.** These must be exposed and brought to our consciousness by the light of the Holy Spirit. This requires that we be **attentive to how we think and feel in situations that trigger those bad attitudes and disorders in us.** These include discomfort, anxiety, fear, anger…

For example, we come in contact with authoritarian and demanding persons and we find that our reaction is to avoid them by running away. We find that we feel fear, insecurity, and inadequacy. Another example: we notice that we are unable to say "no" when we should; then we feel resentment, anger, frustration because we acted just to please.

Ask yourself "Why?"

As we become aware of our disordered tendencies and reactions, the key question we must ask ourselves is "Why?" "Why did I react that way?" "Why did I get angry?" "Why did I avoid that authoritarian person?" "Why did I feel inadequate and insecure?" "Why did I run away?" "Why did I want to hide?" "Why couldn't I say 'NO'?" **By asking the question "why?" we are humbly acknowledging our disorder and giving permission to the Holy Spirit to enter our hearts and unlock the door of our hidden room where our wounds hide.** We ask the Holy Spirit, through the intercession of our Blessed Mother, for the gift of self-knowledge to continue to unfold.

It is not enough to acknowledge our anger or to see that someone's behavior got us angry. We need to ask the Lord why we reacted as we did. Usually, **this question will take us to forgotten memories**. We might remember the harsh, demanding and rigid voice of our father, mother, grandfather, teacher…

Re-Live Memories and Allow Emotions to Surface

Whether the wounds that we remember were self-inflicted, caused by someone we loved, or by an acquaintance or a stranger, we must **re-live the memories with Jesus and allow ourselves to FEEL THE PAIN** that the person caused us. This is hard. We are tempted through nervousness and anxiety to use humor in an attempt to hide or lessen the hurt we feel from those memories.

We first will feel the anger, resentment, hatred and isolation as we remember the harshness of this person's voice and actions. We can think of these emotions as the top layer of a volcano. They are negative emotions, and therefore we cannot unite them with Jesus to suffer them with Him because His heart is incompatible with them. We need to distinguish the negative emotions from the PURE

PAIN of our wound. It is ONLY the pure pain that can be suffered with Jesus.

What do we do with our negative emotions? Most of us were taught since childhood not to show any negative emotions, therefore, we stuffed them but they still oppress us in many different ways. Sometimes they come out in uncontrollable ways. There is a healthy way to have these strong emotions surface—we need to acknowledge that we have them (our anger, resentment, hatred, frustration, irritation…) and expose them all, making ourselves naked before Jesus crucified, asking Him to take them from us. "We submit every thought to Christ" (2 Cor. 10:5).

Name the Wound

Underneath the negative emotions lies the pure pain of our core wound. In order to touch our core wound and own it, we need to ask a second important question: "If I could give a name to my wound that lies under the anger, resentment, and isolation that I feel, what would it be?" The answers could be: "I was not loved; I was not appreciated nor accepted for who I am; I did not count; I was rejected, ignored, abused, forgotten, unwanted or, ridiculed."

Enter the Pain
Feel the Pure Pain and Unite it to Jesus' Pain

Then we must take all the pain coming from our wounds and unite it with the pain of Jesus' wounds. Therefore, as we feel the pain of not having been appreciated, we look at Jesus' wounds of not being appreciated. Jesus, who laid down His life for us, is not appreciated. We suffer our pain WITH the pain of JESUS.

Left on our own, we are self-centered and absorbed in our pain, so we ask the Holy Spirit for this union of wounds. The Holy Spirit changes the center of our attention from ourselves to Jesus. It is through this process that our wounds are healed.

It's hard to get to our wounds. The most difficult part is identifying THE wound, the big one, the core wound. Here's a clue on how to tell if it is the core wound: When you have found it, it is like a punch in the gut that physically knocks you down and takes your breath away, it's a doubling over in pain, sobbing and crying in agony. We resist accepting it. If you can talk about it without reliving it with real emotion, you're not there yet. It is OK. Keep going.

As we face the pain inflicted on us, we may wonder **where was Jesus when this happened.** The truth is that Jesus Himself was suffering as one with us because we are one of His little ones: "Truly, I say to you, as you did it to one of the least of these my brethren, you did it to Me."[109] As we relive our pain with Jesus, we need to touch our wound to the wound that He already bore upon His Body for us. In this way, we also enter into His love that defeats all evil. As we see our wounds upon Jesus' body we must gaze at the eyes of Jesus as He gazes upon us and enters our pain. What is Jesus saying to you? It is through this process that our wounds are healed.

Do not confuse the situations you lived or your behaviors with the wound

Sexual molestation is what somebody did to you—it is not the wound. The annihilation, the trampling of your person, not only of your body—that is the wound. Behaviors such as perfectionism, sexual promiscuity, and drug use numb the pain of the wound but are not the wound.

If you grew up in an environment of alcoholism, it was not your fault and it was not your sin. But you did feel abandonment, neglect,

---

[109] *Mat* 25:40.

and isolation. Those are the wounds. Depression, suicidal thoughts, anorexia nervosa, codependency are consequences but not the wound.

When you find the wound and touch it, you feel like you're dying all over again as when it was inflicted. Be at peace. Don't refuse—Don't pull back This time you are being crucified with Christ on the Cross, wound to wound. He will heal and transform the wound. There is nothing He wants more. But first you need to bring Him the actual wound; not just the events, circumstances, behaviors or consequences. Bringing the wound to Him is your part.

You are not alone

You do not find the wound or bring it to Jesus by yourself. The Holy Spirit brings you to the core wound while Jesus comforts you there. We are deathly afraid because we think we are all alone in a sort of hell in this process. Remember that **Jesus was there when the wound was inflicted.** Truly He was there—every time, but we were unaware. But now, in the healing process, you are very aware of His presence. You realize that He was with you suffering the wound from the beginning and now He is with you healing it.

You cannot "work on" your woundedness. You cannot "discover" your own wounds. We do not direct or control the process—the Holy Spirit does. Invoke the Spirit. Consecrate yourself to the Holy Spirit. I repeat, He will bring you to the wound and then bring you and the wound to Jesus on the Cross. You are not alone. You cannot do it alone. You would accomplish nothing. It is God who "searches the heart" (Jer 17:10; Rom 8:27) and reveals to you its secrets and its wounds in order to heal them. This is Christ's work of redemption applied to your life. Your part is to consent, to allow, to leave the door to your heart open to receive the love and the truth even when it hurts (This is harder than you think).

The Spirit will come in His way, on His terms, when He chooses.

Wounds are the place of encounter with Jesus

Our wounds and the wounds of others need to be treated gently and tenderly as a mother would tend to her hurt child. When we acknowledge that we are wounded, we need to be careful to respect **the process of healing—it is holy ground. This wound is the place we meet Jesus face to face**; this wound will be the source of transformation for us; this wound is the channel of mercy. The transformed wound is the source of light to the world.

— Summary —

1. **My wounds have been infected** and cause disorders in my life (#126).
2. **Only Jesus' wounds can heal me** (#127).
3. **I acknowledge** that I have wounds and seek to know them. (#128).
4. **I have repressed them** and locked them in my "dark room" (#129).
5. **I must bring my wounds to the light of my conscience.** (#129).
6. **Before reaching the wounds, I discover my reactions to situations** (#130).
   a) to discover them, I must be attentive **to how I think and feel** in the situations that trigger then.
7. I ask myself: **WHY** I react in that way? (#131).
   a) I allow the **Holy Spirit to open the "dark room"** where my wounds have been hidden (#131).

8. **I Re-Live those memories and allow the emotions to surface** (#132).
9. **I NAME THE WOUND to enter the pure pain** (#133).
10. **I unite my wound and suffering to the wounds and suffering of Jesus**. I enter the suffering of Jesus. His wounds heal mine (#134).

— Testimony of a Priest —

This is the testimony of a priest who, after witnessing the love between a father and son, was attentive to the sorrow and longing in his heart. As he lives the above process, he comes to touch his core "father wound":

Yesterday, in a celebration dinner for the newly ordained, the father of a new deacon said a few words. In the end, in the midst of applauses, he warmly embraced his son. Seeing them so united in love and, the deacon so affirmed, I had an intuition of what my heart desires.

In the earliest memories, I have of my parents I see them separated, crying and fighting. I have no memory of them together, with mutual affection, living love. So, I grew up in a house where there was no love. In my first personal memories I see myself always alone, playing or just in silence, alone. My parents separated when I was a kid. I experienced a lot of stress, unable to understand or react to what was happening. I just suffered it.

My mom tried to give me love, but I always declined it. I did not like her to kiss me or touch me. Now I understand why: I never saw her being loved by my father, so, unconsciously, I thought she was not loveable. As a result, I thought that I, too, was unworthy of love. When someone loves me, my wounds show up: I think I do not deserve it; I do not trust in myself; I do not know how to take it; I think I will be betrayed.

Several times in my life my father made promises: that he would return, that he would bring me this or that gift. All false: He brought nothing. He simply decided that for him, to live alone was the best. And he did. As a result, my mom went into depression. I remember seeing her for months in bed, weeping, wailing.

My dad did not fulfill any of his two main duties: He did not love my mom (that I remember), nor love me. But it's not his fault: he left his father's house as a youth in conflict with his father. He received no love. He fled. And so he never learned how a father should relate to a son. So he never dedicated time to "explain the world," to "introduce me to the world."

I grew up without receiving the treasure of "experience" and "knowledge" and "training" that a father gives to his son, through long encounters of sharing and fellowship. Compared with my friends, I always felt at a disadvantage: inexperienced, incompetent, insecure, and withdrawn. I never learned to interact with others in a family atmosphere of unconditional love and acceptance. To date, I find it difficult to live with others, although I desire it strongly; and at times I have been able to enjoy it.

This priest, upon finding something stirring in his soul, was attentive to his feelings; he dug deep, he asked himself why, he entered his memories with Jesus and felt the pain. Finally, he got in touch with his core wound and named it: he did not receive the love he longed for. Therefore, he had difficulties receiving and giving love.

Our pain, united to Jesus, elevates us to Him

In a message to Mirjana in Medjugorje, our Lady said: "[I] soothe your pains because I know them, I experience them. Pain elevates and is the greatest prayer."[110] In our pain, we are able to enter into the most profound intimacy with our God. No one else can share in our pain as Jesus can.

Our pain is unique to us. When we try to relieve our pain by sharing it, we are not entirely satisfied because no one is able to enter our pain fully, no matter how close they are to us. That is why the Lord, in this Path, taught us to enter the SILENCE OF THE PAIN. Through this silence we can embrace God Himself and live our pain as one with Him, consoling and soothing our Lord and our Mother as they console us. Through this intimate union of our pain with Christ's we are able, to some degree, to know and live the pain of others and be Christ to them.

Accompaniment

While only Jesus can enter the depth of our pain and heal us, He wants brotherly love to be part of the process. It is important, to have someone we trust who is mature in the faith accompany us in the process of healing; someone who listens to our pains and helps bring our wounds into contact with Christ's wounds. Because we have repressed these wounds, sometimes for a very long time, speaking about them opens the floodgates and releases our pain.[111]

---

[110] 2 Apr., 2016.
[111] Cf. "accompaniment" in our community's website
http://lovecrucified.com/way_life/accompaniment/accompaniment.html.

114

Sacrament of Reconciliation

It is important now to receive the healing graces of the sacrament of reconciliation. When we confess our sins to the Lord, represented by the priest, we also expose our wounds. Not only do we receive forgiveness, but also our wounds are united to Christ's.[112]

— Testimony of Healing the Core Wound—

When I was asked to give a talk, I found myself paralyzed by fear. I had always thought that such reaction was due to my shy personality. However, after digging into my heart, I found that I had many fears. I understood that fear is an acquired disorder and that to blame shyness for my fears is a lie; a coping mechanism that I believed from an early age to cover up many fears I did not want to face. Consequently, I had spent my life distant, quiet, and uncommunicative. Once I admitted to myself my fear in this situation, I began to discover my fear of rejection, of being ridiculed, of making a mistake. Then I had to ask myself, "Why am I so scared to be rejected, ridiculed…?" In this process of asking "why," events of my past that caused fears came to my memory. I remembered my mother's explosive reactions for just about everything, especially if we made a mistake. I remember as a child living in constant fear of my mother's anger. As I began to relive these memories, anger and even hatred were released from the depth of my heart as if a volcano had erupted. First, these intense feelings had to be released so that I could enter my core "mother wound" of not having felt the tender, gentle maternal love of a mother. I

---

[112] Cf. "reconciliation" in our community's website,
http://lovecrucified.com/sacraments/confession/[confession.html.

relived these painful memories with Jesus as I gazed into His eyes and felt my mother's slaps. I could see in Jesus' eyes His deep sorrow for me, but also His deep sorrow for my very wounded mother. I saw not only my wounds on Jesus but also my mother's wounds. The love I could encounter in Jesus' gaze began to slowly melt away my anger and hatred, and with time, healed my "mother wound" completely.

As I began to receive the knowledge that my excessive shyness was a disorder of my personality, a false identity, acquired through my unhealed wounds, the Holy Spirit brought me to an important repressed memory of my father. My father always attended my brother's football games, so I became a cheerleader. I could see my father sitting on the bleachers and, through the whole game, I watched his face, hoping he would look at me, but he never once looked at me. At the end of the game, he made the comment of how the cheerleaders were a nuisance. I repressed my pain and did not cry in front of my father; but, as I relived this memory, I felt intense sorrow, and tears flowed from my eyes. What name could I give my sorrow? My father never looked at me; I was never noticed by my father. Satan planted the lie in my "father wound" that I was not worthy of being noticed by anyone; therefore, I became shy and just hid from the world. I relived this memory with Jesus as I gazed at His sorrow of not being noticed by so many souls. How many notice Him in the Eucharist? I could feel, through my sorrow, His sorrows and through His sorrows touch His love. It is Jesus' love that has healed my "father wound".

As my "father wound" healed in Jesus' wounds, I began to see my father through Jesus. The Holy Spirit brought me eventually to focus on the wounds of my father who was abandoned at a young age by his father. Now I live my wound

116

united as one with Jesus' wound obtaining healing graces for my father. My wound has become God's living chalice of grace for him. This has filled my life with purpose and great joy!

— An Ongoing Process —

One of the fruits of healing the core wound is that you find your heart freer. You can feel emotions that you had only read or heard about, and feel to a more profound depth the emotions you already knew. Another fruit of healing is that we come in touch with our interior life, with our hearts. We come to know ourselves and to be attentive to what is taking place within us. We no longer live disconnected from ourselves and others. When we lived in our wound we were unhappy, afraid, depressed, in bad moods, we lived according to our emotions but were not aware of what was taking place within us. A healed person is "tuned in." This sensitivity becomes the means to live as victim souls receiving the wounds of others and participating with Christ in their redemption. A healed person also lives in INTERIOR PEACE, which is JOY, amidst the pain and sufferings of life, because he has come to know personally the love of God and believes God is present with him in all circumstances of life.

Being healed does not mean that our tendencies, fears, and anxieties vanish. We still have the tendency to fear and to hide. **To be healed means that our weaknesses no longer control our lives.** We know them and we have the power to act against them. The Lord taught us, for the sake of love, to "Choose to live each day according to what is most difficult, not what is easiest." What is easiest for me is to separate myself during a time of conflict; so I have to choose what is most difficult, which is to remain in touch and to communicate.

— Do not Be Afraid —

Satan uses lies and threats to make us live in fear and thus debilitates and oppresses us. Because fear paralyzes us, we do not have the freedom to live the new life in the Holy Spirit. Pope Francis said:

> Fear is an attitude that harms us. It weakens us; it diminishes us. It even paralyzes us. A person who is afraid does nothing, doesn't know what to do. He is focused on himself, so that nothing bad will happen. Fear brings you to a self-centered selfishness and paralyzes you. This is why Jesus says to Paul: "Do not be afraid. Continue to speak."
>
> Fear is not a Christian attitude. It is an attitude, we could say, of a caged animal, without freedom, who does not have the freedom to look ahead, to create something, to do good.[113]

The Lord tells us, "Do not be afraid" because He knows that we are in fact afraid, and it is likely that we don't even know our fears. The enemy has placed us within boundaries and threatens to make us suffer if we dare to go beyond them. He makes us think that our life, as we now live it, is normal. In order to break through those boundaries and fears, we must fix our eyes on Jesus crucified and trust Him even though we do not know where He is taking us. Only then will we be set free; and our knowledge of God and of ourselves will expand. For example, because I thought my shyness was normal, I would not go beyond what was comfortable for me. Yet, as I came closer to God, I could understand that He was asking me to go beyond my fears and to speak in public.

---

[113] Homily, 15 May 2015, w2.vatican.va.

So what should we do with our fears? As we see with St Paul, **our love for Christ must move us to act with courage to cast out fear and to suffer all things with and for Christ.** It is not enough to think we love Jesus; true love moves us to face our fears and to move through them to do what is most difficult.

— Called to Be Wounded Healers —

When the wounds of Christ heal our wounds, ours too become channels of God's healing grace for others. His wounds and ours become one. Not only can we say, "**by His wounds you have been healed**" (1 Pet 2:24), but also "by our wounds, united with Christ's, you are healed."

In St. Faustina's Divine Mercy image, we see blood and water pouring out of Jesus' wound. Our wounds, united to Jesus' wounds and healed, also become channels of His Divine Mercy. We become "living chalices" of Christ's healing blood being poured upon others. Our healed wounds of addiction become a source of healing grace for all addicts, our healed wounds of abuse become healing grace for souls suffering from abuse, our healed wounds of abandonment become grace for the abandoned… United as one with Jesus, we are able to help others come to new life.

— Testimony —
God Used Her Deep Wound
to Heal the Person Who Wounded Her

I was invited to a women's convention the weekend of January 30, 1998. There I met a woman and ended up pouring my heart out to her. I told her how my husband had left me with two small children, had taken every penny, leaving me with a lot of debt and without a job. As I spoke, I could not hold back the tears. She looked at me coldly, and before I had finished, referred me to a priest. I went to him, full of hope, but he also cut me off.

The reason I remember the date of the convention is because it was my wedding anniversary. Being there with women who shared how great their lives were with their wonderfully successful husbands was difficult because, in a perfect world, I would have been celebrating my anniversary—instead, I was divorced because of an abusive husband.

When the woman turned me away, it was hurtful, but when Father rejected me—it was a piercing. I cried for hours and hours. I offered all this to our Lord. If I had known then what I know now, I would have suffered it with Him.

Years later I ran into the same priest though he did not recognize me. Seeing him brought back a flood of emotions and hurt.

When Our Lord brought this to light last week, I recognized I had wounds of rejection. Now I was able to suffer it all with Him—entering His heart when He was judged falsely and rejected. For days, I would feel the pain of the Lord with mine. I begged Him to heal my wounds by allowing me to touch His.

It wasn't until now that I, as a spiritual mother, realized that the Lord was giving me the priest that wounded my heart years ago as a spiritual son. I can now pray and bless him through my healed wound of rejection. I remember hearing in our community that all that happens to us can be used by God for our good. I can already see the good: Through my healed wound and my suffering, Jesus is healing and purifying priests.

— Testimony —
Healing and Forgiving
Through the Wounds of Divorce

Recently, something very simple yet profound happened: I have come to see my family as a family again. With the divorce, my children and I were truly abandoned. The Lord led me to experience a shift in my thinking and understanding of our identity as a family—from a mindset of "we are no longer a family" to "we are a broken family." I don't know if I can explain how important that shift is; but believe me, it is quite different to be nothing than to be broken. Jesus on the Cross was broken, forsaken by His bride. We are also broken but united with Him. I glorify the Lord for that.

I cannot abandon the Cross. Instead, I have realized that God wanted me to continue to pray for my husband's conversion as I did before the divorce; and that, in spite of the civil divorce and separation, I am still entrusted with the duty of helping him go to heaven, as spouses are called to do, through the sacramental covenant of marriage. I, an ordinary woman, have received an incredible expansion of my heart to love with a love that is truly divine. It cannot be of human source.

This is a grace of healing: instead of walking away altogether from a relationship with my husband, I now accept that there is a relationship, which, although broken, still calls for my love and prayers.

This grace was put to the test at my son's graduation. I invited my husband, and he came with a girlfriend. With the knowledge that Jesus loves me and wants me to love others in union with Him, I was ready. Before they arrived at the Mass, I had a moment of desolation. I lived it with Jesus crucified and asked Him for an outpouring of the Holy Spirit, the fire of Love. At that moment, I felt truly alone and abandoned; but when they arrived, I greeted them with a love that was heartfelt. Instead of desolation, I felt the family bond.

I believe the Lord is also working in him because he seems now to appreciate me as the mother of his children and he appreciates the kids as well. For Mother's Day, he sent me roses. Initially, I felt this was surprising and strange; but some days later, after prayer, I was able to open my heart to receive them with gratitude, as a small step towards a willingness to talk. I knew this was the Lord's healing. As I yield to the promptings of the Spirit, even when they are most difficult, the Lord gives me tremendous courage to manifest His love to all. I am able to pray for my husband's conversion with purity of heart. I can see that what is good for my children's father is good for my children. For a person of my temperament and with my faults, it is really and truly miraculous to be able to love with inner peace in all these strange, irregular circumstances. I am most grateful to the Lord for all these blessings and gifts, which are making me into a new creation.

— Testimony —
A priest who lives this Path

Today I saw that I had confusion and shame that came from having tried to cover up my sins by blaming others and the circumstances. I saw this was my pride. I was not trusting in the Lord.

The Lord ASSURED ME that He SUFFERED ALL WITH ME. He knew my sins and still loved me. He was there with me each and every time I fell. He continues to suffer with me in my confusion and shame. Then, He invited me to give it all to Him. He assured me that he wanted to take this burden off my shoulders and heal my heart—He was there! He was always there! I could then acknowledge my sins and repent. I found peace.

35. Suffer all with Me, Diary of a MOC

> *To suffer with Me is to be made pure like Me...*
> *To suffer with Me is to begin to love with Me...*
> *To suffer with Me is to become Love...*
> *To suffer with Me is to enter the fullness of JOY and happiness on earth.* (11/2/11)

3-A-4
— Tears —

Jesus, seeing Mary and the Jews weeping at the death of Lazarus, "was deeply moved in spirit and troubled … and Jesus wept."[114] He wept because He suffered with them. Pope Francis tells us:

> In the Gospel, Jesus cried for his dead friend; he cried in his heart for the family who lost its child, for the poor widow who had to bury her son. He was moved to tears and compassion when he saw the crowds without a pastor.[115]

Jesus weeps for us today, and we need to learn to weep with Him and with our brothers and sisters. When Pope Francis was asked by a twelve-year-old homeless girl why God allows terrible things to happen to innocent children and why there are so few people helping them, he responded:

> Why do children suffer? When the heart is able to ask itself [this question] and weep, then we can understand something. There is a worldly compassion which is useless. … It's a compassion that makes us put our hands in our pockets and give something to the poor. But if Christ had had that kind of compassion he would have passed by, cured three or four, and would have returned to the Father. Only when He cried, and He was capable of crying, did He understand the dramatic reality of our lives.
>
> Dear young boys and girls, today's world doesn't know

---

[114] Cf. *Jn* 11:28-35.
[115] Meeting with young people, Manila, 18 Jan. 2015, http://en.radiovaticana.va.

how to cry. … Certain realities of life we only see through eyes cleansed by our tears. I invite each one here to ask yourself: have I learned how to weep? Have I learned how to weep for the marginalized or for a street child who has a drug problem or for an abused child? Or is my cry the capricious cry of someone who would like to have something more? …If you don't learn how to cry, you cannot be a good Christian… Be courageous, don't be afraid to cry.[116]

As we have learned in this chapter, our hearts can lose their sensitivity and be numbed to their hidden pain, not only through drugs and alcohol but also by burying ourselves in work and constant distractions such as TV, computers, shopping, exercise… We can easily become de-humanized. We need to move in the opposite direction and enter profoundly the pain and sorrow that we carry in our hearts—the pain of being rejected, abandoned, left alone, ridiculed, misunderstood, ignored… As we come to know and feel our own pain, we are able to feel the pain of others; and cry with them. Then our tears become a participation in the mercy and compassion of Christ.

Jesus said to Venerable Conchita:

Those are the tears that should fill this chalice … tears that I cannot find in the world! … the ones I am looking for… those which must exist among souls that truly love Me: tears of gratitude toward Me … tears because of the souls that are lost… tears of love from a thirst for more suffering just to console Me![117]

---

[116] Ibid.

[117] Concepcion Cabrera de Armida, *Holy Hours* (Alba House, 2006), 109.

36. Be My Companion of Love, Diary of a MOC

> *I desire to draw you into the depth of My Sacred Heart to immerse you in Love. Enter into the deep, My little one. Enter into the ocean of My mercy. Come, My little one, and be My companion of love. Be with your God and Savior as I enter My agony again. The time has come when the Father will turn His gaze from the world. My Mother and I will cry for you [humanity]. Who will remain faithful during the great and terrible persecution? Remain with me and collect My tears to present them to the Father.* (2/15/13)

Satan has robbed us of our true identity as men and women created in God's image and likeness. God became man to restore all of humanity. Christ is the new man; free from the shackles of sin, free to love with divine-human love. He cries; He feels; He loves intimately; He touches and allows Himself to be touched; He is passionate; He is courageous in His zeal to do the Father's will; He speaks the truth always; He is consuming tenderness; He is mercy; He is Love. As we collect His tears, suffering with Him, the Holy Spirit restores our true identity. We share in His transformed humanity. To collect the tears of the God-man and to cry with Him is the purest union of hearts. Pope Francis explains:

It is the task of the wise to recognize errors, to feel pain, to repent, to beg for pardon and to cry… corrupted hearts have lost the capacity to cry. …conversion of heart (is) to move on from "What does it matter to me?" to tears.[118]

---

[118] Homily, 13 Sept., 2014, http://m.vatican.va.

Tears are a gift of the Holy Spirit. It is often experienced in places of apparitions and in the baptism of the Holy Spirit. Tears are the movement of a heart that is thawing from a frigid winter. We tend to think that, to be holy, we must repress our emotions. Instead, we must allow God to purify them. Mary is full of grace and is also the Queen of Sorrows, the Mother of tears. That means that she is full of love, ONE with the Sacred Heart of Jesus. She is fully woman as God created woman to be, not ruined by sin.

37. I Come to Console You and to Receive Your Consolation, Diary of a MOC

A statue of the Mystical Rose was releasing the fragrance of roses. Our Blessed Mother told me:

I come tonight, my daughters, to console you in your suffering, but also to receive consolation from you. I desire for you to collect in your pure hands my tears of blood and to unite your tears with mine and raise them to the Father as one with the Blood of my Son.

I come to strengthen you; I come to encourage you; I come to thank you, my daughters, for you have responded to my call. Heaven rejoices seeing the little ones of the Father respond with such courage as each of you have…

Pray tonight with all your hearts, supplicate with me before the throne of the Father; and I promise you that all your prayers will be heard and answered. (4/14/11)

Christ's sorrow goes deep into the agony of the human heart. He wept when He entered as a man the most intense struggle to

127

fulfill His mission. The letter to the Hebrews tells us He called out to the Father for help with "prayers and supplications, with loud cries and tears."[119] When we suffer and weep and find it difficult to gaze upon the Father, we need to remember that "we do not have a high priest who is unable to sympathize with our weaknesses, but we have one who in every respect has been tested as we are, yet without sin."[120]

Christ continues to weep today, and He wants us to accompany Him. Jesus weeps in the Eucharist; He weeps as He enters our wounded and burdened hearts, yet we do not enter into His. We remain near the surface because fear hardens us and we resist a deeper encounter with Him. As He hung upon the Cross, Jesus knew many would not even come to know His love and the love of the Father.

38. Tears Pierce Hardened Hearts, Diary of a MOC

> *My daughter, a hardened heart is not able to receive the grace of God. It is not able to see the glory of God revealed before him. I, God Incarnate, was in their midst yet they were blind. My Heart was grieved to see the condition of their hearts, for I knew that not even My crucifixion would touch their hearts.*
>
> *My daughter, many are called; but it is few that respond. The act of Mary Magdalene and Peter, in which they come to Me with tears of sorrow, is necessary to pierce the hardness of the human heart steeped in sin.*
>
> *My daughter, My Heart continues to be grieved*

---

[119] Heb 5:7.
[120] Heb 4:15.

> *at seeing such hardness of hearts within My Church.*
> *I desire that you awaken the hearts of My sons with*
> *tears and supplications as only a mother can.*
> *(1/14/11)*

Our tears can be a sign of having entered deeply into Christ's oblation to the Father. St. John Vianney would shed many tears upon visiting the Blessed Sacrament. Saint Faustina also cried for love of the Lord:

My body was stretched on the wood of the cross. I writhed in terrible pain until eleven o'clock. I went in spirit to the Tabernacle and uncovered the ciborium, leaning my head on the rim of the cup, and all my tears flowed silently toward the Heart of Him who alone understands what pain and suffering is. And I experienced the sweetness of this suffering, and my soul came to desire this sweet agony, which I would not have exchanged for all the world's treasures. The Lord gave me the strength of spirit and love towards those through whom these sufferings came.[121]

St. Pio of Pietrelcina also cried for love of the Lord and exhorted all to do the same:

Do not depart from the altar without shedding tears of sorrow and love for Jesus, crucified for your salvation. The Sorrowful Mother will accompany you and be your sweet inspiration.

---

[121] St. Faustina Kowalska, *Diary, Divine Mercy in My Soul*, n.1454.

3-B
Bridging the Gap

— St Peter Followed at a Distance —

St. Peter is a great example of how our wounds and fears keep us at a distance from the Lord, but Jesus wants to bring us to filial love, the love of true friends.

After the miraculous catch of fish, Peter "fell down at Jesus' knees, saying, 'Go away from me, Lord, for I am a sinful man!'" (Lk 5:8). Peter manifests his love for the Lord, but later we see that his heart continued to be controlled by the wrong kind of fear. When Jesus tells the disciples that He must go to Jerusalem to suffer and be killed, Peter rebuked Him, saying, "God forbid it, Lord! This must never happen to you" (Mt 16:22). Peter thought that he loved Jesus, but his love was still imperfect, centered in self-love and avoidance of suffering; therefore, he was not able to fathom that Jesus' perfect love will take Him to lay down His life for all.

When they arrested Jesus and took Him to Caiaphas to plot His death, "Peter was following Him at a distance" and "sat with the guards in order to see how this would end" (Mt 26:58). Peter remained as an observer as they condemned Jesus to death, "spat in his face and struck him; and some slapped him."[122]

Peter struggled intensely because he loved Jesus very much. Just before this incident, at the Last Supper, Peter had said, "Lord, why can I not follow you now? I will lay down my life for you" (Jn 13:37). What kept Peter from acting as he really desired? What kept him distant from Jesus, unable to participate in His suffering? It was

---

[122] Mt 26:66-67.

fear, self-love. His fear was greater than his love, so he proceeded to deny Jesus three times with the words, "I do not know that man."

God the Father teaches St. Catherine of Siena about Peter's imperfect love:

> It was with this imperfect love that St. Peter loved the sweet and good Jesus, My only begotten Son, enjoying most pleasantly His sweet conversations; but when the time of trouble came, he failed. So disgraceful was his fall, that, not only could he not bear the pain himself, but his terror of the very approach of pain caused him to fall and deny the Lord with the words, "I have never known Him". The soul who has climbed this step with servile fear and mercenary love alone, falls into many troubles.[123]

We are like Peter. We love Jesus very much, yet there remains, unknown to us, a distance between Him and us. We have not yet become ONE with Jesus' passion of love. For this to happen, the Holy Spirit must transform our hearts, so that our love is greater than any of our fears. "There is no fear in love, but perfect love casts out fear" (1 Jn 4:18).

---

[123] *Dialogue, http://www.catholictreasury.info/books/dialogue/diag46.php.*

131

— How the Holy Spirit Bridges the Distance that Keeps Us from Christ —

The following summary will help us understand:

a) Knowledge of God's Love

As we come to know God's love, fear of God is replaced by a gift of the Spirit called "**fear of the Lord.**" Because of love, we fear offending God and losing our relationship due to sin. We are filled with awe and filial respect. St Paul exhorts us, "work out your salvation with fear and trembling" (Phil 2:12). This is not the fear of our first parents who, after sinning, "hid from the presence of God" (Gen 3:8), or the servile fear of the unfaithful servant that buried his talents.[124] Jesus taught St. Catherine:

> Through love, the imperfection of the fear of the penalty was taken away, and the perfection of holy fear remained, that is, the fear of offending, not on account of one's own damnation, but of offending Me, who am Supreme Good.[125]

Ask yourself:
- Do I really trust that Jesus is committed to me, to love me and take me to heaven or am I afraid of Him?
- Do I try to offer God good works instead of abandoning myself completely to Him?

b) Self-Knowledge

Self-knowledge is crucial to bridge the distance between Jesus and us. We acquire it when we examine our behavior before the

---

[124] Cf. Mt 25:18-26.

[125] *Dialogue, http://www.catholictreasury.info.*

Lord, especially our struggles, sins, and disorders. Through self-knowledge, we know our sins and are able to repent and to follow Jesus closely.

A major obstacle to self-knowledge is that we think we love Jesus but do not realize that our love is tainted with selfishness. Our intentions are therefore mixed. Selfishness is so natural to us that it may be present even when we seek to do good. God teaches St. Catherine of Siena about this imperfect love:

> If they serve Me with a view of their own profit, or the delight and pleasure which they find in Me, [their love] is imperfect. Do you know what proves the imperfection of this love? [When I] withdraw the consolations … This I do so that, coming to perfect self-knowledge, they may know that of themselves they are nothing.[126]

Ask yourself:
- Do I continue to serve with love when I derive no pleasure from it?
- How do I react when Jesus withdraws His consolation from me and permits me to enter battles & perplexities?
- Do I acknowledge my weakness and my need to cling to Him?

c) Suffering All with Jesus, Uniting Our Wounds with His to Be ONE with Him

This practice, which we have already covered, is essential to bridge the distance between Jesus and us.

_____

[126]Ibid., 38, http://www.catholictreasury.info/books/dialogue/diag46.php.

Ask yourself:

- Do I believe that the Lord, in His infinite love, wants to transform all my wounds and sufferings to make me a new creation?
- Do I believe that my healed wounds are the means for God's healing grace to flow to others?
- Do I believe that my wounds, united to Jesus' wounds, become the power of God, the power of the Cross, in my life?

d) Persevere in Prayer and Work

Saint Catherine writes: "If these souls do not abandon the exercise of holy prayer and their other good works, but go on, with perseverance, to increase their virtues, they will arrive at the state of filial love."[127] God warns her that during trials, many tend to "impatiently turn backward, and sometimes **abandon, under color of virtue,** many of their exercises, saying to themselves, 'This labor does not profit me.' Such a soul …has not yet unwound the bandage of spiritual self-love."[128]

Ask yourself:

- Am I faithful to practice what the Lord has asked of me?
- How do I excuse my withdrawal from prayer, confession, community life, etc.?
- Will you allow the Holy Spirit to bridge the gap that separates you from God by transforming your imperfect love to filial love?

---

[127] Ibid., *Dialogue.*
[128] Ibid.

Jesus gives His life to the Father for this union: "The glory that you have given me I have given them, so that they may be one, as we are one" (Jn 17:22). God described to St. Catherine this amazing union:

He who loves Me shall be one thing with Me and I with him, and I will manifest Myself to him and we will dwell together.[129] This is the union of those who love me, for though they are two in body, yet they are one in soul through the affection of love, because love transforms the lover into the object loved, and where two friends have one soul, there can be no secret between them.[130]

---

[129] Cf. Jn 14:23.

[130] *Dialogue, http://www.catholictreasury.info.*

3-C
The Hidden Martyrdom of the Heart
<hr>

3-C-1
— *Jesus' Lifetime Hidden Martyrdom* —

St Gregory of Nyssa wrote: "In this feast of the Nativity ... begins the mystery of the Passion."[131] Fifteen centuries later the Lord told the Ven. Conchita:

> From the first moment of my Incarnation, the Cross already planted in My Heart, overburdened Me and the thorns penetrated it. The blow struck by the lance might have been some solace causing to gush from My Side a volcano of love and of suffering but I did not consent to that until after My death.[132]

This interior cross is the interior martyrdom that Jesus lived all His life because His love for us has no bounds. His Sacred Heart suffers to see us separated from Him. Jesus told Conchita:

> Through the external Cross, which all can see, I was a victim acceptable to the Father by shedding My blood, **but it was above all through the interior cross that redemption was accomplished**. [133]

---

[131] St. Gregory of Nyssa, *Sermon on the Nativity of Christ*, PG 46, 1 (c.335-395), 128f.
[132] http://www.apcross.org/conchita/ConchitaDiary-English.pdf .
[133] Ven. Concepcion Cabrera de Armida, (Diary entry of 7 Sept. 1896), as cited by Marie-Michel Philipon, ed., A.J. Owen, trans. *Conchita: A Mother's Spiritual Diary* (New York, Alba, 1978), 187.

Jesus' heart is pure love and this is why He also suffers infinitely. He bore the crown of thorns on His heart before receiving it on His head. His Heart was wounded, pierced and disfigured as He carried the wounds, brokenness, and sins of all. Jesus saw our wounds and experienced our pain, darkness, spiritual blindness, pride, arrogance… He also sorrowed for the hardened hearts of all who live by the law and not by love. Jesus suffered this torture of His heart in silence, hidden, known only by His Mother who was united as one to His sufferings. It is amazing to ponder that Jesus, as Priest and Victim, suffered His interior martyrdom each day of His ordinary life, offering Himself to the Father for our redemption. **The Cross, therefore, makes visible for us what He had lived all His life.** In fact, Jesus revealed to Venerable Conchita that His interior crucifixion was much worse than Calvary:

> I wish that above all, there be honored the interior sufferings of My Heart, sufferings undergone from My Incarnation to the Cross and which are mystically prolonged in My Eucharist. These sufferings are still unsuspected by the world… There will always be ingratitude, therefore My Heart, overflowing with tenderness, will ever feel the thorns of the Cross. In heaven, as God, I could not suffer. To find this Cross, which above did not exist, I descended into this world and became man. As God-Man, I could suffer infinitely to pay the price of the salvation of so many souls. During my life, I never desired anything except the Cross, and ever the Cross, wanting to show the world that which is the sole wealth and happiness on earth, the currency which will buy an eternal happiness.
>
> I only remained on the Cross of Calvary for three hours, but on the interior Cross of My Heart, my whole life…

These sufferings remained hidden during My life. I smiled, I labored. Only My Mother was aware of this martyrdom, which crushed My loving Heart. My external Passion lasted but a few hours. It was like a gentle dew, a comfort for the other Passion, terribly cruel, which tortured ceaselessly My soul![134]

I found myself relating to Jesus as I read these words from Ven. Conchita: "These sufferings remained hidden during My life. I smiled and labored." I too live my ordinary daily life laboring with the duties of my vocation with my sorrows hidden within my heart. Many times I am asked, "How are you?" and I smile and say, "I'm fine!" Yet, hidden within my heart, are my sorrows. I cannot compare my sufferings to those of Christ, yet these words from Jesus began to reveal to me how to live my hidden sufferings of heart.

Most people can appreciate that love unites hearts "in good times and in bad, in sickness and in health," but Christ's love for us goes beyond what we can naturally understand. That is why **the revelation of His crucified love is the greatest grace, and to respond to this grace is the greatest gift we can offer Him.** When we do not respond to His love, His suffering increases, yet He loves us even knowing that we will betray Him again and again.

We have already seen that, by uniting our suffering with Jesus, we enter a deeper union with Him. Now Jesus asks us to share in the interior martyrdom of His Heart:

---

[134] *Ibid.*: Diary entry of 25 Sept. 1894.

39. Martyrdom of the Heart, Diary of a MOC

> *The martyrdom of the heart is the martyrdom of suffering with Love and for Love. My daughter, if you could only understand the fruit of the martyrdom of suffering, you would desire nothing else on earth. The hidden life of suffering with Love and for Love is of far greater worth than great and small works tainted with human recognition. Believe in the hidden force contained in the martyrdom of the heart. This is the purest fragrance of love that has the power to conquer the enemies of God.* (11/9/12)

At the Cross, Christ reveals the fullness of His love. St. Paul calls this revelation **"The Word of the Cross,"** and teaches that it is **"the power of God and the wisdom of God."**[135] This means that, contrary to the world's view, if we want to have true love, power, and wisdom, we need to go to the Cross with an open and humble heart to be pierced and to follow Jesus as hidden martyrs of love.

We are not going to follow Jesus to the Cross if we have the wrong understanding of redemption. Some believe that we do not need to do anything to be saved, beyond believing that Jesus paid for our sins. For them, redemption is only the legal act of paying the debt. This is a misunderstanding of redemption. The sacrifice of Jesus is indeed absolutely necessary for our salvation, but we still need to put into practice Christ's requisites for His

---

[135] 1 Cor 1:18,24.

disciples: to take the Cross and follow Him. In the words of Pope Benedict XVI: **"Following Christ's example, we have to learn to give ourselves completely. Anything else is not enough."**[136]

Let us now ponder Christ's interior crucifixion through the experience of two saints.

Saint Angela of Foligno:

Already in the womb of His mother, His holy soul began to feel the most extreme suffering as perfect reparation to God, and this not for His own faults but for the faults of humanity... Thus, the whole life of Christ was accompanied by continual sufferings.

How will the unhappy soul, which only wishes to receive consolations in this world go to Him, who is the way of suffering? In truth, the soul perfectly enamored of Christ, its beloved, would not wish to have any other bed or state in this world than the one he had. I believe that even Mary, watching her beloved Son lamenting and dying on the cross, did not ask of him then to experience sweetness but rather suffering. It is in a soul the sign of very weak love to want from Christ, the Beloved, anything in this world but suffering.[137]

Blessed Anne Catherine Emmerich describes in detail the interior crucifixion of Jesus at Gethsemane where His Heart and soul are crushed, as in a wine press, by the sins, indifference and ingratitude of mankind:

After a time, His soul became terrified at the sight of the

---

[136] General audience, 9 Jan., 2013, pontifexcontent.f
[137] http://www.lovecrucified.com/saints/angela_foligno.html.

140

innumerable crimes of men, and of their ingratitude towards God, and his anguish was so great that he trembled and shuddered as he exclaimed: "My Father, if it be possible, let this cup pass from me." But the next moment he added: "nevertheless, not as I will, but as thou wilt"[138] … I saw all the sins, wickedness, vices, and ingratitude of mankind torturing and crushing him to the earth; the horror of death and terror which he felt as man at the sight of the expiatory sufferings about to come upon him…[139]

Who sees Jesus' martyrdom of Heart in Gethsemane? His Apostles are asleep. Only His Abba, His mother Mary, who is united in heart and spirit to Him, and the angel that comes to console and strengthen Him, perceive His agony. Overwhelmed with sorrow and terror, He seeks His friends, Peter, James and John, and asks them to, "remain here, and watch with me" (Mt 26:38). The apostles are alarmed to see their Messiah in such a weak and horrible condition. The appearance of Jesus shocks them. So, they fall asleep. Asleep they are not able to feel the sorrows of the Lord, and therefore, are not able to suffer with Him. **We too, like the apostles, learn ways to avoid being in touch with our own sufferings of heart and the sufferings of others. We also "tune out."**

The hidden force of the interior martyrdom of the heart is still not understood nor known by many. However, Jesus continues to come to us, His friends, asking us to remain with Him and to pray as He continues to suffer in the Eucharist for humanity. To enter Gethsemane with Jesus, to keep watch and to pray with Him, is to

---

[138] Mt 26:38-39.
[139] Blessed Anne Catherine Emmerich, *The Dolorous Passion of Our Lord Jesus Christ*, 103.

participate intimately with Him in His agony of love. Archbishop Fulton Sheen noted: "The only time our Lord asked the Apostles for anything was the night He went into agony. Not for activity did He plead but for an hour of companionship."[140]

40. The Hidden Life Is a Share in the Activity of God, Diary of a MOC

> I feel my Lord in my soul holding His chalice. His tears of sorrow for our brokenness fall one-by-one into the chalice. **He thirsts for my companionship.** His gaze invites me to remain with Him and just to be with Him. I remain next to Him, with Him, as He cries God's tears of sorrow for each of us. I am not called to do, but just to be with Him, to accompany Him in His sorrows. Through the grace of God, my soul is living in the hidden life. The world does not understand the hidden life. It is God who does, Who suffers, Who redeems, but I enter and live within the words of the Mass, "through Him, with Him and in Him." This hidden life is not a state of inactivity but of great activity. It's a participation in the activity of God Himself. I am accompanying my Lord, Who suffers for all. This is peace, and the fruit of this peace is JOY! (2/6/13)

Jesus grants His martyrs the gift of receiving in their hearts the wounds, oppression, and disorders of others, and to suffer with Him for their healing and sanctification, thus participating in the work of redemption.

---

[140] *A Treasure in Clay, the autobiography of Archbishop Sheen*, www.ignatiusinsight.com.

41. Crown of Glory Is the Crown of Thorns, Diary of a MOC

> *The crown of glory is the crown of martyrs. It is reserved for those who enter the King's court. It is for those who enter the interior chamber to dwell with God. Persevere in wearing the crown of many thorns. I am permitting for you to receive the oppression in the hearts of others as one with Me…Suffer those attacks, My little one, with perfect trust and love, obtaining graces for the many who are oppressed. This hidden life of suffering the oppression of other souls with Me will obtain for you the crown of glory.* (12/26/13)

3-C-2
— We Are All Called to Be Martyrs of Love —

— Third Secret of Fatima —

When I first read the Secret of Fatima, I did not think it applied to me. It speaks of martyrs shedding blood. I never thought of myself as a martyr, so I forgot about it. Then I read Cardinal Ratzinger's interpretation of the Secret, which was published by the Vatican. I understood that some will shed blood but all are called to be martyrs and live the Secret of Fatima by living the mystery of Christ's interior martyrdom. In this way, we can all be the hope for the Church and world.

Below is part of the commentary by Cardinal Ratzinger that explains how we are "a Church of martyrs":

Beneath the arms of the cross angels gather up the blood of

the martyrs, and with it, they give life to the souls making their way to God. Here, the blood of Christ and the blood of the martyrs are considered as one: the blood of the martyrs runs down from the arms of the cross. The martyrs die in communion with the Passion of Christ, and their death becomes one with his. For the sake of the body of Christ, they complete what is still lacking in his afflictions (cf. Col 1:24). Their life has itself become a Eucharist, part of the mystery of the grain of wheat, which in dying yields abundant fruit. The blood of the martyrs is the seed of Christians, said Tertullian. As from Christ's death, from His wounded side, the Church was born, so the death of the witnesses is fruitful for the future life of the Church. Therefore, the vision of the third part of the "secret," so distressing at first, concludes with an image of hope: **no suffering is in vain**, and it is a suffering Church, a Church of martyrs, which becomes a sign-post for man in his search for God. The loving arms of God welcome not only those who suffer like Lazarus, who found great solace there and mysteriously represents Christ, who wished to become for us the poor Lazarus. There is something more: from the suffering of the witnesses comes a purifying and renewing power, because their suffering is the actualization of the suffering of Christ Himself and a communication in the here and now of its saving effect.[141]

---

[141] Congregation for the Doctrine of the Faith, "Fatima" 26 June, 2000, www.vatican.va.

42. Grace Through the Hidden Life of Suffering,
Diary of a MOC

> *My little ones, do not be discouraged, for I am doing something new. You are My little servants of love despised and misunderstood by the world. Remain in Me and I in you so that the power of God will flow as living water to My Church. Do not be afraid or discouraged for being rejected and not accepted. Do you not see that this is the way of love, the way of the Cross? It is precisely on this path of rejection and humiliations that you will purchase for the world many graces. I am most pleased with each of you.*
>
> *My Father collected your tears last night as one with My Mother's for the mission I have entrusted to you. Continue on the path of holiness you are walking. My little one, I will make all things new through My Precious Blood and the blood of My martyrs. This spirituality of suffering out of love for Me is not understood even within My Church. Yet here lies the power of God and the power of the Holy Spirit. More grace is obtained for the world through the hidden life of suffering in love than the public life... Live the hidden life to perfection in Me and in the Heart of My Mother.* (9/14/10, Feast of the Exaltation of the Cross)

The secret of Fatima taught us that our interior martyrdom is no less real than the martyrdom of blood because it is our martyrdom of heart—a participation in Jesus' martyrdom of the heart. Many popes confirm this. This is from the homily of Pope Pius XII at the canonization of St. Maria Goretti:

> Not all of us are expected to die a martyr's death, but we are all called to the pursuit of Christian virtue. This demands strength of character though it may not match that of this innocent girl. Still, a constant, persistent and relentless effort is asked of us right up to the moment of our death. This may be conceived as **a slow, steady martyrdom,** which Christ urged upon us when He said: The kingdom of heaven is set upon and laid waste by violent forces. So let us all, with God's grace, strive to reach the goal.[142]

Saint John Paul II tells us that we should have the same spirit of the Roman martyrs:

> We must return to the drama which they experienced in their souls, in which they confronted, face to face, human fear and superhuman courage, the desire to live and the will to be faithful until death, the sense of solitude before unfeeling hatred and the experience of the power that flows from the close, invisible presence of God and of the common faith of the early Church.
>   We need to return to that drama so that the question can arise: **does something of that drama take place in me?**[143]

Pope Benedict XVI encourages us to live a "daily martyrdom in fidelity to the Gospel":

> Celebrating the martyrdom of St. John the Baptist also

---

[142] Pope Pius XII, 24 June, 1950, cited in the Office of Readings of July 6, memorial of St. Maria Goretti.
[143] St. John Paul II, Address, 30 August, 2001, w2.vatican.va

reminds us—Christians in our own times—that we cannot give in to compromise when it comes to our love for Christ, for His Word, for His Truth. The Truth is the Truth; there is no compromise. The Christian life requires, as it were, the **'martyrdom' of daily fidelity to the Gospel**, the courage, that is, to allow Christ to increase in us and to direct our thoughts and actions.[144]

We can see that the martyrdom mentioned by the popes is not limited to the sacrifices needed to avoid sin; Christ's love impels us to accompany Him all the way to the Cross to die with Him.

All the saints are witnesses to the power of living as martyrs with Christ. St. John of Avila writes:

Let us strive with patience to be martyrs, for though our work is not as great as theirs (those who shed blood), it lasts longer. We ought not to wish for a peaceful life but rather for pure martyrdom, as was the life of our Lord and as He wants our life to be also. There have been many martyrs for the faith, and many who, without being so, have gone to heaven, but **we must all be martyrs of love, if we want to go there**.[145]

The martyrdom of the heart is so pleasing to God and holds such great power because it is the purest gift of ourselves to God, the gift that is most like Christ's. Only on earth can we choose to live as martyrs with Christ, victims of love. I often think that at the moment of death our greatest regret will be not having given God totally the gift of ourselves. Wilfred Stinissen wrote:

_____

[144] General audience, 29 Aug., 2012, w2.vatican.va.
[145] _Obras del Venerable Maestro Juan de Avila_, Letter vol VI, #2717.

If we are subject to trials here on earth, if we must struggle to say yes to God, it is because, in eternity, God can say to us: "You have given me something. It is not only I who give, but rather we give to each other. I give myself in gratitude because you have given me something that you could have refused to give. Now you can no longer give me anything, but at one time you did, and it has an eternal value. I never forget."

Theology has always taught that we cannot "merit" anything, either in heaven or purgatory. To "merit," that is, to do something for God, belongs to our earthly life.[146]

3-C-3
— *Mary's Interior Martyrdom* —

Mary participated most perfectly in the interior martyrdom of the heart of her son, and through our consecration to her, she will form us, if we allow her, as Christ's pure martyrs of love.

Pope Francis speaks of Mary's "martyrdom of the heart":

Throughout her life, the Mother of Christ carried out her duties in full union with Him, a life which reached its climax on Calvary. Mary united herself to her Son in the martyrdom of the heart and in the offering of life to the Father for the salvation of humanity.

---

[146] Wifred Stinissen, *Into Your Hands, Father: Abandoning Ourselves to the God Who Loves Us* (San Francisco: Ignatius Press, 2011), 74.

Our Lady made her own the pain of her Son and with Him accepted the Father's will, in that obedience that bears fruit, which gives true victory over evil and death.[147]

St. Bernard writes on Mary's martyrdom:

The martyrdom of the Virgin is set forth both in the prophecy of Simeon and in the actual story of our Lord's passion. The holy old man said of the infant Jesus: "He has been established as a sign which will be contradicted." He went on to say to Mary: "And your own heart will be pierced by a sword."

Truly, O blessed Mother, a sword has pierced your heart. For only by passing through your heart could the sword enter the flesh of your Son… Clearly it did not touch His soul and could not harm Him, but it did pierce your heart. For surely His soul was no longer there, but yours could not be torn away. Thus the violence of sorrow has cut through your heart, and we rightly call you more than martyr, since the effect of compassion in you has gone beyond the endurance of physical suffering.[148]

Mary was united to the "Word of the Cross"[149] (Jesus) ever since she carried Him in her womb. Through her ordinary hidden life she lived united as one to Christ; and in this way, she possessed, with her son, "the power of God and the wisdom of God".[150] She lived her daily trials and sufferings abandoned

---

[147] "Like Mary, the Church Must Bring Christ to the World", General audience, 23 Oct., 2013.

[148] St. Bernard, cited in the Office of Reading, Feast of Our Sorrowful Mother, 15 sept.

[149] Cf. 1 Cor 1:18.

[150] Cf. 1 Cor 1:24.

completely to God. Mary is the "hidden force" united to her Son. Mary is gentle, humble, silent… and also strong. She possesses the spiritual strength that souls can achieve only as they unite to the "Word of the Cross". She is a constant channel of God's strength and consolation for Jesus and the Apostles. It is in this divine power that she participates as Co-Redemptrix in the salvation of mankind.

Pope Benedict XVI said in a homily:

> In the crucified Jesus, the divinity is disfigured, stripped of all visible glory and yet is present and real. Faith alone can recognize it: the faith of Mary, who places in her heart too this last scene in the mosaic of her Son's life. She does not yet see the whole, but continues to trust in God, repeating once again with the same abandonment: "Behold, the handmaid of the Lord."[151]

Mary's sacrifice was perfected in the last years of her life during her suffering of solitude. After Jesus' Ascension, Mary lived in perfect faith and hope as she no longer felt the presence of the Trinity. Jesus reveals her hidden martyrdom of solitude to Venerable Conchita:

> The Heart of Mary obtained these graces in the martyrdom of a solitude in which she was left, not by men (she had St. John and the Apostles and many souls who fervently loved her), not by Me in My Body (she consoled herself with the Eucharist and with her living and perfect faith), but by the

---

[151] Pope Benedict XVI, homily to the cardinals, 21 Nov., 2010, w2.vatican.va.

Trinity, which hid itself from her, leaving her in a spiritual and divine abandonment.[152]

The lives of Jesus and Mary show us that it is not by DOING many great works that we make a difference in the world. What God desires is that we BECOME one with Love. Only then our "doing" bears the fruit He wants.

Mary's life was most fecund in the years of her greatest suffering of solitude. Through her interior martyrdom of heart, she showered an abundance of graces upon the nascent Church. As we begin to live as one with Jesus and Mary through the hidden martyrdom of our hearts, our lives also take on the power of God. We can reach through time and space to help save and sanctify countless souls!

43. The Martyrdom of the Heart Lived with Our Mother of Sorrows, Diary of a MOC

> Again, my heart is consumed in sorrow and I enter this fatigue. I'm struggling to do the simplest tasks. I can't find words to describe this consuming sorrow. I feel I am living the hidden martyrdom of the heart, to a very small degree, I am sharing in Mary's suffering of solitude. Who can understand such a profound suffering but yet so hidden? I try to keep a smile on my face but my soul and heart is crying. At moments, I can't contain the tears from flowing from my eyes. I ponder the words from my Lord,
>
> *"I am the innocent Lamb of the Father Who*

---

[152] Concepcion Cabrera de Armida, as cited by Marie-Michel Philipon ed., A.J. Owen, trans., *Conchita: A Mother's Spiritual Diary*, (New York, Alba, 1978), 178.

> *abandons Himself to be sacrificed so that you may have life. I am Love, incarnated Love..."*
>
> My soul aches knowing who Jesus is and seeing my family live with such indifference. Love is not known; Love is not loved. What sorrow. All I can do is what my Lord has taught me: *"Suffer all with Me."* I feel united to our Mother of Sorrows.
>
> My Lord and my God, receive my tears of sorrow as ONE with Mary's in Jesus crucified for my family, all Your beloved sons and all the hearts hardened to Your love. (12/22/11)

In our relationship with our mother Mary, we assume the role of St. John, the beloved disciple as she takes us to the Cross with her, gives us the power to love the Cross and to enter the love that Jesus forged between her and St. John at the Cross. This union with Mary enables us to be with her at the Cenacle and to be filled with the Holy Spirit. When we take Mary home, we continue to suffer with her. In this way, we are the "hidden force" that is desperately needed in the Church.

3-C-4
— Our Ordinary Life Is a Hidden Force —

In our daily lives, we are given the opportunity to live the hidden martyrdom of love. We can make every one of our acts, including our daily chores, into acts of love. Then we become the "hidden force" of God that has the power to transform hearts and nations and to pierce all darkness. Jesus promised us this power to love through His words to St. Faustina: "great will be your power for whomever you intercede." Venerable Conchita wrote about the same power of love in her hidden life as a housewife:

> Pure love is of far greater apostolic fecundity than the most outstanding works accomplished with less than love. It is at the eve of life, in silence and isolation, in prayer and in sacrifice, that God's Mother attains her maximum of love and her fullness of apostolic fecundity in the service of the Church of Christ, just as Christ Himself did not save the world in the luster of His Word and of His miracles, but on the Cross.[153]

Our human nature seeks to be noticed, to be appreciated, to be important and to do supposedly great things. This is why the world today does not appreciate motherhood. **True motherhood is a vocation of hidden martyrdom, reflecting the perfect motherhood of our Blessed Mother**. Here lies the "hidden power" of spiritual motherhood. This hidden martyrdom, united to Mary, will raise up God's army of holy priests for the reign of the Immaculate Heart of Mary and the new Pentecost!

Pope Francis speaks about **"martyrs of everyday life"**:

> There is also daily martyrdom, which may not entail death but is still a "loss of life" for Christ, by doing one's duty with love, according to the logic of Jesus, the logic of gift, of sacrifice. Let us think: how many dads and moms every day put their faith into practice by offering up their own lives in a concrete way for the good of the family! … They are martyrs too! Daily martyrs, martyrs of everyday life![154]

---

[153] *Ibid.*, 181.
[154] Pope Francis, 23 June, 2013. w2.vatican.va

44. Persevere in the Ordinary, Diary of a MOC

It is through perseverance in living the ordinary of your state in life, in love for Me, that you are perfected in many virtues.

The ordinary duties of motherhood have been greatly attacked by Satan because they are so pleasing to the Father, and when lived in My crucified love, as Mary did, possess the power of God to aid in the sanctification and salvation of many souls. This is why your formation began in the most ordinary of your state in life as a mother (the gentle touch, kiss, blessing, making chocolate milk).

It is here, living the details of the most ordinary that you began to grow in greater love. Living the details of the ordinary became your prayer of blessing and honor to your God. It is in the most ordinary and hidden life that a soul encounters the face of God. I disguise Myself in what the world sees as tedious. That is why all the Mothers of the Cross have begun to encounter Me in the laundry, cleaning, cooking, nursing...

The tasks of ordinary motherhood are precious to the Father because they are the heartbeat of the domestic church. Now you know why Satan has done so much to attack motherhood. Through the restoration of motherhood, I will strengthen the domestic church, aid in the healing of fatherhood, and bring restoration to My Universal Church. (12/12/11)

— Testimony —
A Mother Unites Her Difficult Ordinary Life
to the Love of Jesus Crucified

I will give some details of my life in the Middle East. Women have to wear the traditional Muslim *abaya* (tunic) everywhere outside the house. Women can't go anywhere alone. Hence for anything, I must depend on my husband. At first, I found these situations stifling. But now the Lord has taught me to offer the troubles of such a life for the contemplative priests who live in monasteries shut up from the outside world and for the Middle East.

I used to worry that I don't get enough time for silence and prayer. Here the kids have to reach school at six o' clock. So, however hard I try, I can't get much time in the mornings. But after I was accepted into our family (Love Crucified Community), the Holy Spirit guided me because of your prayers, to make use of the most trivial situations as a time for prayer.

I would like to share with you some of them. Each morning I begin my work in the kitchen by lighting the stove. I would say to the Lord: "Lord, ignite the hearts of your priests with love for you so that they may kindle the same fire in the hearts of all souls entrusted to them." While bathing the kids: "Lord, cleanse the hearts of all your beloved priests from all affections to worldly things." While cleaning the house messed up by the kids, I offer it for the priests who spend hours in the confessional to clean our souls and so on. And thus, the Spirit of God helps me to be in the presence of our Lord throughout the day and makes my daily burdens really light.

45. My Hidden Life, Diary of a MOC

My daughter, the time is short... the will of the Father is to possess you with His love and that through Me, with Me, and in Me you become ONE with LOVE. To do the Will of the Father must become your daily food, your daily life. Nothing else should matter: persecutions, imprisonments, misunderstandings, loneliness, solitude, hunger... for when you live in the Father's will you possess all. Was this not My life here on earth?

My daughter, you must live each moment IN LOVE; then you will live in perfect peace. You must learn to wait upon the Lord, for this is love. Is that not how I lived My life here on earth? Although at the age of twelve I was ready to begin My mission that was already consuming My Heart, I returned with Mary and Joseph to wait upon My Father's time; then My public mission lasted only three short years. But you see, My daughter, My mission had already begun and was being fulfilled throughout all My hidden life from the moment of My Incarnation. The power of God for the redemption of the world was at work in My hidden life, and Mary Most Holy was participating as ONE with Me in My hidden life in the work of redemption. (7/18/11)

Jesus speaks to St. Faustina:

My Daughter, I want to instruct you on how you are to rescue souls through sacrifice and prayer. You will save more souls through prayer and suffering than will a missionary through his teachings and sermons alone. I want to see you as a sacrifice of living love, which only then carries weight before Me. …Outwardly, your sacrifice must look like this: silent, hidden, permeated with love, imbued with prayer. I demand, My daughter, that your sacrifice be pure and full of humility, that I may find pleasure in it.[155]

46. Love as Christ Loves Us, Diary of a MOC

I find myself now in my life striving to live as a Mother of the Cross. Through the immense mercy of my Lord, He has begun purifying my heart in the furnace of His Heart and I find myself loving more purely and also suffering with greater intensity. I see and experience the darkness and the hardened hearts of those that are closest to me, and my heart cries. I go out into the world and I see and experience the spiritual blindness of my brothers and sisters (for now I also see all people as my brothers and sisters in Christ) and my heart is pierced with sorrow. I see so many women of all ages dressed provocatively because this is fashionable, and my heart cries for them.

So many souls do not know the love of the Trinity, and my heart seems to want to offer myself as a living sacrifice even more. My Lord and my

---

[155] *Diary,* 1767.

God, how can it be that so many souls do not know Your love? How can it be that Love is not loved by so many, especially Your beloved sons, Your priests?

The Holy Spirit seems to be drawing me into the hidden life of Jesus and Mary, because here lies the secret of how I can live my life helping to save the souls of my family and many more. I understand with such clarity that it will be through my hidden life that I will be able to live most united to the Word of the Cross, and thus, possess the power of God to save souls as ONE martyr of love in Jesus and Mary. (12/5/10)

Jesus addressed the following words to the Mothers of the Cross, who live their lives as ordinary women through the martyrdom of the heart:

47. One with Mary to Renew the Church, Diary of a MOC

You, My little ones, are the consolation of My suffering Heart because you each have united yourselves to Mary, the Mother of God and the Mother of all. As I gaze at each of you, I see her beauty radiating from you. Allow her to form each of you to perfection.

*I need you, My faithful ones, to bring life to My Missionaries of the Cross. It is My hidden martyrs of love in perfect union with the Queen of Martyrs that will raise up My Apostles of Light. Know that I have taken My abode in each of your hearts; therefore, **radiate the humility and purity of My***

Mother.

Do not grow weary in your hidden life of suffering all with Me, for you are My holy remnant that God the Father will use to purify My Church and pierce the darkness penetrating Her. Therefore, go forth, My daughters, as My holy warriors with Mary to seize the dragon and cast him into hell.

I bless you with My Precious Blood and seal you with the power of My Cross. (4/1/11)

48. Hidden Life of Spiritual Mothers, Diary of a MOC.

It is through the hidden life of the Mothers of the Cross that My army of holy priests will be raised up. These spiritual mothers will live the tears and sorrows of their hearts united as one with My Mother of Sorrows. It is My Mother's sorrows that continue to shower grace upon the world, and as My MOC unite as one with My Mother, the shower will become a living torrent of grace. Therefore, each MOC must be perfected in living her hidden ordinary life with all its trials, sorrows, exhaustion.... with pure love; and in this way she will find her joy: the joy of knowing that she is participating in the hidden sorrows of My Mother for the salvation of many souls.

Allow My Mother to form each of you, My daughters. It is Rosa Mystica who wants to form your gentle hearts. Mary reveals the sorrows of her pierced Heart that continue to remain hidden and the roses of prayer, sacrifice and penance. You must imitate Mary. In this way, your lives will become the

> *sweet fragrance of prayer, and your sacrifices and penances will be lived in the most ordinary of your duties as women.*
>
> *Your lives as My victims of love will go unnoticed by the world but will be seen by the eyes of the Father. He will use your hidden lives of love to humble the proud. Know that you are My consolation.* (5/31/11)

3-C-5
— The Eucharist —

The Passion of Christ encompasses the institution of the Eucharist and Good Friday. They cannot be separated. Saint Teresa of Calcutta wrote:

> The Eucharist is connected with the Passion... When you look at the Crucifix, you understand how much Jesus loved you then; when you look at the Sacred Host you understand how much Jesus loves you now.

When Christ said, "I have earnestly desired to eat this Passover with you before My passion,"[156] He was manifesting His desire to give Himself as Eucharist to His bride, the Church, to become ONE with her. Then He prayed that we too be with Him and remain faithful.[157]

The Eucharist should consume us with such love, gratitude and zeal for the Lord that we forget about ourselves and gladly suffer

---

[156] Lk 22:15.
[157] Cf. Jn 17:24.

any trial for His sake. It would be a contradiction to receive the Lord with love in the Eucharist and then abandon Him by refusing to accompany Him to Calvary. Pope Benedict XVI reminded us of this:

> There is no love without suffering—without the suffering of renouncing oneself, of the transformation and purification of self for true freedom. Where there is nothing worth suffering for, even life loses its value. The Eucharist—the center of our Christian being—is founded on Jesus' sacrifice for us; it is born from the suffering of love, which culminated in the Cross. We live by this love that gives itself. It gives us the courage and strength to suffer with Christ and for Him in this world, knowing that in this way our life becomes great and mature and true.[158]

— Contemplating Jesus' Eucharistic Life We Learn to Love in Our Hidden, Ordinary Lives —

Do you ever struggle to love those that do not love you, do not appreciate you, do not notice all that you do, have been unfaithful, are indifferent to your love, ignore you, criticize you…? Well, that is how Jesus is treated; yet He continues to love us in the Eucharist. He seeks us out regardless of what we have done or how we treat Him.

---

[158] Homily, opening of the Pauline Year, 28 June 2008, w2.vatican.va.

49. I Give Myself to the Good and the Bad, Diary of a MOC

The Eucharist is the power of God in the world. The love of God is the Eucharist and is transmitted through the Eucharist.

Learn about the hidden life by contemplating My Eucharistic life. I am hidden from your human eye but completely present. I am verbally silent, yet My soul speaks to your soul. I am humble, pure, simple, silent, generous, forgiving, merciful, patient, and tender. I give Myself fully to the good and the bad, to the deserving and the undeserving, to those who love Me and to those that persecute Me; for when one is not obedient to the precepts of My Church, I am persecuted. I continue to love those who do not love Me. I continue to love those who use Me. I continue to love the unfaithful. I continue to love those indifferent to My love. I am left alone in the Tabernacles of the world with few who come to be with Me, to adore Me and to give Me thanks. I cry but My tears are hidden. I intercede continuously before the throne of our Father for all. My hidden life in the Eucharist is seen by Abba and blessed by Him Who sees all.

Your ordinary and hidden life through the Cross becomes united to My Eucharistic life. Your hidden life takes on the same power as My hidden life because we are no longer two but ONE. These are My living hosts. In this union of love, you enter and live in the realm of God. Through Me, with Me and in Me your most ordinary life is the power of God. Your thoughts, words, deeds, but most especially

> *your tears and sorrows of heart, possess the power of God to bless the world. Your hidden life not seen by anyone is seen by God and, through Me, with Me and in Me, He blesses many. Your life, as ONE with My Eucharistic life, moves beyond time and space.*
>
> *Ponder My Eucharistic life with the Holy Spirit and Mary. I desire for you to help Me form many living hosts to shine the light of God and to pierce the darkness. You grow in holiness as your hidden life is lived to greater perfection in My hidden life.* (7/5/12)

50. Why I Chose to Remain on Earth in a Host,
Diary of a MOC

> *Why did I choose to remain on earth in a Host? Because, in this way I am present to all, for you to contemplate and to receive Me as living Bread. I remained with you to nourish your life with Divine life; To prepare you, to strengthen you and to become one with you as you journey the path to eternal life in God. I remain in this hidden and ordinary way so that your hidden and ordinary life can be transformed into Divinity and thus participate here on earth in the unity and Divine life of the Most Holy Trinity.*
>
> *The Eucharist is the life of God that has the power to heal and to transform you from within. In the smallness of the Host is revealed the grandeur, majesty and greatness of God. The Eucharist is the greatest miracle of God for humanity. The Eucharist reveals God's faithfulness to His people. The*

Eucharist reveals what each of you is called to become. (7/12/12)

— Horrible Abuses Against the Eucharist Do Not Diminish Our Lord's Desire to Be with Us —

Saint Alphonsus Liguori writes:

(Jesus) foresaw, too, the insults which sinners would offer His Sacred Heart, which He would leave on earth in the Most Holy Sacrament as proof of His love. These insults are almost too horrible to mention: people trampling the sacred hosts underfoot, throwing them into gutters or piles of refuse, and even using them to worship the devil himself!

Even the knowledge that these and other defamations would happen did not prevent Jesus from giving us this great pledge of His love, the Holy Eucharist. ...Should we not melt with love, as do the candles, which adorn the altars where the Holy Sacrament is preserved? There the Sacred Heart remains burning with love for us. Shall we not in turn burn with love for Jesus?[159]

The Angel of Fatima told the children:

Make everything you do a sacrifice, and offer it as an act of reparation for the sins by which He is offended and in supplication for the conversion of sinners... Above all, accept and bear with submission the sufferings sent you by

---

[159] *From the Heart of Saint Alphonsus: Excerpts from Saint Alphonsus Liguori* Ed. Norman J Muckerman. (USA, Liguori Publications, 1 May, 2002).

Our Lord.

In the next apparition the angel said that those sacrifices and suffering are effective **"by offering them in union with the Eucharistic Sacrifice."**[160]

51. Trust, I Am the Power of the Hidden Life, Diary of a MOC

Trust and place all your confidence in the power of the hidden life being revealed to you now in My Eucharistic presence. I am the power of the hidden life. I want to possess you with My hidden life, which is the Eucharist, transforming you into living hosts. This transformation will take place as you live your hidden and interior life united to My interior crucifixion, suffering all with Me and in Me. In this way, the power of the hidden force will intensify with the fire of the Holy Spirit. (6/15/11)

52. Form My Hidden Martyrs, Diary of a MOC

You must form My hidden martyrs of love, for God the Father is using them to fulfill His plan of salvation during these decisive times. Live your hidden life as ONE with Me in My hidden life in the Eucharist and you will grow in the power of God, which is LOVE. This is the HIDDEN FORCE that will sweep through the face of the world to conquer Satan's darkness. The Eucharist is the power of God in the world, and God desires to make you living

---

[160] As cited by George W. Kosicki, Gerald J. Farrell, *The Spirit and the Bride Say, "Come!"* (Ami Pres, Dec. 1991), 72.

Hosts. (6/30/11)

53. One with My Eucharistic Son, Diary of a MOC

> Mary speaks: *It is my army of victim souls that I am preparing for these decisive times, for it is their hidden lives, as One with my Eucharistic Son, that are being given the power from heaven to defeat Satan and all his principalities and to raise My Son's cohort of holy priests to usher in my reign.* (6/16/11)

3-C-6
— Living Hosts —

When a soul, filled with the Holy Spirit, is united to Jesus so profoundly as to share His sufferings and joys, in total abandonment to the Father, she is a "living host."

The Venerable Archbishop Luis Maria Martinez observed that the sacrament of Holy Orders unites a priest to Jesus in such a way that, at the moment of the consecration, Jesus—in the priest—changes the substance of bread and wine into Himself by the power of the Holy Spirit. But "total transformation" into a "living host" required something more: It required that a human being—priest, religious, or lay—make the "marvelous exchange" of his independent human will for the Divine Will by allowing the Holy Spirit to unite him to Jesus in all of his acts. "Then, in every moment, we can offer the two victims united in one same immolation, we can renew unceasingly the sacrifice of Christ."[161]

54. My Living Hosts, Diary of a MOC

*My daughter, I am alive and present in the world in My Eucharist. But My living presence takes on human form in My living hosts. When I become alive in you, through the power of the Holy Spirit, it is no longer you but I who live and take My being in you.[162] I am able to speak through your lips; My voice becomes audible through yours; My hands touch and heal through your hand... **I move outside the Tabernacle through you**, thus reaching out to the four corners of the world. The power of God is spread through My living hosts, and new life is given to many through My living chalices of My Most Precious Blood.*

You must proclaim from the housetops what you hear Me whisper in your heart.[163] This is My hidden force that will sweep through the world and that holds the power of God. (7/9/11)

---

[161] Archbishop Luis Maria Martinez of Mexico (1881-1856), cited by Hugh Owens in *New and Divine: The Holiness of the Third Christian Millennium* (John Paul II Institute of Christian Spirituality, 2001), 39.

[162] Gal 2:20.

[163] Cf. Mat 10:27.

55. Participate in My Body and Blood, Diary of a MOC

> *Most people **partake** of My Body and Blood, but few desire **to participate** in My Body and Blood.*
>
> *"The cup of blessing that we bless, is it not a **participation**[164] in the blood of Christ? The bread that we break, is it not a **participation** in the Body of Christ?"*[165]
>
> *In order to become One Body in Me you must respond to participate in living in My Body and Blood. In the Eucharist, I give of Myself fully to you and you partake, meaning that you receive Me; but then you must respond to this gift of Love by giving yourself to Me. You must give Me your blood in sacrifice and your body, which is your will.*
>
> *In the Eucharist, I Am the Victim of Love. In order for you to become ONE BODY, ONE BLOOD in Me you must respond to become My victim of love, a victim united as ONE to The Victim. What is required of My creature is her response, her "Fiat," then the power of My Spirit, the Holy Spirit, brings about this perfect union. It is at the foot of the Cross with My Mother that you receive the outpouring of the Holy Spirit from My pierced side. It is He who will lead you through the narrow path of My Cross to perfect union in Me.* (The perfect narrow path from the feet of Jesus crucified to His kiss). (6/26/11 Solemnity of Corpus Christi)

---

[164] "Participation" or "communion" in Greek: "**koinōnia.**" It refers to the union effected by the Eucharist: we are the body and blood of Christ (nuptial union.) This is what constitutes Christian community. See:
http://lovecrucified.com/bible/homilies_audio/ord23_saturday-en-sp.html.

[165] 1 Cor 10:16.

Advice from St. Cajetan:

Do not receive Christ in the Blessed Sacrament to use Him as you judge best, but give yourself to Him and let Him receive you in this Sacrament, so that He Himself, God your Savior, may do to you and through you whatever He wills.[166]

56. Remain Small, Diary of a MOC

My daughter, desire to be only My insignificant vessel, for it is in your humility and poverty of spirit that I have found great joy. Remain small, and I will reveal My power. Desire only the Cross, and My love will triumph through you. Believe in the power of My hidden force as ONE with the power of My Eucharistic life. This is the force that God is strengthening for the decisive battle. Perfect your family in the hidden life I have revealed to you. (7/6/11)

---

[166] *Letter to Elisabeth Porto*, Office of Readings, feast of St. Cajetan, 7 Aug.

— The "Hidden Force" is Not a Romantic Idea —

The "hidden force" truly suffers a martyrdom of the heart. At first we suffer from our own daily struggles, sorrows and sins, but as we grow in union with Christ as martyrs of love and drink directly from His bitter chalice, we also suffer with Him the wounds and oppression in our brothers and sisters.

We are living in the midst of a real and great spiritual battle. Satan and his principalities are constantly working to oppress the work of God. Our Lord's martyrs are God's warriors of love sent directly into the battlefield. They receive in their hearts the burden of the sin of those Satan is attacking.

These warriors of love many times experience physically the battle through great fatigue and exhaustion, which may last for a few days, even when a visit to the doctor shows that they are in good health. We have come to understand that this fatigue is spiritual. During those periods of exhaustion, we are receiving the burdens, sins or oppressions of other souls, in order to help obtain the graces they need. We should not be afraid of this experience because we are in God's hands. We have learned the value of this fatigue; so instead of fighting against it, we enter it and live it with patience and deeper prayer for souls.

"See, I am making all things new" (Rev 21:5)

Saint Arnold Janssen wrote, "The Lord challenges us to realize something new, precisely when so many things in the Church are crumbling."[167] The Lord said to our community, "I am doing something new, believe that the martyrdom of the heart is a hidden force!"

---

[167] St. Arnold Janssen Joseph. Priest founder of the Congregation of the Divine Word.

57. We are Purified Through Situations and Persons,
Diary of a MOC

> *The purpose of the Path is to make all of you My living hosts. As My living hosts, you are God's warriors for the great battle at hand. Countries will rise up and fight this battle with missiles and arms, but the evil will only continue to intensify. Allow Me to possess you with My life.*
>
> *Ponder every relationship and situation in your lives where you are not loving with Me, through Me and in Me. Ask yourselves, "Why is it so difficult to love this person or to love in these situations?" It is precisely in those situations and with those persons where you need to be purified. It is only in this way that you can become ONE with My Eucharistic life and be transformed into Love. My pure victims of love are God's warriors for these decisive times.* (9/1/14)

Longing for intimacy of hearts in marriage

Through years of speaking heart-to-heart with many married women, God revealed to me a deep and very hidden suffering in their hearts: the pain of not being able to live the intimacy of heart they long for with their husbands. Many times they live with the hidden fear that they do not feel love towards their spouse. These deep sufferings are rarely acknowledged and much less spoken about. Some men suffer the same situation, especially when they have entered deep into the spiritual life and their wives have not. When this pain is not acknowledged, but buried, it will manifest itself in anger and resentment towards the spouse. Yet, by living what the Lord has taught us through this Path, these deep hidden sorrows can become the means to enter the hidden life of Jesus' suffering in the Eucharist. This interior suffering is the path for our true femininity and masculinity to reach its greatest potential to love to the extreme of the Cross.

— Testimony —
Our Interior Suffering Can Transform Us into Living Hosts

I shared with a friend my sorrow in seeing how our Lord is so abandoned. I lamented that He cannot be mentioned in many places. He is not loved; He is not called upon. Even His own, who believe in His Real Presence, do not visit Him; few want to go deep into His Heart. I placed myself in His position and thought of how sad I would be if my children did the same to me, not wanting to be with me, not calling upon me, not loving me. I remembered a teaching about our Lord being a prisoner in the tabernacles of the world, alone in a world full of people.

Then, my thoughts turned to my husband. I didn't expect to speak about our relationship, but the words flowed from the depth of my heart. I realized that there is great sorrow in my soul regarding our relationship. We are faithful to each other, and there is even peace and joy at the surface of our marriage; but there is also a certain solitude, an emptiness that I have come to accept as a normal part of marriage.

I am very much aware that he is a good man, a good husband, and a good father. I am also aware of the wounds in his heart and how he guards his emotions and lives on the surface, unable to leave this place where he feels safe.

As I spoke, the words that came out from my mouth were of resentment, disappointment and anger. I shared how I dislike greatly that my husband is present for the kids in body, but not with his feelings, conversations, or the sharing of his heart. I resent that I am alone in teaching them the faith. I resent not being able to share my heart with him. He knows general things about my life, but has no idea what is deep within my heart, what is in the depth of my soul.

It is difficult for me to enter and to live this pain. I am not even sure I know the depth of it. So I had kept my feelings hidden or perhaps turned off, like a computer that shuts down when not used. Even though my heart desired to find intimacy with him, I felt that I couldn't reach him. I even wondered if I truly loved him or if we had reached a point in our marriage where we resigned ourselves to taking care of our daily duties without ever sharing the depths of our hearts.

Then the Lord, with my friend's help, reminded me that He also felt my distance from Him and remained alone in the tabernacle. I saw how often I approached the Eucharist as a duty, instead of joining with Him as ONE to console, to truly accompany Him in His solitude.

This brought me to see how deep was my wound, how hidden, often expressed with damaging emotions. I understood that I must go to the Lord to accompany Him in His solitude and to allow Him to accompany me in mine. As His wounds touch mine and I allow Him to unite me to Himself, He makes me His Living Chalice, a Living Host for my husband, our children and others.

My dear sister told me that many women live the same hidden loneliness. I see the importance of being united to our Mother of Sorrows. I feel she truly understands this hidden suffering that many women do not talk about. Our Blessed Mother lived her solitude to perfection, bearing much fruit for the Church. She will be our teacher, our source of strength and help as we move through this necessary process.

In the testimony of this valiant woman who exposes her deepest hidden suffering, we see that, through her husband, Jesus is perfecting her in love. As she embraces her hidden pain, by suffering with Jesus in the solitude of the tabernacle, her suffering is transformed into victim love; and the anger and resentments gradually melt away in the fire of the Holy Spirit. Then, her suffering, as one with Jesus', receives the power of God to bless her husband, children and the whole world! Remember that a log in the fire takes time to be consumed; so too, the anger and resentments that have grown out of our pain, take time to melt away in the fire of the Sacred Heart. It is PERSEVERANCE in suffering all our hidden sorrows with Jesus' interior crucifixion that brings forth our transformation into love!

58. The Triumph of the Cross Is Fulfilled in Me,
Diary of MOC

As I gaze upon the glorious Cross and come into contact with Love, my search for truth, love and happiness is complete. I see my life as the triumph of God's Cross. As I die with my Lord and Savior, my life, insignificant as it is, becomes the triumph of the Cross, the triumph of love. The triumph of my Lord's Cross is fulfilled in me, His body and bride. In this intimate union of love, I participate in my Lord's sorrows and tears as I suffer with Jesus the horrible reality of my own sin and the sin of humanity. This union of sorrows heals me of my self-love and selfishness as it draws me to know Love. My femininity finds its identity in my Mother of Sorrows, for pure love moves us to bear all for the Other and with the Other.

The union with my Love Crucified stretches me as Jesus' Body was stretched on the Cross. The tent of my heart is stretched and expanded as God calls me to love beyond my human capacity or desire. I feel the spiritual and physical reality of my life and body being blessed, broken continuously, and given so that others may feed and be nourished from the Bread of Life that lives in me.

It is in this docility of heart in which we voluntarily allow God to stretch us in Jesus crucified that we become transformed in Love, so that it is no longer we that live but Jesus crucified who lives in us! (9/14/12)

The litmus test to know if the Eucharist is truly transforming our lives into living hosts is the question, "**Am I responding to evil with good in my life** when a spouse, daughter, son, father, mother, friend, boss… hurts me?"[168]

Let us pray that each time we participate in the Eucharist we "**offer ourselves as a living host** to the One who lovingly gave Himself up for our sake."[169]

3-C-7
— *Living Chalices* —

At the wedding at Cana (Jn 2:1-11) there were six jars, but they were unnoticed as they seemed to be unnecessary for the present need. Those jars represent God's hidden, insignificant victim souls. There are few jars, only six, yet they each had the capacity to hold thirty gallons of water. Once Jesus performs the miracle of turning the water into wine, the wine is poured out from the jars and all the people in the wedding party drink. The multitudes, thus, receive the graces of Jesus' miracle.

We, as God's insignificant victim souls, allow ourselves to be emptied, purified, as we journey through the narrow Path of the Cross. The Lord is transforming us into His pure chalices of gold that are filled with His Blood, which is His very life. Our lives are then poured out upon many souls, the multitudes, bringing Christ's healing grace and new life.

---

[168] Cf., Rom 12:51.
[169] Pope Benedict XVI, homily in Havana, Cuba, 28 Mar., 2012.

59. Allow Me to Fill You with My Precious Blood,
Diary of a MOC

> *I am preparing My pure holy vessels by cleansing them with My Precious Blood. These living chalices will be filled with My Precious Blood as I unite them to the Word of the Cross and they suffer with Me. My Blood will be poured upon My Church to cleanse Her through them.*
>
> *You have been given the particular mission of cleansing My priesthood.*
>
> *"Woe to you, O Jerusalem. How long will it be before you are made clean?"[170]*
>
> *To receive My Blood is to receive My suffering, My love and new life... As My martyrs of love you are called to suffer with Me so that you can love with Me... In this way, you become My living chalices of healing grace for many...* (10/7/2010)

The Gospel tells us that the jars were meant for the "Jewish rite of purification" (Jn 2:6). This too has a significant symbolism for our lives as victim souls. We, as Christ's vessels, receive the wounded dirty hearts of souls to be washed by our tears united in Christ crucified.

---

[170] Cf. *Jer* 13: 12-27.

60. God Will Bless the Multitudes Through His Victim Souls, Diary of a MOC

> *I want you to live with all your love, with all your strength, with all your might as My living force. Suffer with Me in the hiddenness of your heart. Cry with Me for your brothers and sisters, sons and daughters. Do not grow weary in living with Me the sorrows for a humanity that has lost their way.*
>
> *God in His infinite mercy will bless the multitudes through His holy remnant of victim souls. Do not fear to proclaim the power in suffering with the Victim of Love.* (6/9/13)

The jars that hold the wine are not noticed by the people—what they notice is the "good wine" (Jn 2:10). This is the JOY of victim souls—our lives are hidden and unnoticed and many times are unappreciated; yet, through our sacrifice, we bring to many the grace of noticing Christ. We are little victim souls; but as ONE with Love Crucified and Mary, we are vessels of abundant grace poured out as a libation upon the multitudes.

> But even if I am being poured out as a libation over
> the sacrifice and the offering of your faith, I am glad
> and rejoice with all of you (Phil 2:17).

Collect the Lord's Tears in the Chalice of Your Heart

While the Blood of Christ pours out from His Body, tears flow from His Heart. He gives Himself for us entirely, with all the faculties of His soul. The Lord invites us to receive His gift of self by becoming *Living Chalices*, able to collect His tears—tears of love and sorrow—that flow from His most-sensitive Heart. We are called to collect Jesus' tears in the chalices of our hearts with gratitude and veneration. **This is our most hidden, interior life: the union of sorrows with God.**

61. The Power of Tears, Diary of a MOC

Our Lord revealed to me His face in the center of the Eucharist. It was His crucified face, and He was shedding tears. I then saw myself place a golden chalice under the Eucharist to collect His tears. I felt that the chalice represented my heart.

*Will you **participate in My tears**? Will you cry with Me, for My people have gone astray? The justice of God is at hand. Be My living hosts in the world. A time of great justice approaches. My presence will be seen for a time only through My living hosts. My sons and daughters, the time is short; please multiply My living hosts in the world, My living chalices. Who will listen? Are you willing to suffer with Me, like My Mother, so that you can redeem with Me? Many will be lost.*

Suffer with Me, My family. You will have to undergo many trials. Your only safety is in My Cross. Bring many into My crucified embrace where I can protect you. Keep your eyes fixed on My crucified gaze; and I will be your strength always, everywhere, and in all things. Have perfect hope in the God who loves you. Love one another as I have loved you. I bless you tonight with My tears and the tears of My Mother; and I invite you to cry with us and present your tears, as ONE with ours, to the Father for the salvation of many. You are My people and I am your God. Do not forsake Me. (2/9/2012)

—The Transformation of Our Wounds into Living Chalices—
Insights of a Mother of the Cross

Regardless of the kind of wound, it is always a deep hole in the heart. This deep hole in your psyche, this piercing of your heart, God wants to transform into a perfect chalice to receive the tears and blood of your crucified Lord, the flood of Divine Mercy that has nowhere else to go unless a wounded heart is there to receive it. We have nothing else to offer but our wounded hearts.

The deep wound must be attended and must be cleaned so that it becomes the chalice. It must be utterly cleaned out so that it can be filled with the Precious Blood and Tears of Jesus, so that the Mercy of God can overflow onto our territory of souls. As the deep wounds are turned to chalices, our martyred hearts are filled with God's mercy for the multitudes.

We are transformed into living chalices according to our individual capacity, understanding, willingness, and commitment. It is only the wounded heart made vulnerable, open, powerless, and receptive to Him that becomes the living chalice.

Jesus tells St. Faustina, "My Heart finds disappointment; I do not find complete surrender to My love. So many reservations, so much distrust, so much caution."[171]

---

[171] Diary, n.367.

— Jesus Gives Himself as Eucharist —

The gift of becoming living chalices is the full communion with the Eucharistic Lord. He is the gift of love from the Father that fills our chalice and enables us to become a gift for each other. Jesus in us gives Himself in our ordinary and hidden lives as men and women. The Eucharist holds the power of the hidden life of Jesus Christ; yet He is hidden in a humble, ordinary appearance of bread. The Eucharist reveals how God lives "for" us and patiently longs for His Bride, century after century, to come to Him in thanksgiving, praise and adoration.

He gives of Himself to the good and bad, the deserving and the undeserving. Jesus asks each of us in the Eucharist, "Will you love as I love you? Will you love those who don't appreciate you, who condemn, misunderstand, abandon and reject you? Will you love and wait with patience for them? Will you give yourself as a gift to those who ridicule and ignore you?" Men and women, husbands and wives, are you willing to love in this way? This is the LOVE OF THE CROSS. This is the love of all victim souls, our hidden and ordinary life that transforms us into the "HIDDEN FORCE" through union with Christ. This hidden force will penetrate and conquer the darkness that consumes the world and that has seeped into our families.

There is an URGENCY IN OUR TIME, and God NEEDS us to be His martyrs for these decisive times, His living chalices. Our Lord wants us to be living hosts, blessed, broken and given to many.

Speaking about Catholic families, Fr Hardon observed:

They must either be holy—which means sanctified—or they will disappear. **The only Catholic families that will remain alive and thriving in the twenty-first century are**

181

the families of martyrs. Father, mother and children must be willing to die for their God-given convictions… What the world most needs today is families of martyrs, who will reproduce themselves in spirit in spite of the diabolical hatred against family life by the enemies of Christ and His Church in our day.[172]

---

[172]Fr. John A. Hardon, S.J, *The Blessed Virgin and the Sanctification of the Family*, cited in http://www.markmallett.com/blog/a-priest-in-my-own-home-part-ii/.

Chapter Four

In the Sacred Heart of Jesus

---◆---

4-A
Purification in the Sacred Heart

On the Path to Union we are always moving to a deeper level, growing and maturing in our spiritual life. Now the Lord draws us into His Heart. As with children, He takes us from the visible to the invisible, to the heart of the mystery. St Paul teaches: "But I, brethren, could not address you as spiritual men, but as men of the flesh, as babes in Christ. I fed you with milk, not solid food; for you were not ready for it."[173] The Path to Union now brings us to a more solid food, a greater participation in love and suffering with the Lord, so that our hearts gradually become one with His.

A few years ago, as I reflected upon the Gospel story of the rich young man I asked the Lord: "What is the main thing I still need to let go of?" To my surprise the Lord answered quickly, "your reputation." I was stunned. Wow, how difficult it has been to let go of my reputation—to let go of how others perceive me, like me or

---

[173] 1 Cor 3:1-2.

accept me. This has been a long and difficult process for me. I now realize how much my attachment to my reputation is connected to the lies I have come to believe about myself. My low self-image has kept me in bondage to the need of pleasing everyone, to doing what is right in the eyes of others in order to be accepted, liked and loved by all. I have been all my life a woman "less free, less spontaneous, less playful and heavy"—like the older son in Henri Nouwen's book, *The Return of the Prodigal Son.*[174] I realize that all my life I have secretly envied men and women whom I perceive as free—free to laugh, to be spontaneous, playful and free to love—without being concerned about what others think.

Tenderly, the Lord continues to lead me through the difficult process of crucifying with Him my attachment to my reputation, so that the new woman can emerge—the woman who has been deeply touched and embraced by Love and now has the freedom and courage to love others as God has loved her; a love that does not fear to touch and be touched, to embrace and be embraced, and to gaze deeply into the eyes of others; a love that has the freedom to speak the truth; a love that is vulnerable and intimate, and ultimately, as the Lord has said to me from the beginning, a love that is willing to be misunderstood, judged and persecuted.

Pope Francis speaks about the importance of this love:

A society without proximity, where gratuity and affection without compensation —between strangers as well— is disappearing, is a perverse society. The Church, faithful to the Word of God, cannot tolerate such degeneration. A

---

[174] Henri J.M. Nouwen, *The Return of the Prodigal Son: A Story of Homecoming*, (New York: Doubleday, 1996), 71.

Christian community in which proximity and gratuity are no longer considered indispensable is a society which would lose her soul.[175]

As the "new Adams" and "new Eves" living in the purity of Divine Love here on earth, we will be misunderstood, judged as improper and scandalous, and persecuted. The Path of Divine Love leads us to the third nail, which is persecution, the nail that crucifies us as one with Christ so that Love can triumph.

This Path in the Sacred Heart will bring us to a complete dying of our old selves; a dying of our own perceptions, prejudices, desires, tendencies; a dying to our self-righteousness that is so hidden in each of us under the disguise of obedience, duty, adherence to the law, hard work, respect, admiration, eloquence, and piety. As the Holy Spirit exposes the lies that have become part of who we are, the "older sons" living in each of us will be exposed. The older son of the parable of the Prodigal Son lived as the perfect, good son until the return with his younger brother exposed his hidden lie. The love of the father permitted this situation so that his son could be freed from the resentment, pride and selfishness that remained deeply hidden in him.

Through the Path, especially when we are in His Sacred Heart, we will each live personally the parable of the Prodigal Son. God, in His infinite love for each of us, will permit many situations in our lives where the "resentful saint" that hides behind our desires to be good and virtuous, will be exposed; then we will find ourselves at the crossroad of the Path. Like the older son, we may obstinately remain in our self-righteousness and pride, or we may come to know our own hearts, acknowledge the darkness of our hidden pride, and prostrate ourselves before our Father, in order to

_____

[175] General audience, 4 Mar. 2015, w2.vatican.va.

repent and enter His embrace and the joy of His celebration.

62. My Fire Purifies, Diary of a MOC

> *My little one, I want you to understand what takes place in a soul that enters the fire of My Sacred Heart. My fire purifies* (your soul) *as gold is purified. As glass placed in the fire, it is softened so that it can be molded into the shape desired. My fire, the fire of the Holy Spirit, purifies all hardness from your heart making it soft and pliable. I then am able to form you and make of you a new creation, the creation you were meant to be from the beginning of time, pure and radiant in the image and likeness of God. This process of purification in My Heart is different from the purification at My feet and side.*
>
> *The fire of My love, the Holy Spirit, is making you pure, radiant chalices of gold.* (9/2/11)

What is the difference between the purification in the Sacred Heart and the purification at His feet and side?

We began the Path by kissing Jesus' feet. Our hearts began to open and become vulnerable. It brought us to knowledge of God and self and the gold of precious repentance so that we could receive mercy. It was the beginning of the Path of intimacy with Christ. Now that we are in the Heart of Jesus, we are taken to His feet again; but this time the Lord wants to crucify our feet with His. We no longer walk according to our self-will or our desires, which are rooted in our ego. Christ now crucifies us to His Divine Will.

4-B
The Three Nails
that Crucify Us with Jesus

In the Sacred Heart, we live three types of mortification and dying to self. These represent the three nails that crucified Jesus. Through the gift of His nails, we are crucified with Him to be no longer two but ONE.

4-B-1
— The First Nail Pierced Jesus' Feet —
Fruit: Purification of Our Desires

63. The Purification of Your Desires, Diary of a MOC

> *The purification of your desires is the first stage of purification in My Sacred Heart. **You begin to move only according to My desires** and not yours. You no longer do what you want to do, nor go where you want to go; but now, you go only where I take you. You choose to live each day according to what is most difficult, not what is easiest. This will require a greater discipline of your will, greater silence and stillness of soul in Me.*
>
> *You have come to recognize My voice and the promptings of My Divine Spirit. At times God requires immediate obedience; at others, your obedience is lived as you wait upon the Lord. The latter obedience requires greater abandonment and trust, and therefore, is more pleasing to Abba, Our*

> *Father. This is a complete dying to moving in your will.* (1/16/14)

Based on the above message, let us ponder step by step the first stage of purification in the Sacred Heart:

You begin to move only according to My desires and not yours. You no longer do what you want to do, nor go where you want to go; but now, you go only where I take you.

This raises important questions: What keeps us walking according to our own will and desires? How do we discern the difference between our desires and those of Jesus? As we begin humbly to live this purification, we discover the answers. Jesus tells us what each of us must do to enter this purification: *Choose to live each day according to what is most difficult, not what is easiest.* Then He tells us what is required in order to choose the most difficult: *A greater discipline of your will and greater silence and stillness of soul in Me.*

— Silence, Trust, and Gratitude —

These are essential virtues to live the discipline of the will. **Silence** is in section 5-B.

— Trust —
To expose our lies and begin to trust

We have learned that the narrow path of the Cross takes us through the healing of our wounds, purification, and liberation. Now we must face a more difficult task: to expose the lies that we believe about ourselves so that we can know the truth of who we are. This is difficult because Satan planted those lies in our wounds, and we have integrated them into our personalities and into the way we see ourselves. They have defined our identity. We have also covered up these lies with false humility. For example, if I believe the lie that tells me I am good for nothing, I may think that acting as such is being humble. In this way, Satan keeps us in bondage. The lies are lived out in timidity, anxiety, fears, comparisons…

Only when we have discovered and rejected those lies and accepted the truth about ourselves, can we trust ourselves and the Lord who wants us to come home. Henry Nouwen, reflecting on the parable of the Prodigal Son, writes:

Without trust, I cannot let myself be found. Trust is that deep inner conviction that the Father wants me home. As long as I doubt that I am worth finding and put myself down as less loved than my younger brothers and sisters, I cannot be found [these are the lies]. I have to keep saying to myself, "God is looking for you. He will go anywhere to find you. He loves you, he wants you home, he cannot rest unless he has you with him." [These are the truths].

There is a very strong, dark voice in me that says the opposite: "God isn't really interested in me; he prefers the repentant sinner who comes home after his wild escapades. He doesn't pay attention to me who has never left the house. He takes me for granted. I am not his favorite son. I don't expect Him to give me what I really want."[176]

We are all familiar with this voice within ourselves. It is the voice of Satan, the Prince of Lies, which speaks to us loudly through the lies we have come to believe. Through the Path up to this point, we have been growing in trust through the knowledge that we are the beloved of God and He desires for us to live in His embrace. **Now we need to exercise this trust through the discipline of our will to crush the lies and choose to live in the truth.** The lies MUST come to light in our consciences as we embrace the TRUTH of who we are in Christ. The truth is the power that casts out the lies into the "refiner's fire" (Mal 3:1-4).

Because this inner struggle requires great spiritual energy, the Lord tells us we need to enter silence and stillness of heart. This part of the process of purification through the Cross transforms us little by little into a new creation, pure and radiant in the image and likeness of God, forming our new identity.

An important exercise at this point is to begin to journal on the wounds which you have discovered in yourself and the lies from these wounds which you have come to believe about yourself. Next to each lie write the truth. Practice speaking the truth out loud to yourself. Satan cannot create anything; he can only twist the truth. Therefore, once we identify the lies, they can give us clues about the truth about ourselves, and we can praise and thank God for the truth. For example, if Satan made you believe that you are not

---

[176] *Return of the Prodigal Son* (The Crown Publishing Group, 2013). 84-85.

lovable, now you can see that you are indeed lovable.

Often, when you begin to tell the truth, you believe it with your intellect but not yet with your heart. The truth feels foreign to us because the lie has been our lifetime identity. We need to understand this and persevere in the truth.

WOUND	LIE	TENDENCIES - DISORDERS	TRUTH
*Paternal wound- rejection.	*I'm ugly. *I'm Stupid, useless, incapable of doing anything well. *I am not worthy of being loved.	*Timid *Seek attention of men through my language, bodily expression, sensual dress, "in style." *This continued during my conversion although only in social events, while in Christian circles I dressed modestly. *Bulimia. *Alcoholism. *Insecurity in all relationships, especially with men. *Co-dependency, especially with men and close friends.	*I am a beloved daughter of God, capable of loving and being loved. *I have talents, beauty, intelligence. **NEW WAY OF LIFE** *I am free to give and receive love. *I do not seek attention. *Knowing that I am not the most intelligent, most beautiful no longer bothers me.

— Examples of Lies We Have Come to Believe —

- I am not lovable.
- Vulnerability is a sign of weakness.
- If I am intimate and show tender love, I will be hurt.
- Intimacy of hearts is not for men.
- Real men do not cry.
- They will love me only if I do what they want, if I am intelligent, if I produce, if I am perfect…
- I need to be self-sufficient in everything.
- I am a bad person.
- My sins are too many and too grave to be forgiven.
- I have to be in control.
- God is not going to guide or protect my life.
- God's love is dependent on my response.
- I am not good enough.
- I have nothing to contribute, to say.
- I am ugly.
- I am stupid.
- I don't make good decisions.
- I am useful only if I do things for others.
- I am not wanted.
- I am being rejected.
- To be humble is to live as a "doormat."
- I am not important.
- When someone comes to know me, they no longer love me.
- I can't defend myself if I'm misjudged or accused.
- I can't say "no" because I must please everyone.
- I'll never be appreciated.
- Making a mistake proves I am stupid.
- I have to be perfect.
- My opinion or what I feel does not matter.
- I am not listened to.

- I am not worthy of being taken care of.
- It's all my fault; the wrongs others did to me are my fault.
- Men cannot be trusted / Women cannot be trusted.

— Testimony —
A Mother Who Practiced the Above Exercise

My mom told me she didn't want me and that she cried the entire nine months she was pregnant with me. When I was born, she and my Dad had the flu for the first two weeks of my life; and we went to my grandmother's house. My brother was a year older, and we shared a baby bed as soon as I could hold my own bottle—he would drink his bottle and then take mine. I would be fussed at because I was crying—they told me it took them a long time to figure out what was happening. So, the feelings of not being cared for, loved, listened to or wanted began at an early age and the lies followed: I'm not wanted. I'm not lovable. I don't have anything important to say.

My mom wanted two children and a career. She was given eight children—I'm the second oldest. From a very young age, I tried to please everyone—hoping to get a little attention and affirmation. My Dad constantly asked me to give in and change my plans, to please Mom, my brothers and anyone else who came along. I loved my Dad and wanted to please him—so I gave and gave and gave. After a while, it was hard for me to tell what I wanted because it never mattered to anyone and I wasn't going to get it anyway. The lies followed: I'm not important, I have to do what they say if I want to be loved by them, I'm useful only if someone needs me to take care of them.

I constantly tried to make my Mom happy. I cleaned the house, washed the dishes, hung out the clothes, took care of my brothers—it was never enough. There was never a thank you. It was usually a criticism about something not done perfectly. I've never felt loved by her—only manipulated and controlled. She expected me to be perfect. When things went wrong it was often my fault—she never defended me. She was very critical and often made fun of me in front of others; so, it's not surprising that my brothers, cousins, aunts, uncles and others joined in to poke fun at me too. My brothers took turns making fun of me about being a girl, being ugly. The lies followed: I'll never be good enough; I'm not worth anything to anybody; I'll never be appreciated.

I grew up in a family that didn't communicate. I wasn't allowed to be angry or express any kind of disagreement. I was only allowed to say "Yes, Sir," "No, sir," "What, sir?" When I was in college, my brother took my new car without my permission—a car I worked very hard to buy myself—and wrecked it—it was totaled. I was given an old beat up car in its place and was told I should be happy he wasn't hurt in the accident—and that was the end of the discussion. The lies followed: I don't have anything important to say or anything to add to a conversation.

Everything got stuffed. I had no one to turn to ask questions, get advice or share my feelings. Looking back now, I can see why I was taken advantage of, mistreated, ignored and abused. It's not surprising that I was molested by the high school coach. When I turned to a priest friend for help, he said that it didn't happen and, when I insisted it did, he said he didn't want to get involved; again, I felt I wasn't worthy of being taken care of. When I was raped on a date, I made the mistake of going to my Mom for help; and she told me it was all my fault. I suffered terribly for this and didn't feel worthy a decent guy. So, it's not surprising I fell for a guy who gave me lots of compliments and attention at first. When things started to change, I told my Mom I didn't want to marry him, and she said it was too late—she had ordered the invitations, and so I was "sold" for $100.00. My sister-in-law made all the decisions about the details of the wedding, and I just went along with whatever was decided. I told my Dad, "I don't want to marry him," and he said, "It's you having cold feet." That was the end of the discussion. I couldn't get either of them to listen to me. The priest who wouldn't help me in high school was the one who performed the ceremony— I didn't bother to go to him for help. On the altar, I couldn't focus on what was said because I wanted to leave; but I was stuck, and before I knew it, I was married to a guy I didn't even like let alone love. I cried the whole honeymoon night, and it was downhill from there for the next eight years. He was very abusive, physically and emotionally. We moved to another state with nothing, and we knew no one.

A week after my daughter turned three and my son turned one, my husband left us; he took every penny we had, and I was without a job. I asked my Mom to keep the kids for just a couple of months so I could get back on my feet and she said: "It's your little red wagon—you pull it." It was the hardest thing to take my children to a day care and just leave them with strangers. I was nursing my son at the time and didn't have time to wean him; I had to leave him there crying. That was very hard for me.

As a result, when I started this process of healing my wounds, it took me the longest time just to admit and speak about my hurts. I wasn't sure I could trust anyone. I wasn't sure they would accept me or like me or let me come to the retreat if they knew even a little of the mess I was. It took me even longer to name the wounds—I just couldn't figure it out. The sister that accompanied me named the wounds; then I could see it and say "Yeah, that's it." It's the "Mother wound," the wound of being rejected, abandoned and betrayed, and the wound of not being loved.

For the longest time, I've felt a block in my relationship with our Lord. I've spent hours in adoration loving Him as best I could, but it wasn't until I started this process of understanding my wounds that I saw how I was acting and reacting out of these core wounds and true healing began to take place. But at first, it was very painful!! Once I started looking at the wounds, a whole volcano of emotions erupted; and I had to face my hidden sins of hatred, bitterness, resentment, pride and most of all, my unconscious un-forgiveness. I thought I had forgiven for each of the hurts, but I hadn't even touched the surface. I went to confession over and over and over, asking our Lord to forgive me and to heal me for each of these hidden sins as the emotions came up and I recognized their many faces. I'm not saying I'm completely finished with this process, but recognizing and admitting there's a problem was the first step for me because I had lived my whole life in denial.

For me, digging deep was the process of going back to the beginning with Jesus and in my heart, looking at my parents individually and expressing the hurt they have caused me and with Our Lord naming each hurt and forgiving them from the heart. It has taken several times of doing this before I was able to move to the next step and ask them to forgive me for holding a grudge against them and for my unconscious bitterness and resentment over the years. I asked our Lord to heal every emotion I was experiencing and through the power of the Holy Spirit to consume each of the negative feelings that are deeply repressed and to heal our relationship. I trust He is and will continue to do this for as long as I need Him to. I also realized my parents were doing their best. Our Lord has allowed me to see into their hearts and to see their hurts and their pains and to understand that they were working out of their wounds. This was such a gift, and it had never even crossed my mind.

Throughout the years, I have always been close to our Lady and have often gone to her, but this time I asked Our Lady to be my Mom, to go back and allow me to be born in Bethlehem and have her hold me and give me the love I wanted and needed throughout my life but especially through the hard times. This process of healing is setting me free because it's the light of the Holy Spirit that is shining on my wounds and exposing the darkness.

I see my need for humility and purity of heart. I see how much time I have wasted in self-concern and self-absorption. It's not pretty, and I beg His forgiveness for this. But I'm also realizing how much I need to understand His true love for me; He loves me in spite of myself and has been so patient with me. I can't help but truly praise and thank Him for everything, the good and the difficult, for always being there with me and never leaving me. I understand a little more of what dying to self means.

I'm seeing how the lies that I have been taught throughout my life have shaped and have become who I am. I've lived my life in bondage to fear and self-hatred. As I try hard to walk our Path, I am learning to suffer each of these experiences with Our Lord, to suffer no longer two but one in His sacrifice of love; and this has been very powerful.

I'm spending time with Him, seeing His suffering—gazing into the eyes of Jesus and seeing His pain of being used, abused, unloved, unwanted, rejected, abandoned, betrayed, alone, stripped, forgotten, unappreciated, taken for granted. I'm uniting my pain to His wounds and pouring out this blood of mine with His, for their healing and salvation, as well as for the healing of my family tree. Jesus was there with me even though I didn't recognize Him. What a great privilege this is, that He wants to heal all those who have hurt me, through my suffering. I want to be truly transformed into a new woman. I beg Him to set me free and to fill me with His love so that I can truly be His and love others as He loves me.

— Fake Saints —

This process will bring us to authenticity. We no longer pretend to be holy and perfect because we know that God loves us as we are. Now we can honestly acknowledge our sins without fear and allow the Lord to continue healing us.

Pope Francis warns us about the lie of being "fake saints":

God "generously forgives" …, but what he doesn't forgive is "hypocrisy and fake saints," … God prefers "sanctified sinners"—people who, despite their past sins, learn how to do a greater good. "Fake saints" are people who are more concerned with appearing saintly than doing good. …

We are all clever and always find a path that is not right, to seem more virtuous than we are: it is the path of hypocrisy. They pretend to convert, but their heart is a lie: they are liars! It is a lie … Their heart does not belong to the Lord; their heart belongs to the father of all lies, Satan. And this is fake holiness. Jesus preferred sinners a thousand times to these. Why? Because sinners told the truth about themselves. "Get away from me, Lord, I am a sinner!" Peter once said.[177]

Fake holiness is a common lie that results from believing that, if we appear to be holy, we will be loved and accepted. Then we do what looks good exteriorly but do not face the lies by which we live. As we begin to bring to the light of our conscience the lies embedded in our identity, we are also able to identify our inordinate desires and tendencies that are rooted in the lies. Now we can discern the difference between the desires of God and our desires

---

[177] Daily meditations, 3 Mar. 2015, Radio Vaticana, http://en.radiovaticana.va.

and tendencies. Love moves us to the obedience of choosing to live according to God's desires regardless of how difficult or impossible it might seem.

64. Death to Our Human Desires, Diary of a MOC

> *With this first nail, you begin to be crucified with Me. My desires begin to override your desires and tendencies. Obedience is the virtue that now moves you to act according to My Will, despite your desires.* (1/18/14)

Wounds and lies lead us to many tendencies: To compare ourselves, to segregate and to judge others. When we **"compare"** ourselves to others, we end up feeling inadequate, unworthy, anxious and insecure. We then put on masks to portray outwardly what we think we ought to be in order to be loved and accepted.

We also fall into **"segregation"**: We separate from God and each other. Think about the consequences of segregation in our country—anger, hatred, division, deep wounds and suffering. We too can live segregation in our hearts and suffer the same effects. **When we feel hurt by people, we tend to separate ourselves from them emotionally and physically. Murmuring (complaining) and lies follow immediately.** These are defense mechanisms we learned at a young age to enable us to bury our wounds and justify our false self-image. We fall into this trap because we have not come to believe the truth of who we are in God.

Another tactic of the enemy is to incite us to judge. Pope Francis explains:

Feeling shame and blaming oneself, instead of assigning fault to others, judging and condemning them. This is the first step on the path of Christian life which leads us to ask the Lord for the gift of mercy. …

However, we are all masters, we are all experts when it comes to justifying ourselves…when I find envy in my heart and I know this envy is capable of speaking ill of another and morally killing him, I have to ask myself: "Am I capable of it? Yes, I am capable!" This is precisely how this knowledge begins, this wisdom to blame oneself. …

When one learns to blame himself, he is merciful with others; and he is able to say: "Who am I to judge him if I am capable of doing worse things?" …

The Lord is clear: "Stop judging, and you will not be judged. Stop condemning, and you will not be condemned. Forgive, and you will be forgiven." **It is certainly not an easy road, which "begins with blaming oneself, it begins from that shame before God and from asking forgiveness from Him."**[178]

---

[178] Daily meditations, 2 Mar. 2015, w2.vatican.va.

— Gratitude —

Gratitude is another important virtue necessary to live in the discipline of our will. It is the opposite of resentment. Henry Nouwen writes:

The discipline of gratitude is the explicit effort to acknowledge that all I am and have is given to me as a gift of love, a gift to be celebrated with joy. Gratitude as a discipline involves a conscious choice. I can choose to be grateful even when my emotions and feelings are still steeped in hurt and resentment. It is amazing how many occasions present themselves in which I can choose gratitude instead of a complaint. I can choose to be grateful when I am criticized, even when my heart still responds in bitterness. I can choose to speak about goodness and beauty, even when my inner eye still looks for someone to accuse or something to call ugly. I can choose to listen to the voices that forgive and to look at the faces that smile, even while I still hear words of revenge and see grimaces of hatred.[179]

To live in silence, trust and gratitude, not comparing or judging, is very difficult. This is why the Lord tells us we must choose to live each day according to what is most difficult and not what is easiest. We must discipline ourselves to believe that we are loved and to love one another!

---

[179] Henry Nouwen, *Return of the Prodigal Son*, (The Crown Publishing Group, 2013), 85.

— Obedience —

The practice of these virtues leads to loving obedience to God.

65. The Virtue of Obedience Is Perfected in the Sacred Heart of Jesus, Diary of a MOC

> *Obedience is the fruit of trust, of surrender and of pure love. Obedience is the virtue that is perfected in My Sacred Heart. I did only the will of My Father because I live in Him and He in Me. In our unity, oneness, I could never act outside of Him. This is love. This pure love moves you to obedience to the Father's Will. Therefore, a sign of genuine love in the Heart of the Trinity is perfect obedience to My Holy Will.* (1/16/14)

Hebrews 5:8-9

Although He was a Son, he learned obedience through what He suffered; and being made perfect, He became the source of eternal salvation to all who obey Him

66. Obedience Is the Fruit of Interior Transformation,
Diary of a MOC

The virtue of obedience is the fruit of a great interior transformation, for it requires you to see with the eyes of your soul and hear the voice of your God leading you. It is the virtue that grows from humility and purity of heart. It requires much abandonment of your will. It requires for a soul "to believe" in the way I have already taught you.

Obedience is the fruit of trust. Obedience is the fruit of love. That is why I am perfectly obedient to the will of My Father. My every breath here on earth was in perfect harmony and obedience to the Father because I live in perfect union with the Father and Holy Spirit.

To grow in obedience is to grow in a deep attentiveness to the movements and stirrings of the Holy Spirit in your soul. That is why I have taught you so much about silence. Perfect obedience to My will is your response of love to Me. Poverty brings forth chastity and chastity brings forth obedience, which is the essence of Love. (12/14/11)

— Testimony —
Responding to Christ's Desire
that We Love to the Extreme of the Cross
Letter from a mother to her community's sisters

As I sat this morning pondering these words [the above message], it hit me how very much of a channel of grace is the routine life of a mother. Our very lives serve as the nail in the foot of Jesus. This is an example:

I cannot be this morning where I would like to be, with you all. Instead, I am sitting in the parking lot of a soccer field waiting for the game to start. I cannot choose another place, or I would be disobedient to my duties as a mother.

What a blessing that it is so very clear what I need to do; it makes self-denial much easier to bear. At times the duties of mothering are so many, so intense, so unrelenting that I come to a point where I wonder if I —the person—, even exists anymore, or if I am only a body that works endlessly serving the needs of others.

But this morning I saw that each of us loves in a unique and personal way and that the Sacred Heart is not only the source of this love but that the flames of His love mold each of us into a particular channel of love. There is nobody in the world who loves like me. There is nobody who loves like you. Only I know exactly how much milk to pour into the cereal bowls of my children; only I know how tight to tie their shoelaces or exactly where to put the ponytail on the back of my daughter's head. So I am not just a body, but another Christ to that child and that child is the Christ Child to me.

I must go now. The game is about to start, and I need to be on the sidelines smiling. It's too embarrassing for her if I yell.

As we begin to live in the Sacred Heart of Jesus, we see with the eyes of Jesus how self-centered and self-absorbed we are. Through the long process of "suffering ALL with Jesus," the Holy Spirit gradually moves our gaze from self to others. Now, the woundedness in the hearts of others becomes more important than our wounds. We begin to live for others as we begin to live for the Other. Love moves us to suffer the brokenness of others with Jesus to obtain healing for them. This is particularly difficult when others offend us; but we can do it when Jesus' desire to save and transform souls becomes the deepest desire of our own hearts, a desire that moves us beyond ourselves.

We cannot overcome our self-centeredness and pride on our own. We must allow others to tell us our defects, even though it is a humbling experience.

— Testimony —
A Mother of the Cross Discovers Her Wounds

My soul was torn by a decision I had to make with my husband. My spiritual director helped me see that my wounds and sins had distorted my identity. When these wounds are touched, I react with anger, resentment, and unforgiveness.

As a child, it was hard for me to adapt to the frequent family moves. Though my parents loved me, my father was emotionally absent, and my mother was overbearing. One way this affected me is that, when I need to make a big decision, I am torn between what I think is right and what I think my parents will approve. For many years, I had a double life between the "real me" and the "pleaser."

When I became a married woman, my family moved close to my parents; which is not something I wanted to do. Being far, I only had to "act" my life in front of my parents a few times a year. But my husband and I knew the move was part of God's plan to face and heal my family wounds. I had to choose between being the Christian victim of love God wants me to be and the woman my parents wanted me to be.

Walking the Simple Path to Union, the process of healing began to take place. I entered the narrow path. Full of suffering and challenges, it is very uncomfortable because I had to encounter and confront the darkness in my own soul. Many of my wounds and sins were very difficult to acknowledge, but I could now allow my husband, with his love, patience, and faithfulness, to travel with me through my wounds and help bring them to the light.

My first reaction was to deny my wounds, but the Lord gave me the grace to confront my pride. I could see the wounds I had ignored for years. They were infected with sins and were ugly. **I realized that one of the most painful parts of this narrow path is when someone brings to light the darkness of our souls. Then we must also confront our pride. This is the key. Our pride is the beast guarding the darkness of our souls. This pride must be killed in order for the light of the Holy Spirit to penetrate the depth of our soul, to heal our wounds and remove the infestation of sin.**

— No Humility without Fraternal Correction —

Fr. Raniero Cantalamessa explains why:

We must not make the mistake of thinking we have attained humility just because the word of God has led us to discover our nothingness and has taught us that it must show itself in fraternal service. We see the extent to which we have attained humility when the initiative passes from us to others, namely when it is no longer we who recognize our defects and wrongs, but others do so; when we are not only able to tell ourselves the truth, but also gladly let others do so. … In other words, **the point we are at in the struggle against pride is seen in the way we react, externally and internally, when we are contradicted**, corrected, criticized, or ignored. To claim to kill your pride by striking it yourself, without anyone intervening from outside, is like using your own arm to punish yourself: you will never do yourself any real harm. It is as if a doctor tried to remove a tumor from his own body on his own.[180]

---

[180] Fr. Raniero Cantalamessa O.F.M. Cap., *In Love with Christ, the Secret of Saint Francis of Assisi*, (Zenit books, 2014), 56.

4-B-2
— The Second Nail of Purification Crucifies Our Emotions —
The Darkening of Our Interior Senses

Since the beginning of the Path, our hearts have been growing in the ability to interiorly "see" and "hear" Jesus. Now we no longer feel His consolations as we used to and we must walk in the darkness of faith in perfect trust. We still have emotions, but now, having experienced profound intimacy with God, our union is no longer contingent on consolations. We are now one in pure love.

67. My Flame of Love Has Now Possessed Your Faculties, Diary of a MOC

> *You now live in peace in the darkness of faith without My sweet consolations. My flame of love has now possessed your faculties of sight, touch, hearing and, speaking. It is My Spirit in you who sees into the hearts of others; it is God's touch moving through your hands; you live now in the "silence" of the Trinity, and your words are wisdom and understanding itself.* (5/26/14)

68. Flame of Love, Diary of a MOC

> *My flame of love is the Holy Spirit. Through My Path, My flame of love has possessed your minds, hearts, and faculties so that it is no longer you who live but I who live in you. In this way, I live in you as you live in Me and the Father lives in us. Do not be afraid to be sent out as My heralds of hope to usher in My era of peace. Do not be afraid to*

> *confront the forces of evil as My Light, for it is the light of My holy remnant that will conquer the forces of darkness. Believe that you are the Light of the world and hold the power of God.* (5/26/14)

69. Desolation United to Me, Diary of a MOC

> *In times of desolation, your life has the greatest power and is most fecund. In My desolation on the Cross, My life shone most brilliantly the love of God the Father. My desolation made My faith in My Father radiate its perfection.*
> *-Through My desolation, I gave birth to My Church and all her sacraments.*
> *-Through My desolation, I gave birth to all My sons, My priests.*
> *-Through My desolation, the Holy Spirit expanded the maternal Heart of My Mother to embrace all of humanity.*
> *-It is in your times of desolation that the Holy Spirit and My Mother wish to unite you more intimately to Me.*
> *-It is in your times of desolation that you are given the opportunity and grace to suffer with Me.*
> *-It is through your desolation that you can come to know the pain, suffering and love of My Heart.*
> *-It is through your desolation united to Mine that your life will also be most fecund.*
> *My desolation was so important for the salvation of the world that the Father willed for My Mother to continue suffering My desolation on earth. Her suffering of solitude was her continuation*

> *of My desolation, and it produced and continues to produce a shower of graces for the world.*
>
> *I desire for the souls who love Me to live their times of desolation united to Me and completely abandoned to the Holy Spirit. In this way, My hidden force will acquire the power of God to overcome the darkness in the world. My Cross is not My Cross without the power of desolations lived with perfect faith.* (3/2/11)

— Testimony —
A Wife and Mother Living the Process of Purification in The Sacred Heart

I think it all began months ago when I felt nothing but dryness. It's as if our Lord left me. I could no longer feel consolations, nor hear our Lord's voice… I only felt a death in my spiritual life. Several months later, words were spoken by two sisters in the community that pierced my heart… the words touched a wound. I didn't talk about it to them, nor to my accompaniment (the person in my community that walks the Path with me), which was a mistake, as it moved me to isolate myself. I heard the words, which had come into my wound, over and over for weeks. This was, I think, an opening for Satan to enter, which he did.

One day, a couple of sisters of my community prayed over me with much love and concern. Shortly after that, I broke my silence: I opened my heart one Saturday at a mothers' meeting. They prayed fervently over me and for me and then began my process of healing.

Through the community's prayer for me and spiritual

accompaniment, I began to see that I had fallen into a deep darkness that I had allowed, but that the Lord had allowed as well so that many things could come to light. Jesus wanted to bring to light all the lies that the enemy had been feeding me and that for years had become a part of me, creating a false identity. For years, I had been told that I am not lovable, that I am not good enough, that I am a failure and many more lies.

Satan takes advantage of our woundedness and sin, coming in for the kill by feeding us lies in order to infect our wounds. The Lord wants to remove all those lies that have become a part of us and speak the truth in our hearts, giving us our true identity in the process.

I've had an image in my mind of my heart like a rock that is crumbling and breaking down. I feel that this is what God is doing: crumbling away all the lies, breaking down the old self and making a new creation. I feel as if I am being thrown off balance, but, in reality, I am being given a new center of gravity. My center of gravity had always been myself... my wounds, my disorders, my selfishness, the lies that hold me in this center creating a false identity, a false center of gravity. Our Lord wants to be my center of gravity, where there is order and not a false order or a false identity. Because of this feeling of imbalance, I feel I am falling and I try to hang on to the old self I have always been. However, He is chiseling me as a sculptor chisels a rough piece of marble to make a new creation. I can't see the finished product yet—I can't even imagine it; so I am holding on for dear life to the old self because it is what I know. What I need to do is let go, but here is where my faith is weak. At the same time, Satan knows what is going on and sees an opportunity. He amplifies the lies and the battle becomes fiercer. He is working harder because I am being liberated, set free from the lies that have kept me oppressed for years.

The other image I keep seeing is that of the port that was surgically implanted when I was sick with cancer a few years ago, which was used to administer chemotherapy. This port has sunken deeper into my chest with time, and there is now a thicker layer of flesh on top of it. To remove it now, the cut has to be deeper because the port is deeper within. I see the same thing with the lies. I have heard these lies for so long that now they are deep within me and are a part of my flesh. In order to root them out, I must be profoundly pierced, our Lord has to go deep within me to remove them. One can't do it alone, just like I needed a surgeon to remove my port, I also need Jesus to heal my spiritual wounds.

To dig deep into the depths of my soul, to the deepest recesses of my heart, to my core wound, is tremendously painful! So much so, that I had to stop all extra activity and do only my daily duties. I had to find "a greater silence and stillness of soul" as the Lord purified and continues to purify me.

This purification is a crucifixion of our old selves, of our desires and tendencies. It is a deliverance from all evil that keeps us oppressed. Our Lord told us in the community: "My desires begin to override your desires and tendencies." What I see happening is that my will is being perfected. This, as one can imagine, can be a lengthy process because the person we have been all our lives can no longer live, and we have to will to move in obedience to God.

For a long time, I have been oppressed by the many lies, and the Lord wants to set me free, to make me new to be a "pure chalice." He wants to remove all these lies that created in me a false identity and replace it with my true identity that He planned for me since the beginning of time.

The process of living through the first nail is very difficult, very painful and requires complete obedience and a greater strength of will. Our Lord tells us: **"Obedience is the virtue that now moves you to act according to My Will, despite your desires."** I confess that at first, I rebelled. I believed the lies because they were so perfectly crafted to fit my wounds. Therefore, they were so very believable. I find myself fighting these lies constantly, trying to cast them out. The lack of consolations makes it even harder. I now have to choose to follow Christ, to be a victim soul, to stay in the community, to do what is most difficult, to love when I don't want to love. I move out of obedience rather than by emotions. I have been in a great spiritual battle for months. I am constantly fighting against my own tendencies and against the many demons that fill me with their lies. Occasionally—actually quite often—I fall, but the Lord continues to strengthen me and send me our Mother to lift me up, just as she helped to lift Him up when He fell on the way of the Cross.

It is important to say that our Lord has not abandoned me throughout this process. In fact, looking back now, I see that to write down all He has done for me in the past few months, would be too lengthy. Jesus has lavished me with so many gifts. He has provided for my family in such beautiful ways. It is strange because although I have felt no consolations, He has answered many prayers and has given me many, many, many gifts. The greatest gift to come, I think is that of a new identity.

4-B-3
— The Third Nail
Brings Us to Perfect Unity —

The Nail of Persecution

70. As They Persecuted Me…, Diary of a MOC

As they persecuted Me, they will persecute you. As they hated Me, they will hate you. This last nail fuses your heart to My Sacred Heart: you love as one with Me all the enemies of God, and thus complete your crucifixion in Me; and the triumph of God's love is manifested through you in the unity of My Body. Prepare yourself in silence and prayer to live the last stage of My Divine Path. (5/26/14)

71. All Will Be Called to Suffer Persecution,
Diary of a MOC

The time is at hand when all will be called to suffer persecution for My sake. This time of persecution will divide My followers into two camps: those with Me and those against Me. Few will remain with Me in the time of the great tribulation. You, My little ones, are being prepared for this time. Your lives lived in humility and purity of heart, united to Me, will be the light in this darkness. Your lives hidden and transformed in My crucified love will usher in the New Pentecost for the world. (2/25/14)

St. Paul writes to the Hebrews regarding persecution:

> But recall the former days when, after you were enlightened, you endured a hard struggle with sufferings, sometimes being publicly exposed to abuse and affliction, and sometimes being partners with those so treated. For you had compassion on the prisoners, and you joyfully accepted the plundering of your property, since you knew that you yourselves had a better possession and an abiding one. Therefore, do not throw away your confidence, which has a great reward. For you have need of endurance, so that you may do the will of God and receive what is promised.[181]

---

[181] *Heb* 10:32-36.

72. The Ecstasy of the Love of God Transforms the Pain into the Sword of the Spirit, Diary of a MOC

Some saints received the stigmata with the physical pain of the nail wounds, but ALL My saints were crucified with Me mystically through My nails. The mystical crucifixion is no less real and painful than the physical one, just as the white martyrdom is no less real and painful than the red martyrdom.

Unity in the Holy Trinity is the fruit of becoming one with Me in My crucifixion, for this is perfect love. The ecstasy of the love of the Father, Son, and Holy Spirit transforms the pain into the Sword of the Spirit that pierces the darkness of Satan. This union of Love is achieved by few because of lack of perseverance and selfless love.

A saint who becomes one in My crucified love has the power to transform an entire society. I am raising up My saints for the decisive times at hand to fight My holy war and usher in the era of peace. (12/28/14)

4-C
True Intimacy in Suffering
──•❖•──

4-C-1
— *True Intimacy is to Suffer as One Heart with the Beloved, to Enter a Union of Sorrows* —

In the Garden of Gethsemane Jesus expresses the immense sorrow of His Heart. He says to Peter, James, and John, "My soul is very sorrowful, even to death; **remain here and watch with me**" (Mt 26:38). Our Lord then goes out to pray, "My Father, if it be possible, let this chalice pass from me; nevertheless, not as I will, but as You will" (*Mt* 26:39).

73. To Love Is to Suffer, Diary of a MOC

> *The love of the Father, Son, and Holy Spirit was fully contained in My human heart. In My humanity, the Word Incarnate, My love was manifested in My suffering. My ocean of mercy flowed from My love in suffering for you.*
>
> *Because of sin, to love here on earth is to love in suffering. Only in heaven does love exist without suffering. You desire to become ONE Heart with Me. Do you then desire to suffer with Me? To love is to suffer. I suffer the condition of each of your wounded and broken hearts because I love you.*
>
> *You were created from the beginning of time to know LOVE and to live in LOVE. This is happiness, but sin came into the world, and the darkness has overcome the Light in the hearts of many of our*

> *children. My Sacred Heart, consumed in the Fire of*
> *Love, continues to love and desires to set the world*
> *ablaze with My fire. This is love.*
>
> *Do not be fooled, My daughter; My death and*
> *resurrection have defeated sin and darkness. The*
> *darkness of Satan can never extinguish My fire of*
> *love within you. It is My fire within you that has the*
> *power to extinguish the darkness surrounding you.*
> (7/1/11)

Our Lord desires that we remain with Him and partake of His chalice, which is the cup of His sufferings for the sins of the world. The fire of love of the Holy Spirit that consumes the Sacred Heart of Jesus also consumes our heart, and we begin to desire to drink and partake in our Lord's suffering. This is pure love. This intimacy in suffering is expressed in the prayer of St. Gemma Galgani:

Do grant, oh my God, that when my lips approach Yours to kiss You, I may taste the gall that was given to You; when my shoulders lean against Yours, make me feel Your scourging; when my flesh is united with Yours, in the Holy Eucharist, make me feel Your passion; when my head comes near Yours, make me feel Your thorns; when my heart is close to Yours, make me feel Your spear.

In this oneness, our desires are those of the Lord. The soul desires desolation before consolation because the chalice of our Lord's suffering is filled with desolation. The soul desires hardships before pleasures because our Lord's chalice is filled with hardships. The soul desires exhaustion before rest because our Lord had nowhere to lay his head. Our soul desires tears before laughter because His chalice is filled with the tears of His sorrows for every soul. Who will drink from our Lord's chalice and suffer with Him solely to be ONE with Love?

Devotion to the Sacred Heart of Jesus will not be a superficial piety if we enter His Passion. St Paul reminds us: "If one member suffers, all suffer together; if one member is honored, all rejoice together. Now you are the body of Christ."[182]

74. Enter into the Sacred Heart of Jesus, Diary of a MOC

> *To enter into the Sacred Heart of Jesus is to enter more intimately into His agony of love. To enter into the Heart of Jesus is a most intimate participation in His bitter chalice. To come to love with Jesus is to share His sorrows and participate in His tears. To enter into the Sacred Heart of Jesus is to receive directly His tears into our hearts as His living chalices. Our tears and the tears of Jesus are one. Our sorrows are His sorrows. Our desolation is His desolation. Our solitude is His solitude. We are no longer two but ONE. This is life in the Sacred Heart of Jesus. It is life in God's agony of love for souls. It is participation in Jesus' interior crucifixion. It is the martyrdom of the heart, and in this union of suffering is the most perfect union of love, a love that is the fulfillment of our soul's desire.* (5/9/12)

---

[182] 1 Cor 12:26-27

4-C-2
— *Receiving the Crown of Thorns* —

Saint Margaret Mary saw the Sacred Heart of Jesus
As if on a throne of flame, more radiant than a sun and transparent as crystal, with its adorable wound. It was surrounded by a crown of thorns, which signified the pain which our sins inflicted on it, and was surmounted by a cross, which signified that from the first moment of His Incarnation, when the Sacred Heart was formed, the cross was planted there, and His Heart felt all the bitterness which would be caused by the humiliations, poverty, grief, and dishonor which the Sacred Humanity would suffer through the course of His life and during His Passion.[183]

Notice in St. Margaret's vision that the Sacred Heart of Jesus is crowned with thorns and surmounted by the Cross. Therefore, for us to be united in the intimacy of the love of the Sacred Heart, we must also be willing to partake in His thorns and Cross.

Saints, such as St. Rita and St. Faustina,[184] were so united with Christ's passion that they mystically suffered His thorns. These thorns were a sign of the thorns that they endured in the trials and temptations of their everyday life. St. Paul prayed to be freed of the thorn afflicting him, but the Lord told him: "My grace is sufficient for you, for my power is made perfect in weakness." St. Paul then saw his thorn as a powerful grace. He received self- knowledge to face all adversity relying in the Lord. He exclaimed: "I will all the more gladly boast of my weaknesses, that the power of Christ may rest upon me. For the sake of Christ, then, I am content with

---

[183] Jesus to St. Margaret, second revelation, 1674, as cited in www.catholic2000.com.
[184] Cf. Saint Faustina Kowalska, *Diary, Divine Mercy in My Soul,* n.1399.

weaknesses, insults, hardships, persecutions, and calamities; for when I am weak, then I am strong" (2 Cor 12:9-10).

When St. Therese of Lisieux suffered the thorn of a bitter disappointment, she accepted it as a gift from Jesus. She wrote to her sister:

Oh, what a blow! But I feel that it is struck by a hand divinely jealous. … It is Jesus who has guided this affair; it is He, and I have recognized His touch of love. … It is not a human hand that has done this; it is Jesus; His eyes have fallen upon us. **Let us accept with a good heart the thorn that Jesus presents to us.**[185]

75. My Heart Is Crowned with Your Sin,
Diary of a MOC, Solemnity of Christ the King

Jesus tells us: *Receive the crown of glory, the crown of thorns. The King of Kings allows Himself to be crowned with the crown of thorns. I permitted this so that all of humanity would know and see the thorns crowning My human and divine Heart.*

My interior crucifixion I lived through the thorns of ingratitude, rejection, ridicule, murmurings, lies, disloyalty, unfaithfulness, deception, arrogance, pride in all its disguises... My Heart is crowned with the darkness of your sin (humanity's). This is how I lived My Kingship on earth and it is how I continue to live My Kingship in the Eucharist, for this is Love.

To share in My Kingship on earth is to share in My crown of thorns. ... You must receive with

---

[185] Therese of the Child Jesus, (as cited in Nosert, *Joy in Suffering According to St. Therese of the Child Jesus*, Rockford: Tan Books and Pub. 2006), 67.

greater docility, abandonment and love My thorns through the darkness in the hearts of our sons and daughters. This is the perfect participation in the life of your Beloved, the life of Love. (11/24/13)

76. Mary Receives the Thorns, Diary of a MOC

See the Heart (Immaculate Heart of Mary) that has loved Me and her tears shed for love of Me and you (humanity). This Heart (Mary's) being revealed to you is the Heart of a victim soul. **Receive each thorn I present to you as a gift more precious than jewels,** *as My Mother has done. Cry tears of love (tears of blood) for Zion...*

A time is drawing very near when the sounds you hear will be of wailing and terror. ... But know that My Bride (Church) is being cleansed through the justice of God, My Precious Blood and the Tears of My Mother as ONE with the tears of all My victims of love.

Are you willing, My little ones, to allow your hearts to be pierced as ONE with My Mother's for the cleansing of My priesthood and the salvation of many? Do not grow stubborn, but persevere in love by suffering all as ONE with My Pierced Sacred Heart and the pierced Immaculate Heart.

Encourage one another as My martyrs of love, for the battle is fierce. My little ones, know that the

> *crown of glory awaits you.*[186] *Do not grow weary as*
> *My martyrs of love, but be strong and steadfast in*
> *the power of God as ONE with the Word of the*
> *Cross.*[187] (10/20/11)

Recently, as I was praying the rosary, an image of Mary was revealed to me. She was sitting with her face in her hands crying, as our Lady of La Salette. She then lifted her face and looked at me. She had a large crown of thorns on her head. She said nothing, but the words "provided you suffer with Him" came to my mind. I understood that Mary is the one who suffered with her Son most perfectly because she is also the one who has loved Him most perfectly.

She also gave me the image of a tractor plowing with large blades an open field. I could see the blades entering deep into the earth. **Our hearts are like a field; they must be tilled in order to produce an abundance of fruit.** The reason that we produce little is that sin has made our hearts hard as rocks so that the Word of God and His grace cannot enter them. Every thorn of suffering serves to plow our hearts, making them docile, humble, and soft in tenderness and patience, perfected in obedience, steadfast in faith and hope, and expanded in love. Every thorn we receive is a source of healing for others and ourselves.[188]

---

[186] Cf., Rom 8:17.
[187] Cf., 1 Cor 1:18.
[188] Cf., Heb 5:9.

4-D
Participation in the Groans of the Sacred Heart

God seeks to bring us to such depth of union that we can participate in the very groans of the pierced Heart of Jesus. St. Paul wrote: "The Spirit helps us in our weakness. We do not know what we ought to pray for, but the Spirit himself intercedes for us with groans that words cannot express" (Rom 8:26).

What the heart contains cannot always be expressed in words, but the Spirit can do so with groans. The Lord crucified, filled with the Holy Spirit, expresses His passion of love with ineffable groans. We too are moved by the Spirit to listen and to participate in His passion and groans of love.

77. Listen to My Groans, Diary of a MOC

> *Can you hear My groans that come forth from the depth of My Crucified Heart? The groans of My agony of love. Listen to My groans of love.* (3/11/12)

78. Living Tabernacle of God, Diary of a MOC[189]

> *To be one with Me means that you become the living tabernacle of God. My loving, pulsating Heart lives in you as one with you. You feel My sorrows and participate in My groans for the fulfillment of humanity's transformation into LOVE.*
>
> *The martyrdom of the human heart is the intimate union of love in My Sacred Heart. You live the sorrows of the Heart that is love in as much as you allow Me to share My chalice with you. It is usually only a sip of one drop until your being acquires the taste of My Blood and it loses its bitterness in the Divine sweetness of My love.*
>
> *My daughter, My Heart overflows with the sorrows of rejection. Share in My rejection as you share My words and are not ashamed.* (10/15/12)

This union of love in suffering, sharing the groans of Jesus' agony of love, is a powerful prayer before the throne of Abba and always brings forth new life. As we begin to hear the groans of the Sacred Heart of Jesus and willingly participate in them, our intercession for souls brings us to the battlefields, the dying, the widows and orphans… **St. Benedicta of the Cross** explains:

The world is in flames. The conflagration can also reach our house. But high above all the flames towers the cross. They cannot consume it. It is the path from earth to heaven. It will lift one who embraces it in faith, love, and hope into the bosom of the Trinity.

---

[189] Cf., Mk 8:31-38.

The world is in flames. Are you impelled to put them out? Look at the cross. From the open heart gushes the blood of the Savior. This extinguishes the flames of hell. Make your heart free by the faithful fulfillment of your vows; then the flood of divine love will be poured into your heart until it overflows and becomes fruitful to all the ends of the earth.

Do you hear the groans of the wounded on the battlefields in the west and the east? You are not a physician and not a nurse and cannot bind up the wounds. You are enclosed in a cell and cannot get to them.

Do you hear the anguish of the dying and would like to be a priest and comfort them?

Does the lament of the widows and orphans distress you and you would like to be an angel of mercy and help them?

Look at the Crucified. If you are nuptially bound to Him by the faithful observance of your vows, it is your precious blood that is being shed. Bound to Him, you are omnipresent as He is. You cannot help here and there like the physician, the nurse, the priest; but **in the power of the Cross, you can be at all fronts, wherever there is grief. Your compassionate love—the love of the Divine Heart—takes you to every place where the** Precious Blood is being poured, everywhere soothing, healing, saving.

The eyes of the Crucified look down on you asking, probing. **Will you make your covenant with the Crucified anew in all seriousness?** What will you answer Him?

Lord, where shall we go? You have the words of eternal life.[190]

---

[190]*Collected Works of Edith Stein*. III.2, Meditation on the feast of the Elevation on the Cross, 14 Sept. 1939.

Our lives, in our ordinary homes and workplaces, transcend time and space. The Lord allowed me to experience this reality years ago when one morning my young son woke up and walked into the kitchen. I immediately went to him, as I do every morning, to give him a good morning kiss. Then, as if time had stopped for an instant, as I knelt to embrace my son, I knew without a doubt that another child somewhere in the world, who desperately needed a mother's kiss, received mine. The Lord allowed this experience, in His infinite mercy, so that I could believe that the simplest gesture of love in my ordinary life as mother, united with Him, could transcend the confines of my world. I knew that someday in Heaven I would meet this child.

4-E
Becoming One

— Jesus' Heart Longs for Us —

Jesus revealed to **St. Margaret Mary** the deep longing of His Sacred Heart for our response. She wrote: "He made me repose for a long time on His Sacred Breast, where He disclosed to me the marvels of His love." Then Jesus said:

My Divine Heart is so inflamed with love for men, and for you in particular that, being unable any longer to contain within Itself the flames of its burning Charity, it must spread them through you, and manifest itself to them (mankind).

St Margaret continues,

After this, He asked me for my heart, which I begged Him to take. He did so and placed it in His own adorable Heart where He showed it to me as a little atom which was being consumed in this great furnace.

During the fourth apparition, Jesus said to her:

Behold the Heart which has so loved men that it has spared nothing, even to exhausting and consuming Itself, in order to testify Its love; and in return, I receive from the greater part only ingratitude. … But what I feel most keenly is that it is hearts which are consecrated to Me, that treat Me thus.[191]

— How Do We Respond? —

Christ wants to draw us to Himself to become ONE with us, but we often limit Him to the role of **benefactor**. We want benefactors to help us, to finance our projects, but we do not want them to take over our lives. In a similar way, we want to be close to Jesus and benefit from Him, but we are afraid of a love that calls for total surrender.

It is not enough to be consecrated to Jesus or to say that we have Jesus in our hearts. We have many things in our hearts. Rather, the question is, **who is on the throne of our hearts**? Are our hearts so inflamed with love for Him that He has full authority over everything in our lives? Can we say with St. Paul "I have been

---

[191] *Autobiography of St. Margaret Mary Alacoque*,
   https://www.ewtn.com/library/CHRIST/FIRSTFRI.TXT.

crucified with Christ; it is no longer I who live, but Christ who lives in me?" (Gal 2:19-20) The love of Christ on the Cross was his passion, the driving force for all he did. This is the fusion of hearts that Jesus wants with each of us.

People may unite for a cause, a project, a mission, but **only through a fusion of hearts can we become truly one**. St. Paul could suffer all things without discouragement because he knew Christ loved him: "I live by faith in the Son of God, who loved me and gave Himself for me" (Gal 2:20).

— Fusion of Love —

Fusion of love with God brings about communion among persons. Those who are united with God share the same fire and thus are able to be united to each other. This is why saints grow in bunches. They experience a deep love for one another such as the world cannot understand. However, this fusion does not annihilate their uniqueness. Just as the body is one but has different organs, each part contributes its uniqueness to the whole.

79. The Fusion of Hearts Is the Kiss of Union,
Diary of a MOC

> *The fusion of hearts takes place through the sword of suffering as ONE. It is through the union in suffering that you die more-and-more to self until it is no longer you who live but I Who live in you... The fusion of hearts is the kiss of union, the embrace of the Holy Spirit, the embrace of Love.* (12/3/12)

— Testimony —
A Mother of the Cross Who Entered the Sacred Heart

For a long time, the Lord has been calling me to love with all my heart a family member who is in grave sin and to trust that love casts out darkness. However, it was difficult for me to love, mostly out of concern of exposing my children. I was burdened with doubts and fears. I knew deep within me that our Lord was calling me to love those most difficult to love. I also knew that He would take care of my children if I decided to love. Finally, my heart was transformed in Lent.

80. Abandon Yourselves, Diary of a MOC

> *Abandon yourself simply by accepting all, the way that it is given to you… Give yourself completely, serving all for love of Me. The mission will move forward according to My plan and Will. You are called to be love by sacrificing yourself completely for Love. This simple abandonment in each of the circumstances of your lives that I have placed you in will produce the hidden force needed to conquer the darkness covering the earth. Abandon yourselves to love the most difficult ones closest to you. Kiss My pierced feet each morning; and set yourselves out like warriors on a mission to serve with love, patience, tenderness—be slow to anger.* (2/26/11)

The testimony continues:

Immediately, the Lord allowed me to recognize that I had

taken my eyes off Him, like Peter who took his eyes off Jesus and fell into the water, after having walked on it. At that very moment, I made a conscious decision to join Jesus in the Garden of Gethsemane, where He had been inviting me to enter; in my weakness, I had been careless and hadn't fully responded as He desired. As I entered the Garden, I immediately felt so very united to His sufferings for being unjustly accused, misunderstood, rejected, betrayed and abandoned. He was alone. It was then when I understood that our Lord allowed this situation in order to strengthen me, to show me that I should depend only on Him, to gain self-knowledge and also to enter a deeper union with Him, as St. Margaret Mary Alacoque tells us: "Every time that some punishment, affliction or injustice comes your way, say to yourself: 'Accept this as sent to you by the Sacred Heart of Jesus Christ in order to unite yourself to Him.'"

81. How to Enter His Sacred Heart, Diary of a MOC

To enter My Heart is to enter the consuming fire of God, which is the Holy Spirit. To enter My Heart is to drink from My bitter chalice of love. To enter My Heart is to be consumed into God, to become ONE with God, no longer two but ONE. (3/4/12)

The testimony continues:

The moment I joined my Beloved in the Garden, He began to lead me straight into His Sacred Heart, although I didn't know it at the time. I picked up my *Path to Union* manual and began to read and meditate as He lovingly directed me. I entered His sufferings to such a degree... I lived His Passion right along with Him. I wanted to reach out to others in search of consolation, but instead, I was drawn into a deep silence, where I could better hear His Voice and truly partake in His sufferings. Our Lord then led me to these words:

82. Silence, Diary of a MOC

> *In the fire of My Sacred Heart, you come to know personally the Holy Spirit. Now you have ascended into the silence of the Trinity. In the Holy Spirit, you possess Me and the Father as One. The Spirit now lives in you and you in Him. You are ONE.*
>
> *This divine dimension is SILENCE. When you enter this divine union in silence, the soul must be careful to nurture it. Careless speech and careless activity can bring the soul out of this divine dimension of silence.* (7/22/11)

The testimony continues:

After reading these words, I understood that I had "ascended into the silence of the Trinity," that I had entered the "Divine dimension of silence." Here, I began to ponder this mystery that is the Holy Trinity. I began to ponder Jesus' selfless sacrifice, a sacrifice of pure and holy love for the Father and for humanity. I pondered our Heavenly Father's gift of His Only Son to be put to death; He gives Him up to be crucified for love of us. The love of the Father and the Son for each other is the Holy Spirit—love that is an immeasurable, perfect and holy sacrifice. When we live in the Holy Spirit, we live united to Jesus as a sacrifice of love to the Father and share in that love and salvation with all of God's children. He loves us all and wants to bring us all Home safely. I am amazed by this incredible work of redemption.

Having received this gift, this knowledge, I feel as if something is different in me. I am no longer the same. I feel that I have entered a deeper union with our Lord. I have entered the Sacred Heart of Jesus. And what is the Heart of Jesus? LOVE. Pure LOVE. Sacrificial LOVE. Selfless, abandoned LOVE. And if we are no longer two but one, then this love is the love in my heart… sacrificial, selfless, abandoned, pure… love for ALL. Here in the Heart of our Savior, I am being called to be love to all. I am being called to go out into the darkness to bring His light and love to everyone He places in my life. And as He sends me out on a mission to love, I must trust that He will take care of my children. He has asked me time and time again to entrust them to His care and the care of our Blessed Mother. He has expressed His grief for my lack of trust in Him, because, you see, I have not fully given my children to their Savior. All He asks is that I be obedient to His call to love and He will handle the rest. This is who we are called to be and is at the core of our mission: Living chalices, one with the Sacred Heart.

83. Be My Clear, Pure Chalice, Diary of a MOC

Just as you can see the liquid through a clear glass, you are called to be My clear, pure chalices. You are chosen to hold My Precious Blood.

My Blood is My life. My Blood is healing fire. Therefore, first, My chalice must be emptied and purified. This is what I have been accomplishing in you at My feet and in My pierced side. It is now, in My Sacred Heart, in the furnace, which is the fire of the Holy Spirit, that you are formed as My living chalices.

My fire purifies all blemishes and tarnishes. You are of pure glass; but when filled with My Precious Blood, you radiate to the world the golden light of the Holy Spirit. My Blood always heals, restores, refreshes and brings new life. Therefore, the gaze of your eyes will radiate pure love, the touch of your hands will heal and your words will pour forth the wisdom, knowledge, and understanding of God. This is how you put on your Lord, Jesus Christ so that you are the light of the world.

My little ones, help Me and My mother form many victims of love by radiating the pure love of the Trinity. (10/7/11)

The testimony continues:

As His chalice and victim of love, I cannot run away from a sinful world, but rather I am called to be His channel of grace to flow to others. Yes, this is very difficult, but how can I not show the same mercy and love to others that He has shown to me? Our Lord continues to reassure me. The words below really touched my heart and have helped me to truly love with all my heart, to love with the Sacred Heart of Jesus.

84. I Desire for You to Be My Companion, Diary of a MOC

I desire for you to be My companion in this time of great suffering; to remain with Me... To collect My tears shed for all of humanity. You have been chosen to be ONE with Me, My consolation during these end times. This is your identity as a Mother of the Cross.

I asked Jesus how to live as His companion of love. It is easy when I am in prayer and He allows me to feel His presence and see His gaze, but during the day there are so many distractions.

Be attentive to each person you encounter in your life. I live in them. I suffer for them and with them. "This is My Body" (Mt 35:31-41). My little one, have the docility of heart to receive the brokenness of all people into your heart as ONE with Me. This is participation in the love of the Trinity: to receive the wounds of your brothers and sisters and to give the sacrifice of your life, as ONE with Me, for their salvation and sanctification. This is Love. (2/18/13)

The testimony concludes:

I have come out of this powerful experience with greater strength and assurance of who I am—I am a Mother of the Cross[192], a woman of love, living in the furnace of His Sacred Heart, united to our Blessed Mother! I just have to be and live who I am; and by doing so, I will witness the love and mercy of God to those our Lord places in my life, including my children. St. John Vianney said, "Virtue goes easily from mothers into the hearts of their children, who willingly do what they see being done."

I have also come to a greater understanding of what our Lord is asking of me. First, He is asking me to TRUST and to BELIEVE. So often I doubt as He guides me and speaks to me. He is asking me to trust, as Abraham trusted when our Lord asked him to sacrifice his only son Isaac. Abraham believed and trusted in the Lord, and in the end, our God provided the sacrifice and saved the son He earlier asked Abraham to give up.

Our Lord wants an intimate union, a sacred union with each one of us personally, but so often we just do not truly believe nor do we trust!

Second, the Lord is asking me to love everyone with all my heart, especially those most difficult to love; and this, in fact, is very, very difficult! I feel that He has granted me a certain spiritual growth and strength to do so, BUT with this comes a greater responsibility. I no longer belong to myself. I now must respond to our Lord with selfless love. I must choose to love, as He tells us in this Path. He is now sending me out like He sent the apostles, placing me in certain difficult situations; and He is

---

[192] http://lovecrucified.com/a_branches_comm/mothers_cross/_motherscross.html.

asking me to step out of myself, trust and set out to LOVE. He is asking us all to love, and with not just any love, but to love with the One and Only Trinitarian Love, the perfect Love in the Sacred Heart of Jesus. Then, as He did with the apostles, Jesus will perform miracles through us as well.

I now live in the Sacred Heart of our Lord Jesus Christ, united as ONE with Him, suffering all with Him for the salvation of souls. To confirm this, our Lord had my young daughter pick up a children's book on the promises of the Sacred Heart of Jesus. The book tells of the 12 promises given to St. Margaret Mary for all those who honor His Sacred Heart. A prayer follows each promise for the child and the family. What an amazing, beautiful and tender confirmation! If I now live in His Sacred Heart, will He not personally make me these promises as well? Will He not look upon my children with mercy and make them the same promises? And this is why I should not and cannot despair… this is my strength and my help.

4-F
Drawn into the Unity of the Trinity

Jesus told the Father that He was giving His life for the sake of unity with us:

> That they may be one, as We are one, I in them and You in Me, that they may be brought to perfection as one, that the world may know that You sent me, and that You loved them even as You loved Me (Jn 17:22-23).

Venerable Conchita writes about her personal experience of this unity:

> The secret for arriving at unity is to let yourself be conducted by the Holy Spirit since it is He who brings about unity in God Himself.[193]

> All that you do and practice, cast it as often as possible into this Unity (God)… Your pains, your sufferings, your joys, your acts of renunciation, your desires and your hopes, your needs and your feelings, cast them all into this Unity which by its contact will simplify your life.[194]

---

[193] Ven. Concepcion Cabrera de Armida, as cited in *Conchita, A Mother's Spiritual Diary*, 230.
[194] Ibid., 230.

85. What Is True Unity? Diary of a MOC

*What is true unity? First and foremost, unity is union with the God-Man. I, the Second Person of the Trinity, became man so that you could come to know personally your good God. I became man to set you free from the bondage of your sins so that you can see with the eyes of My angels the glory of God before you. But **I was not incarnated in the womb of Mary only to save you and set you free but to become ONE with you.***

The Father and I are ONE; the Father in Me and I in Him with the Holy Spirit (cf. Jn 17). The union of the Trinity is pure love. I came upon the earth to draw you into union with the Most Holy Trinity through the Cross—no longer two but ONE.[195] It is in this union that love exists.

Only from this union of love with your Triune God can unity exist in My Body, the Church. It is through My life in the Eucharist that I become One with you, but it is only through your participation in My Eucharistic life that you become One in Me. This participation can take place only by entering the Cross of new life, My crucified love. (11/23/11)

---

[195] Cf. *Eph* 2:15-16.

86. **Unity**, Diary of a MOC

I long for unity in My Body, the Church. My Body has been torn to pieces as a savage dog tears to pieces its prey. This work Satan accomplishes by keeping My members away from the Cross. Unity and love can be accomplished only through the Cross and in the Cross.

It is My martyrs of love who will wage war against the principalities of darkness during the final and decisive battle. Bring Me many victim souls, My true and only victims of love. Only they satisfy My thirst for love. Only they soothe the pain of My suffering Heart and My Mother's. Only they can penetrate the hardened hearts of My priests.

Live during the time of the great and terrible persecution in perfect faith in the triumph of My Cross. The triumph of My Cross is the triumph of love. (9/9/11)

87. **How to Respond to Christ's Desire for Unity**,
Diary of a MOC

I desire to draw you into true unity, the unity of the love of the Most Holy Trinity. The union of sorrows will bring you into the union of Love. The gaze of the Father is upon you. Be love. Live solely for Love, forgetting yourself.

My Lord, how do I live solely for Love, forgetting myself?

Live to please Me. To live in the unity of the Trinity is to live gazing at the Father, through the

Son, to please Him in all things. (3/18/12)

4-G
The Light of the World

— The Light of Christ in Us —

Christ is the Light of the world. As we receive His Light, our eyes are able to see Him and see the beauty and purpose that God intended for all things. **People then need to see the light of Jesus in us.** Pope Benedict XVI said, "Many today are asking: 'Who will show us what is good?' We can answer: 'those who reflect God's light and face with their lives.'"[196] He also tells us how we can do so:

Faith, which sees the love of God revealed in the Pierced Heart of Jesus on the Cross, gives rise to love. **Love is the light**—and in the end, the only light—that can always illuminate a world grown dim and give us the courage needed to keep living and working.[197]

---

[196] Letter to Cardinal Gianfranco Ravasi, 23 Feb. 2013.
[197] Message for Lent, 2013, www.vatican.va.

88. The Light of Jesus Christ Is Love that Suffers All,
Diary of a MOC

> *Only love radiates the light of God, for His light is Love. The light of Jesus Christ is love that suffers for all and with all: Love in pain and sorrow, Love that enters into the brokenness of humanity and receives her brokenness into Himself to heal and restore her in God. Love receives her wounds and bears them upon His Body to heal her with the balm of His tenderness in mercy. This is the Light of the world. This is Love, the Word Incarnate.*
>
> *Receive My wounds, the sin, brokenness and oppression of your brothers and sisters, so that you can radiate My light in the darkness. This is love. The love of the world is self-seeking and self-centered, but the love of God is self-giving.* (12/31/12)

We may believe that we are the light of Christ in the world, but do we really understand what this means? Jesus, in the above message, tells us that, to be His light, we must receive in our bodies the wounds and brokenness of the people He places in our lives and suffer them as one with Him. This is true love, but to practice it, we must overcome our primary reaction to go against it.

Pope Francis

When we have external enemies that make us suffer so much, it is not easy to win with love. There is the desire to take revenge, to turn another against him. … Love: the meekness that Jesus taught us … this is our victory, our faith. Our faith is precisely this: believing in Jesus who taught us love and taught us to love everyone. And the proof that we are in love is when we pray for our enemies.[198]

The pope also said:

I see clearly that the thing the church needs most today is the ability to heal wounds and to warm the hearts of the faithful; it needs nearness, proximity. I see the church as a field hospital after battle.[199]

Only souls illumined by Christ can fight the "decisive battle" and pierce the darkness consuming the world. It may seem that the world is in hopeless chaos, but the Word of God tell us that "The light shines in the darkness, and the darkness has not overcome it."[200]

89. Your Life Now Holds the Power of God, Diary of a MOC

The darkness of Satan will not conquer the Light of God. It is the Light of God that will extinguish the darkness of Satan.

Consumed in His Heart, you have entered the hidden power of God. Your life now holds the power of God. It is through your love in suffering that your life will conquer the forces of evil. Live in My Hidden Force, unnoticed by all, but seen by Abba, our Father. Believe who you are through the mercy of God who loves you... Now WE—for we truly have

---

[198] Daily Meditations, 24 May, 2013, w2.vatican.va.

[199] Antonio Spadaro S.J. interviews Pope Francis, "The Church Is a Field Hospital After Battle," *America*, 30 Sept. 2013.

[200] Jn 1:5; cf. Jn 1:1-18.

> *become ONE—must enter the pains of Calvary for the salvation of many.* (4/12/14)

— The Love of God Is a Consuming Fire —

We are tempted to sit comfortably near the fire so that we can enjoy the light and warmth without getting burned. However, Jesus' Heart is a consuming fire,[201] which it is painful to enter because it constantly burns away all our impurities; yet those who persevere in the flames of love cannot help but desire to be consumed in them, to become one with the fire and to be able to spread it to others.

St. Catherine of Siena prayed with these words:

My Lord set me on fire with love for you. Let me think of nothing, crave for nothing, yearn for nothing, search for nothing, but you. How I wish to be caught up in this scorching fire of love! How I wish it would consume every obstacle that blocks my path toward you! Make my love for you grow stronger each day of my life.

---

[201] Cf. Lk 12:49-53.

90. Do Not Be Afraid to Be Consumed by the Fire,
Diary of a MOC

I have been seeing Jesus' chest as a consuming fire. Moses approached the burning bush but could not enter the fire of God. Now, through Jesus Christ, we are able to enter the fire and be fully consumed in the unity of the Holy Trinity.

My mercy, in My blood and water, is being poured upon the world, but I find very few hearts open to receive My grace. It is as the parable of the seed.[202]

There are very few hearts docile, humble, pure, cultivated in patient suffering, and open to receive My gift of infinite mercy and love. This Heart (Sacred Heart), which has loved you (humanity) so much, is not loved. I promise you, My little one, that those who come to Me in the last stage of My mercy will ascend perfection quickly, for the Father and I, and the Holy Spirit love you and want to restore humanity in Us...

Do not be afraid to be consumed in the fire of My Sacred Heart. The fire of My Sacred Heart is the Holy Spirit. As you are consumed in the fire of My Sacred Heart, you are consumed with the fire of the Holy Spirit. My hidden force is the fire of the Holy Spirit moving out in the world. The passage to enter the fire of My Sacred Heart begins with My Mother, who is the gate to enter My Cross; therefore, she is the gate to enter heaven. (7/13/11)

---

[202] Cf. Mat 13:1-23.

This consuming fire can sometimes even be experienced as a burning heart or a fire within us. This fire is the Holy Spirit, which has united us to the heart of Jesus. Now we are no longer two but one heart on fire. The **men and women who enter the painful process of being consumed in the fire of Christ will bring forth the New Evangelization:**

91. What is Evangelization? Diary of a MOC

What is evangelization? Evangelization is the witness of the Good News to all people: God is with you! Father, Son, and Holy Spirit are present, alive, in the world. I came from heaven to evangelize the world. I came to reveal the Father through the Son and to bring you the Holy Spirit to protect, guide, teach and lead you through transformation into Love.

I am the Evangelizer, for I am One with the Father and the Holy Spirit. My every thought, word, and deed was one with the Father in the Holy Spirit. I am Love and therefore can draw all into Love. What is required to evangelize? To come to know Love; to come to hear, see and touch Love; to receive the embrace of our Father through Me, with Me, and in Me.

The Evangelizer is the Holy Spirit who is the love of the Father and the Son. It is the power of the Holy Spirit who witnesses the love of the Father through the Son. Without the Holy Spirit, there can be no evangelization. The world is being prepared for the new Evangelization: men, women, and

> *children consumed in the fire of the Holy Spirit through My Cross.*
>
> *New men and new women are required for the New Evangelization. This is why I plead with the thirst of God for victim souls, for it is only My victim souls that abandon themselves completely to Me, who can be made a new creation in the image and likeness of God.* (12/17/14)

— Testimony —
Coming to Light, Healing, and Forgiving

My dear Jesus, when I went up to be prayed over for healing, my mind went blank as Father asked me what I wanted them to pray for. I truly felt that the Holy Spirit was prompting me to go up, but I just could not think of anything to say. Why? Was it Satan playing on my heart? Was it my own insecurities? Either way, Father decided to just thank God and praise Him with me for all He has done in my life. My vulnerabilities kept playing in my mind... why am I not "special" enough to be healed? I actually went back to my seat feeling kind of dejected, thinking that something was wrong with me. I completely overlooked the fact that the past year had been one of the most difficult, yet completely blessed, of my life. How quickly do I fall back into the traps of doubt, fear, and anxiety over God's love for me. The rejection I lived in my youth still plays strongly in my head. Father was also spot on: Why am I not thanking You more? Why don't I continually see my life as a beautiful confirmation of mercy?

My year since then has been completely about growth, love, and abandonment to Your heart. My Jesus, You have used my pain and my past to bring much grace through both my physical motherhood and my spiritual motherhood. Yes, those fears of not mattering, of my actions not being good enough, of being rejected, still come to my heart. In those moments, weakness sometimes overcomes me. But **You have used my wounds and experiences to give me a heart able to suffer with You in deep intercession for the wounds of my family and the priesthood; to suffer with You the rejection and isolation that You feel daily as You sit enslaved in the monstrance… forgotten and neglected just as I was in childhood.** You let me share the pain that You suffer to intercede for Your children, especially Your priest sons who do not understand the love You have for them, the great calling they have to lay down their lives as priests and victims… and the deep fear (many are unaware of it) that Your priests feel of not being good enough—just as I felt in childhood.

You chose me, the littlest of the little for this great grace. And to think You call me to all of this in the great isolation and hiddenness of my life as wife and mother! To truly understand the significance of that, I have to go back and look at my past, because that was exactly what I was running from for so many years, my Jesus. Yet, through my past, You were training my heart to do the beautiful work you have called me to…

I grew up in a home with a lot of rejection, isolation, and neglect. I did not grow up with a true, authentic concept of what a loving father and mother are. Both of my parents were in the picture of my childhood; and you could probably say that, on the outside, we even resembled a family… but only in the physical sense of the word. My Dad was, and still is to this day, a severe alcoholic. A case of beer to him was like a snack. He would move from one case to another, or grab a box of wine, like a child eating a handful of candy. My mom was the typical enabler who shut down, got angry at the world, and blamed everyone else (including us kids) for the things wrong with her life.

When I was in elementary school, my Dad's secretary and her daughter moved in with us because her husband left her and she had no place to go. It was supposed to be a good thing, and temporary. However, it quickly turned into a permanent situation. They lived with us for many years and quickly became more important, and more loved, by my Dad than his own family. The three of them became inseparable while we became more ignored, isolated, and neglected. My childhood consisted of a lot of hiding in my room, praying that Dad would pass out in the living room after a long day of work and drinking, instead of screaming, being immodest, inappropriate or abusive.

As I look back, my Jesus, I think that Your loving heart spared me a bit because the days Dad passed out became more and more frequent the older I got, but it was still late at night by the time that happened, and the damage was usually done. When his car pulled into the driveway each evening, we should have all been excited, saying, "Yay, Dad's home." Instead, most of the time, I ran to my room praying I was not bothered or found. I also hid during my parent's drunken parties because they never saw the way their friends looked at me. I hid on Easter Sundays because we spent them celebrating the fact that Dad could drink again after a long, abusive Lent, during which he gave up drinking just to prove he wasn't an alcoholic.

I now see, as an adult, that my Dad does have a genuine, yet DEEPLY wounded heart; but at the time, it was yet another opportunity for me to hide from all the drunken, inappropriate behavior of my Dad and his friends.

This was my childhood. It was lonely… I never brought friends over because I did not know what my Dad would do. There was never a "good job" or an "I love you" from my Dad that I can remember. On my first date, as the boy was coming to the door, my Dad said that I was ugly and, "who would want to go out with you?"

Report cards… I was in the top handful of students in my class, but my Dad wanted to know why I didn't have higher grades. He was drunk and criticizing at my high school graduation. When I graduated from college, he told me that I probably wouldn't succeed and I was worthless. Even my wedding day, although beautiful and blessed, was filled with drunkenness and backhanded comments. Yes, it was a life of abandonment, isolation, and neglect; and I became very good at hiding and shutting down.

As for self-inflicted wounds, I've got those too. At the age of 13, I started "watching what I ate." At our dinner table, you got hit with forks if you ate the wrong way or if you ate too slowly. By the age of 15, I was anorexic and remained that way for many years. What brought me out of it, with Your grace, my sweet Jesus, was love, your love shown through my husband. One day after we were engaged, my husband looked at me with tears in his eyes and said, "I truly love you and want to grow old with you by my side." That was one of the first moments I saw a glimpse of Your true love, my Jesus, and how transforming it had the potential to be.

All of this only scratches the surface, my Jesus; but somehow, in that nightmare of my childhood, I can now see that You were quietly forming my heart. You were sparing me, protecting me, and setting me apart to learn, and take on, a kind of love that no one knows but You. With each child You have blessed us with, my heart has expanded. With each year that passes, You are drawing me closer to You through Your great mercy. With each year, the beautiful gift, grace, and privilege of physical motherhood only deepens and expands in union with my spiritual motherhood for the priesthood. I still sometimes struggle with my worth and God's love for me. It is definitely Satan's "go to dig." But this year has been about expanding my notion of what love truly is at the foot of the cross with You, Jesus.

After my last child was born, You started "taking" things from me (even those that were good and holy), to bring my heart to a place of constant desire and intercession for You within the simple life I am called to as wife and mother. The dear friends I saw frequently, the distractions I created, and the things I did at church were slowly "weeded" from my life for a time, to help me grow. These were things I was using to keep "hiding" from You. It was painful to stay home, in the isolation and hiddenness you wanted for me.

There was a time when You asked me to deal with the wounds and fears that led to my insecurity and isolation. You made me aware of the wounds from my relationship with my father and asked me to give them to Your Father. I couldn't fully do that until last year because my heart needed more work to be emptied and to have enough room for You to work, to be ready in humble confidence to live the life You asked and use your gifts—not as the wounded child, but as your daughter. That lesson gets easier as I learn to live what You ask of me despite my worries of what others may think. You are transforming me as You strip me of all that I thought love was, to teach me the love of the Father. I am learning to attach my heart to His with a vulnerability and trust that I know I could not handle or understand on my own.

My Jesus, You have opened my wounds, cleaned them with Your own blood, and transformed them into a merciful sacrifice given for others. I have learned through this loving mercy that, when I get out of the way and step out in faith with a complete vulnerability, You use my hidden intercession to heal the wounds of others. Many of them I know as You bring them across my path. However, You place many others on my heart which I do not know, yet I feel in prayer that they also share my wounds. My heart is grateful for this work You have asked me to participate in, and I continue to give you my "fiat" like our dear Blessed Mother—no matter how broken mine sometimes is. You have called me to this life of hidden abandonment and intercession, Jesus. At times, that has been so difficult after the life I grew up in; however, I know that the Father is loving me through this and I am confident and truly believe deep in my heart that You are using me in this life as wife, mother, and spiritual mother for your priesthood… in the times when I do not know it and also in the beautiful times when I do.

As for my Dad, You have allowed me to live, suffer, and mourn his wounds that run much deeper than mine. With Your grace, my Jesus, I see how his wounds, his guilt, pride, and anger have consumed his heart, especially after I was critically injured as a child due to a grease fire explosion. Doctors did not think I would live, nor did they think I would ever see again, yet I do. You have helped me to understand that I am the "miracle" (literally) You are using to heal my family if I just continue to trust with patience. My Dad's heart does not yet know how to forgive; but with Your help, my Jesus, mine does. Thanks to Your complete and utter forgiveness, the union of my heart with Yours, and the trust that my sorrows and sacrifices matter and are used for Your glory, I have been able to forgive. After interceding for my Dad at many, many Masses, and offering his wounds to the Father through my intercession, last week, for the first time that I can remember, my Dad voluntarily told me that he loved me.

I do not know most of the merits of my intercession and sacrifices, nor do I want to… that is only for You, my sweet Jesus. That is the complete and total giving of a victim soul and spiritual mother… a life that is not mine to keep, but only to give. However, sometimes You do give me the grace to know and understand what that total oblation does in the hearts of others. Then, it is like a small consolation of the heart that humbly reminds me, sanctifies me, and gives me the strength to continue in the work You ask of me. All I can do for You, my Jesus, is to love You with the complete and selfless love of the Cross, even though I am weak and sinful. I can comfort You through those I offer my life for and through those I bring to You, especially from my family and the priesthood. All thanks to the gifts that you have given me. I can offer You myself nailed there right beside You. Only then do grace and mercy flow, and Your heart is satiated.

4-H
Spousal Union with Jesus

Fall ever more in love with the Lord Jesus, our Bridegroom[203]

God reveals His infinite love to us gradually, taking into account our limited capacity and receptivity. First He revealed Himself as our Father; then He taught us that He also loves us as a mother. Isaiah writes: "Even these may forget, yet I will not forget you."[204] Finally, God reveals Himself as our Spouse, with a love beyond natural human understanding.

Dr. Brand Pitre's excellent book, *Jesus the Bridegroom, the Greatest Story Ever Told*,[205] demonstrates, based on Sacred Scripture, that the fundamental revelation of salvation history is that God seeks an eternal marital love covenant with us. Although we had rejected Him, He did not give up on us. Throughout the Old Testament, we see God preparing the way and longing for our response. Each covenant was a step towards greater intimacy with His people, but the Lord laments the unfaithful responses: "But you trusted in your beauty, and played the harlot."[206] God remains faithful to His Bride in spite of all. He sends His prophets to promise a new Marriage Covenant:

---

[203] Pope Francis, Angelus, 17 Jan. 2015. w2.vatican.va/
[204] Isa 49:15.
[205] Brand Pitre, *Jesus the Bridegroom: The Greatest Story Ever Told,* (New York: Crown Publishing Group, 2004).
[206] Ezek 16:15.

Isaiah

As the bridegroom rejoices over the bride,
so shall your God rejoice over you.[207]

I will make an everlasting covenant with them… as
a bridegroom decks himself with a garland, and as
a bride adorns herself with her jewels.[208]

In this section of the Path, we seek to know Jesus as Spouse, not only of religious women but of all the baptized. We are more accustomed to relate to Jesus as Redeemer, Lord, and King. It is more difficult for us to believe that Jesus wants to be our Spouse, to give Himself and to possess us so intimately forever.

St. Thomas Aquinas wrote, "Through faith, the soul is united to God, and by it **there is between the soul and God a union akin to marriage.** 'I will espouse thee in faith.'"[209] The Catechism teaches that "the entire Christian life bears the mark of the spousal love of Christ and the Church. Already, Baptism, the entry into the People of God, is a nuptial mystery; it is, so to speak, the nuptial bath which precedes the wedding feast, the Eucharist."[210] We need to realize that it is in this spousal union with Christ and in nothing else, that we find the foundation of our true fulfillment and happiness. Everything else finds its meaning in this union with Christ. St Therese of Lisieux believed that, "without the spousal love of Jesus, fidelity is impossible, both in marriage and in consecrated

---

[207] Isa 62:5; cf. Isa 54:5-7; *Ez* 16:59-60;63.
[208] Isa 61:8;10. Cf. See also the *Song of Solomon,* the story of the bride longing for the bridegroom.
[209] Thomas Aquinas, *In symbolum apostolorum,* 1,I, citing Hos 2:21-22.
[210] *Catechism of the Catholic Church,* n.1617, cf. Ef 5,26-27.

celibacy."

— Nuptial Union with God Is Fulfilled in Christ —

I have given you in marriage to one Husband,
presenting you as a chaste virgin to Christ
– Saint Paul[211]

John the Baptist said, referring to Jesus, "He who has the bride is the bridegroom."[212] How great is the amazement of all upon hearing these words! Jesus is the Bridegroom prophesied by Ezekiel and Isaiah. He "has the bride," the people of God that He came to espouse in a new and eternal covenant.

John overflows with joy: "The friend of the bridegroom, who stands and hears him, rejoices greatly at the bridegroom's voice; therefore, this joy of mine is now full."[213]

92. Know Who You Are, Diary of a MOC

> *Know who you are, as John the Baptist knew who he was and the gift given to him from heaven to accomplish his mission. He was the Bridegroom's best man (prophet) preparing the heart of the bride (the Church) to recognize, know and love the Bridegroom. When the Bridegroom appears, John understands he must decrease. His joy is made full.*
>
> *You, on the other hand, are My bride, the Church, as one with My Mother, the perfect, pure, holy Bride. Your mission, as one with Mary's, is to*

---

[211] 2 Cor 11:2.
[212] Jn 3:29.
[213] Ibid.

> *bring souls to the foot of the Cross to contemplate the love of their Bridegroom, to look and gaze at the One who has been lifted up and to be healed, restored and made new.* (4/28/11)

Jesus said He was the Bridegroom who will be "taken away."[214] The unfaithfulness of the bride takes Him to the Cross, but this will become the occasion for Him to manifest the greatness and power of His love for her.

— The Last Supper —

The Last Supper was the Lord's wedding banquet, where He, as the Bridegroom, established the everlasting covenant. He gives the bride (us) His Body and Blood. St. Mathew wrote: "Jesus took bread, and blessed, and broke it, and gave it to the disciples and said, 'Take, eat; this is My Body.'"[215] By doing so He fulfills His desires to be ONE with us. He prays to the Father:

> Father, I desire that they also, whom thou hast given me, may be with me where I am, to behold my glory which thou hast given me in thy love for me before the foundation of the world.[216]

Jesus then goes to prepare a place to be forever with His bride:

> In my Father's house are many rooms; if it were not so, would I have told you that I go to prepare a place

---

[214] Mk 2:20.
[215] Mt 26:26.
[216] Jn 17:24.

for you? And when I go and prepare a place for you,
I will come again and will take you to myself, that
where I am you may be also.[217]

Dr. Pitre points out that, in Jewish tradition, the bridegroom built the house before the wedding could be celebrated. Therefore, before taking us to heaven, Jesus "prepares the house" by going to the Cross to give His life for the bride.

The "house" that Jesus prepares is His own Body. Jesus had referred to the Jerusalem temple as "My Father's house" and spoke about a new temple. This temple is His own resurrected and glorified Body. He is the "House" where we become ONE in divine nuptial union, and dwell in communion with the Father. This is the union in the Holy Spirit that we received in Baptism and live through the Eucharistic sharing in His Body.

However, the bride must respond by loving and following the Groom wherever He goes. Jesus says: "Whoever loves Me will keep my word, and my Father will love him, and we will come to him and make our dwelling with him."[218]

— Calvary —

Pope Benedict XVI called the Cross of Christ "the expression of his 'marriage' with humanity."[219] At the Cross, Christ's love is an all-consuming oblation for His bride. The Cross becomes His marriage bed where—having given all—He surrenders His naked body and seals the marriage covenant with His blood. He is the Bridegroom who truly gives Himself forever in "good times and in

---

[217] Jn 14:2-3.
[218] Jn 14:23.
[219] Apostolic Exhortation, *Sacramentum Caritatis*, n.27, w2.vatican.va.

bad."

Dr. Pitre's research reveals that there is a nuptial story in the Biblical account of the Passion, especially **John chapter 19**:

Verse 2: "**Crown of thorns**" In a Jewish wedding, the bridegroom wore a crown, meaning that he is king that one day. Jesus wore the crown only one day: His wedding day. But it was a crown of thorns that reveals how far He goes to love His bride, even taking upon Himself all her sins.

Verse 23: His "**tunic was without seam, woven from top to bottom.**" This is the description of the tunic of the bridegroom in a Jewish wedding.

Verse 26 and 27: "**He said to his mother, 'Woman, behold, your son!' Then he said to the disciple, 'Behold, your mother!' And from that hour the disciple took her to his own home.**" Those who share the Passion of Jesus, whether they are women or men, mother or son, also become His mystical bride fused to Him and to each other as one to form one body.

Verse 28: "**I thirst.**" Jesus thirsts for the bride's response to His love, and for each of us to become His spouse.

Verse 30: "He said, '**It is finished.**'" In the Latin Bible (Vulgate): *CONSUMMATUM EST*. Christ consummated His marriage covenant at the Cross. Having fulfilled in this way His mission on earth, and so that we could respond as His bride, "He bowed His head and gave up His Spirit."

Verse 34: "**One of the soldiers pierced his side.**" Saint John Chrysostom noted that God formed Eve from the side of Adam and Christ gave life to His own spouse from His pierced side: "God took the rib when Adam was in a deep sleep, and in the same way Christ gave us the blood and the water after His own death. Do you understand, then, how Christ has united his bride to himself?"[220] The first marriage is natural; the second is a participation in the divine life of the Spouse and is capable of sanctifying the first. An ancient homily for Holy Saturday confirms it: "I who am life itself am now one with you. … The bridal chamber is adorned, the banquet is ready, the eternal dwelling places are prepared."[221]

— Cana Is Fulfilled at Calvary —

Commenting on the wedding at Cana, Pope Francis said:

Jesus reveals himself as the spouse of the People of God, proclaimed by the prophets, and reveals to us the depth of the relationship that unites us to Him: it is the new Covenant of love. What is at the foundation of our faith? An act of mercy by which Jesus binds us to him. And the Christian life is the response to this love; it is like the history of two people in love. God and man meet, seek, find, celebrate and love one another: just like the lovers in the Song of Songs. Everything else comes as a result of this relationship.[222]

Jesus provided wine for the wedding party as was expected of the Jewish bridegroom. He miraculously turned water into wine. At Calvary, when the "hour" came for His own wedding, He went much further: He turned wine into His Precious Blood becoming

---

[220] Catechesis on the power of Christ's blood, cited in the Office of Readings, Good Friday.

[221] Anonymous ancient homily, cited in Office of Readings, Holy Saturday.

[222] Pope Francis, General Audience, 8 June, 2016. w2.vatican.va

Eucharist for the sake of the Bride. Pope St. John Paul II concludes that the Eucharist "is the sacrament of the Bridegroom and of the Bride."[223] The two become one. Jesus gives us His body, and we give Him ours. Being Christ's Body, we make Him visible. "The body, in fact, and only the body," wrote the pope, "is capable of making visible what is invisible: The spiritual and the Divine."[224]

St. Peter of Alcantara affirms:

> The Bridegroom would not have His bride lonely during such a long absence. He wanted her to have a companion. And the best companion he could leave her was Himself in the Eucharist.[225]

— The Bride Must Respond —

The Bridegroom has given His all, but there cannot be a marriage without the Bride's consent.

We must join Him at Calvary and have our hearts pierced like Mary's. The Bride there becomes the Spouse by uniting herself as a victim to the Victim of Love, no longer two but ONE in His sacrifice of love.

But the Bride is incapable of responding without first receiving the Spirit of the Groom. The bride needs to be redeemed by Christ. This does not mean a return to the state before the Fall. Paradise was certainly a wonderful place, full of delights; Adam and Eve loved God and each other, but their love had not yet known trials that require sacrifice. They lived in a state of innocence and loved much as children do. We could say that their relationship with God

---

[223] Pope John Paul II, Apostolic letter, *Mulieris Dignitatem, n.26*. www.ewtn.com.
[224] Pope John Paul II, General audience, 20 Feb. 1980, w2.vatican.va.
[225] Peter of Alcántara, *Treatise on Prayer and Meditation*.

was like an engagement, as they had not yet committed their lives to Him. They were not yet "married" to God. Being engaged is wonderful and romantic, but does not yet have the depth of unity that grows from living the total self-giving of the covenant of marriage.

The day came when God allowed them to be tested. For the first time, love and fidelity required self-denial for the sake of the other. It was the moment of decision to commit to love, to enter the marriage covenant with God. But Adam and Eve did not trust God and broke the engagement with Him. Then they turned against each other. This was the Fall, the first sin. Since Adam and Eve represent all mankind, their sin alienated us all from God.

Jesus is the new Adam. He too was tested to the depth of His soul. But He said, "YES" to the Father's love all the way to the Cross. He sacrificed everything for love of the Father. He is the faithful Son in whom the Father is well pleased. Through His obedience, Jesus not only restored the damage caused by Adam and Eve, but He also opened for us His heart so that we may abide in Him.[226] Consequently, even though we live in a valley of tears and not in paradise, as Adam and Eve, we have in Christ what they failed to receive: the nuptial union of love with God—a joy, a love that far surpasses any delight of the old paradise. If we respond, we will no longer be engaged to God; we will be ONE with Him, able to love as Christ loves.

Mary is the greatest exemplar. Pope Benedict explains it well:

The Covenant with Israel was like a period of courtship, a long engagement. Then came the definitive moment, the moment of marriage, the establishment of a new and everlasting covenant. As Mary stood before the Lord, she

---

[226] Cf. Rom 5:17-19.

represented the whole of humanity. In the angel's message, it was as if God made a marriage proposal to the human race. And in our name, Mary said yes.

In fairy tales, the story ends there, and all "live happily ever after." In real life, it is not so simple. For Mary, there were many struggles ahead, as she lived out the consequences of the "yes" that she had given to the Lord.[227]

— To Understand Christ as the Bridegroom, We Need to Understand Redemption —

Think of a young man who risks his life to save a woman from drowning. That would be a wonderful story, but what if he then falls in love with her and they marry? This is what Jesus did. He did not come just to rescue us from hell, nor just to give us paradise. He came to give Himself in a marital covenant with us forever. Only then can we be happy. Jesus told St. Teresa of Avila: "If I had not created heaven, I would create it for you alone." What spouse can say that? Heaven is nothing other than to be united with Jesus, the Bridegroom.

Pope Francis said that Jesus is like a groom saying to his bride: 'when we are together, when we get married…" This is the "dream of God." The Pope then asked: "Have you ever thought: 'the Lord dreams about me? He thinks about me? I am in the mind, in the heart of the Lord? The Lord is capable of changing my life?'"[228]

The bride of the Song of Solomon was not afraid to respond to

---

[227] Benedict XVI, Angelus, 20 July, 2008, w2.vatican.va.
[228] Daily meditations, 16 Mar. 2015, w2.vatican.va.

the beloved:

> O that you would kiss me with the kisses of your mouth!
> For your love is better than wine…
> I am my beloved's, and his desire is for me.[229]

The time, however, had not arrived for the nuptial union because Christ had not yet come. Now that He is with us, what is the obstacle to the spousal union? St Theresa of Avila taught her daughters regarding the text above: "We practice so poorly the love of God that we think a soul cannot speak with God in such expressions.[230] Our sinful condition makes us think that a holy, passionate spousal love with Jesus is impossible. Saint Theresa was able to live it because her heart was purified by contemplating and responding to the crucified love of Jesus. She could love and suffer as one with Him.[231]

Saint Theresa went on to explain to her daughters that to give Jesus a kiss in the mouth is to experience His love in such a way that one is capable of all things for His sake: "We stop at nothing, but rather we shall forget about ourselves to please such sweet Spouse. His Majesty makes Himself, in many ways, perceived by those who enjoy this favor … Oh powerful love of God! To the one that loves, nothing seems impossible!"[232]

The goal of this *Simple Path to Union* is to help us enter the bliss of union with God through spousal union with Christ. The Community of Love Crucified prays that you will persevere,

---

[229] Song 1:1; 7:10.
[230] Theresa of Avila, *Concepts of the Love of God*, ch.1
  http://digital.library.upenn.edu/women/teresa/perfection/perfection.html#dl
[231] Jesus' love is both agape and eros. See Fr. Raniero Cantalamessa, *The Two Faces of Love: Eros and Agape.* (St Pauls Publishing, 31 Oct, 2012).
[232] Saint Theresa de Avila, *Concepts of the Love of God*, ch.3.

allowing the Bridegroom to take you to the Cross with Him. May we say, "Yes, my beloved Spouse, I suffer all with you, no longer two but One, in your sacrifice of love."

93. Be My Spouse, Diary of a MOC

It is My victim souls abandoned to My crucified love that possess the power of God to defeat Satan and usher in the reign of the Immaculate Heart of My Mother. Do not be afraid to be My voice. Do not be afraid to be crucified with Me. Be My spouse. A bride follows her spouse wherever He goes. Will you follow Me to My Cross where our love will be consummated in the power of God? Suffer all with Me, your Spouse, through the embrace of the silence of the Holy Spirit. This is most pleasing to Me. Trust, for there isn't a suffering I permit that will not bring you into the union of love I desire. Trust in the power of suffering all as ONE with Me. It is this power that will set the world on fire with My Spirit. Raise up My victims of love for these decisive times. (7/9/12)

— **The Bride Finally Says, "Yes"** —

Throughout the entire history of salvation, God seeks His unfaithful Bride. In the last chapter of the Bible, the heavens at last burst with joy and exultation because the Bride is finally ready to say 'yes' and the celebration of the wedding feast of the Lamb is about to begin.

Book of Revelation

Let us rejoice and exult and give Him the glory, for the marriage of the Lamb has come, and his Bride has made herself ready; …Blessed are those who are invited to the marriage supper of the Lamb.[233]

The entire people of God and each of us personally are the Bride, made ready through openness to the Holy Spirit:

The Spirit and the Bride say, "Come." And let him who hears say, "Come." And let him who is thirsty come, let him who desires take the water of life without price.[234]

Jesus on the Cross said: "I thirst." Now the Bride is also thirsty! This is the work of the Holy Spirit: To enkindle in us thirst for the Bridegroom, to give our lives as victims of love with Him. When we gaze at Jesus crucified and behold the act of love of the Bridegroom, we thirst. This is the power of the Cross—the power of love. This is what moved St. Paul to say: "He loved me and gave Himself for me!"[235]

_____

[233] Rev 19:7,9.
[234] Rev 22:17; cf Rev 21:2)
[235] Gal 2,20.

Ask yourself: "When I go to the Eucharist, do I realize that I am the bride, going to join the Bridegroom to become one oblation of love with Him?" "When I gaze upon Jesus Crucified, do I see my Bridegroom?" "Do I thirst for Him?"

94. As My Spouse, You Will Satisfy My Thirst,
Diary of a MOC

> *My daughter, as My spouse, you will satisfy My thirst for your love, as you lay down your life for the mission I have placed in your heart... This thirst of love moves Me to pour out My Precious Blood for you so that your thirst for love can be quenched. But I continue to thirst and seek souls to quench My thirst for love. (6/12/12)*

95. I desire to remain with you, Diary of a MOC

> *I live in you. I have come to remain in you as My living tabernacle. In this way, I am not alone. You can feel Me, see me, touch Me and I can hear your words of love and tenderness towards me, your God and Spouse. I can feel your touch, and receive your kiss of love and purity. I desire to remain with you as One with you in this embrace of love. For your part, protect this union through the purity of your lips. Remain and live in the embrace of the silence of the Holy Spirit. My little one, love Me and be attentive to Me. (7/17/12)*

96. As a Spouse, Your Life Must Be Lived to Console Him,
Diary of a MOC

> During the Consecration of the Mass, I felt God the Father speak in my soul. He said, *"Are you now ready to become My Son's sacrifice of love? …You can no longer be concerned about what others think of you nor your reputation, you can be concerned only with pleasing My Son. You are no longer His handmaid but His spouse. As His spouse, your life must be lived to console Him and to be faithful out of love to His desires."* (2/19/11)

But how can men identify themselves as brides? In relation to Jesus, we are all "brides" because all are Church. We need to allow Christ to enter us and possess us. He longs for a profound intimacy also with men, according to their manly nature. In fact, it is only through an intimate union with Christ that men discover true manhood. As men grow to be one with Christ, the Bridegroom, they live His identity and mission as their own. They lay down their lives to love the bride with the love of Jesus. An example of this is St. Paul, he "put on the Lord Jesus Christ" [236] and spent his life giving himself as priest and victim for the bride Church. In his letter to the Ephesians, he calls men to do the same for all and especially for their wives: "Husbands, love your wives, as Christ loved the church and gave himself up for her."[237]

Inspired by Paul's letter, St. John Chrysostom writes to husbands about the implications of becoming a new man in the image of Christ:

---

[236] Rom 13:14.
[237] Eph 5:25.

269

Pay attention to love's high standard. If you take the premise that your wife should submit to you as the church submits to Christ, then you should also take the same kind of careful, sacrificial thought for her that Christ takes for the Church. Even if you must offer your own life for her, you must not refuse. Even if you must undergo countless struggles on her behalf and have all kinds of things to endure and suffer, you must not refuse. Even if you suffer all this, you have still not done as much as Christ has for the church. For you are already married when you act this way, whereas Christ is acting for one who has rejected and hated him. So just as he, when she was rejecting, hating, spurning and nagging him, brought her to trust him by his great solicitude, not by threatening, lording it over her or intimidating her or anything like that, so you must also act toward your wife. Even if you see her looking down on you, nagging and despising you, you will be able to win her over with your great love and affection for her.

Tell her that you love her more than your own life, because this present life is nothing, and that your only hope is that the two of you pass through this life in such a way that in the world to come you will be united in perfect love. Say to her, "Our time here is brief and fleeting, but if we are pleasing to God, we can exchange this life for the Kingdom to come. Then we will be perfectly one both with Christ and each other, and our pleasure will know no bounds."[238]

---

[238] St. John Chrysostom, homily on Ephesians 5. 20.5.25.

Part II

Aspects of Living the Path

Chapter Five

Virtues of a New Heart

———— ◆ ————

Remember what we learned at the very start of *The Simple Path to Union*: "The new life we received in baptism is like a tiny seed meant to grow into a full life in Christ. **The purpose of our time on earth, then, is to pursue this growth along a path of continuous transformation.**"

In this path, our virtues must be perfected. It is important therefore to study the virtues, gifts, and fruits of the Holy Spirit, as found in the Catechism.[239] It teaches that "a virtue is a habitual and firm disposition to do the good. It allows the person not only to perform good acts, but to give the best of himself."[240] According to St. Gregory of Nyssa, "The goal of a virtuous life is to become like God."[241] In other words, to be virtuous is to become one with Christ.

---

[239] *Catechism of the Catholic Church*, n.1830-1835.

[240] Ibid, n.1803.

[241] St. Gregory of Nyssa, *De beatitudinibus,1*, 44.

In previous chapters, we learned that the path to union with Christ is through suffering all with Him for love. In this chapter, we will learn virtues and practices that must become our way of life in order to live in the fire of the Sacred Heart.

5-A
Prayer

— Prayer Begins with Listening —

Through prayer, we "incline our ears"[242] to the Lord. Prayer is the opening of the doors of our hearts through which we invite our Beloved. Prayer is the "yes" of our hearts to our Lord's gentle pleading.

Our loving Father longs for us to go to Him, but for us, prayer is difficult because our ears and hearts are hardened, and many interests distract us. To overcome this condition, we need to persevere gazing upon the Lord. *"Through humility and purity, you will quickly attain perfection in all the virtues if you persevere in prayer."*[243]

---

[242] Cf. Sirach 2:2, Ps 78:1.
[243] Diary of a MOC, 4 Mar. 2011.

— Prayer Has the Power of God —

In the book of Revelation, we see the power of the prayer of the saints (that includes the faithful on earth):

> The smoke of the incense rose with the prayers of the saints from the hand of the angel before God. Then the angel took the censer and filled it with fire from the altar and threw it on the earth; and there were peals of thunder, loud noises, flashes of lightning, and an earthquake (Rev 8:4-5).

We see in this image that God is not indifferent to our prayers; He intervenes and makes his power felt, and His voice heard on the earth. He makes the systems of Evil tremble and disrupts them.

Our prayers—with all the difficulty, poverty and imperfections they have—reach the heart of God. Therefore, there are no useless or lost prayers. "They find a response—even if it is oftentimes mysterious—because God is Love and infinite Mercy."[244] Prayer makes our weakness fruitful. (Cf. Rom 8:26-27).

Pope Benedict XVI

As Christians, we can never be pessimists; we know well that along life's journey we often encounter violence, falsehood, hate, and persecution, but this does not discourage us. Above all, prayer teaches us to see the signs of God, of His presence and action; indeed, to be lights of goodness that spread hope and point out that the victory is God's.[245]

---

[244] Pope Benedict XVI, General audience, 12 Sept. 2012, w2.vatican.va.
[245] Ibid.

— Prayer Brings Us to Life —

To pray is to open ourselves to an intense passion of love for Christ. St. Paul's union with Christ was so profound that he could say: "It is no longer I who live, but it is Christ who lives in me" (Gal 2:20). This union brings him to a supernatural joy that nothing could take away. While in prison and great danger of death, he encouraged all to share his joy: "Rejoice in the Lord always; again I will say, Rejoice" (Phil 4:4). Reflecting these words of St. Paul, Pope Benedict XVI tells us that, through prayer, we too can become one with Christ, "able to think, act and love like Him, in Him and for Him. Putting this into practice, learning the sentiments of Jesus, is the way of Christian life."[246]

— Prayer Is a Way of Life —

Many of us might spend some time each day in prayer, but how is it possible to live our lives as a continuous prayer? Lovers are constantly united in their hearts though they may not be able to speak. How much more when our beloved is God! This depth of union is a grace that God wants to give us.

Prayer takes different forms and engages our entire being. According to Pope Benedict XVI, prayer "is composed of silence and words, of singing and of gestures that involve the whole person: from the mouth to the mind, from the heart to the entire body."[247]

St. Therese of Lisieux writes of her life as a prayer, "For me, prayer is a surge of the heart; it is a simple look turned toward heaven, it is a cry of recognition and of love, embracing both trial

---

[246] Ibid., 27 June, 2012, w2.vatican.va.
[247] Ibid.

and joy."

Pope Benedict XVI

Prayer is the encounter of God's thirst with our thirst. God is thirsting for us to thirst for Him. In prayer, we must turn our hearts to God, to consign ourselves to Him as an offering to be purified and transformed. In prayer we see all things in the light of Christ, we let our masks fall and immerse ourselves in the truth and in listening to God, feeding the fire of love.[248]

What Pope Benedict is describing above is fulfilled if we go to Mass with the right disposition. We "consign ourselves" as one with Christ to the Father. This is why the Sacrifice of the Mass is the most perfect prayer.

Have you ever considered your sufferings as a prayer that has great power before the throne of the Father? For Venerable Conchita, the crosses of her life became a prayer, a kiss of Jesus, seeking to draw her to Himself. In the message on the next page our Lord explains how to live our daily sufferings as a prayer.

---

[248] Ibid., 22 Aug. 2007, www.vatican.va.

277

97. Your Life Is a Prayer, Diary of a MOC

When I say your life is a prayer, [I mean that] your life is an offering. To offer Me your life is the perfect prayer. Your thoughts directed to Me, directed to love, is a prayer. Your desire to know Me, love Me, and serve Me is a prayer. Your touch is a most beautiful prayer. Your words of encouragement and love to others are a prayer. Your efforts to bring peace and unity to your families are a prayer. Your smile is a prayer. But your most perfect prayer is your pure suffering united to Me and My Mother.

*The **prayer of pure suffering is the sweetest fragrance that reaches and delights the Heart of our Father**. This is also the prayer that produces an abundance of fruit. This is the prayer that is most united to Mine as I intercede before the throne of My Father.*

This is why My Mother's suffering of solitude produced and continues to produce showers of graces upon the world. I wish the Mothers and Missionaries of the Cross to be perfected in the prayer of suffering.

But my Lord, what about contemplative prayer and the prayer of praise?

It is through contemplative prayer that you come to know Me and the prayer in which I fill, guide and form you, but it is the prayer of suffering in which you honor, console and love Me, and participate in the redemption of souls. The prayer of gratitude and thanksgiving should be your every breath. (8/23/10)

278

98. Mary Explains the Power of the Life of Spiritual Mothers United to Her Fiat, Diary of a MOC

The mothers of the cross (spiritual mothers) are my maidens who, united to me, will renew the priesthood. Your "fiat" to be victim souls will be perfected in my "Fiat." Your lives will be a holy cloth that soaks up the Precious Blood of Jesus. In this way, you will become pure living chalices filled with the Blood of Jesus. You will live your hidden lives like me in prayer, sacrifice, and suffering. Your hidden lives lived in your domestic monasteries will be a source of grace for the sanctification of priests.

You will imitate to great perfection my virtues of humility, simplicity, gentleness, silence and charity. You will be women of an intense prayer life centered in the Eucharist. Your lives will be a continuous prayer offering as you offer up your daily sacrifices and duties on the altar of your homes. As you love in suffering, imitating Jesus and me, you will be our joy and consolation. (6/13/09)

99. Allow Everything to be a Prayer, Diary of a MOC

> *My daughter, pray, pray, pray. I know how much you love to be in prayer before My Son in the Blessed Sacrament, but I desire for you to pray continuously. Allow your every word, thought, and deed to be a prayer. It is in this way that you will come to know the promptings and whispers of the Holy Spirit and live in peace.* (1/29/10)

Jesus speaks to St. Faustina:

My Daughter, I want to instruct you on how you are to rescue souls through sacrifice and prayer. You will save more souls through prayer and suffering than will a missionary through his teachings and sermons alone. I want to see you as a sacrifice of living love, which only then carries weight before Me.[249]

Mary is the model of prayer because her fiat held nothing back, even when this meant that she was interiorly crucified with her Son. That is why God could do great things in her. She will help us enter ever deeper into her fiat so that the Lord can use our prayers to bless the world.

---

[249] St. Faustina Kowalska, *Diary, Divine Mercy in My Soul,* n.1767.

100. Your Prayers Shower Immense Graces on Earth,
Diary of a MOC

> *I have chosen My simple and humble servants to do great things… You have the mission to evangelize and intercede… Your prayers of intercession, praise and thanksgiving are showering immense graces upon the earth.* (11/26/08)

5-B
Silence

Silence is the embrace of love between God and the soul. The Lord tells us, "Be still, and know that I am God" (Ps 46:10). He wants us to enter His embrace to make us His forever. Ponder the silence of Mary and how it allowed her to be receptive to the Word. Ponder the example of Jesus who went regularly to a deserted place to pray. Pope Benedict teaches us the importance of silence:

> **Inward and outward silence is necessary if we are to be able to hear the Word.** And in our time this point is particularly difficult for us. In fact, ours is an era that does not encourage recollection; indeed, one sometimes gets the impression that people are frightened of being cut off, even for an instant, from the torrent of words and images that mark and fill the day.[250]

Mary's receptive silence allowed the Holy Spirit to

---

[250] General audience, 7 Mar. 2012, w2.vatican.va.

overshadow her. Pope Francis tells us that the Spirit now wants to overshadow us so that we can encounter Him and the mystery of our life with Him:

> This overshadowing in us, in our lives, is called silence. Silence is the cloud that veils the mystery of our relationship with the Lord, of our holiness and of our sins…
>
> It is a mystery that we cannot explain. But when there is no silence in our lives, we lose the mystery, it goes away. Hence the importance of guarding the mystery with silence: this is the cloud, this is God's power in us, it is the strength of the Holy Spirit.[251]

Mary, the Pope said, guarded her heart with silence:

> I think about how many times she remained silent, how many times she did not say what she felt in order to guard the mystery of her relationship with her Son… (Mary) was silent, but within her heart, how many things she said to the Lord in that crucial moment in history… (She) veiled in silence the mystery which she did not understand. And, through silence, she allowed the mystery to grow and flourish, thus bringing great hope to all.[252]

In the teaching below Our Lord tells us that **silent prayer is like ascending a ladder that takes us to an increasing union with God.** The first steps are the most difficult and tedious because we cannot easily quiet our minds. However, if we persevere in the prayer of silence, we will encounter the divine visitation. This

---

[251] Ibid.
[252] Pope Francis, homily, 20 Dec. 2013, w2.vatican.va.

encounter will lift us up the ladder towards God's embrace. The closer we come to union with God, the more silent we are and the more we allow God to speak to us.

101. Silence Is Like Ascending a Ladder, Diary of a MOC

Silence is the realm of God. Silence is a state of being in union with God. Silence is like ascending a ladder. You must begin on the lower steps to reach the highest. A human soul must begin to enter silence through the mortification of the tongue, thoughts, and internal noise.

Daily periods of silent prayer help the soul come to know silence. The beginning steps of entering and living in silence are the most difficult and tedious. If a soul perseveres in mortifying her senses, the Father will bless her with experiences of coming in contact with the divine. The human heart and flesh will experience Me. These divine visitations will serve to awaken the human heart to a greater desire for Me. These visitations will encourage her weak human nature to continue climbing the steps of silence, mainly through perseverance in prayer.

The journey can be very hard depending on the strength of will of the soul, and at times she might find herself descending the steps, but her thirst for My love and visits will be the fuel that keeps her ascending. My Spirit is the One that is her companion at each step. My Spirit is her help, guide and inner strength; but as of yet, she does not know Him. His life and light are growing in her being, and with her ascent, through the abandonment of her

> *will, the life of the Spirit is strengthening in her. But it is in the fire of My Sacred Heart that she (the soul) comes to know personally the Holy Spirit. It is now that she has ascended into the silence of the Trinity.*
>
> *In the Holy Spirit, you possess Me and the Father as One. The Spirit now lives in you and you in Him. You are ONE. This divine dimension is SILENCE. When you enter this divine union in silence, you must be careful to nurture it; careless speech and careless activity can bring the soul out of this divine dimension of silence* (7/22/11).

Silence allows us to get in touch with our sorrows so that we can enter them and unite them to the sorrows of Jesus. Then our sufferings are no longer obstacles in our path to God but actually become the path to union with Him.

When Mary embraced her Son as in the Pieta, she embraced and received the brokenness of all of humanity. When we join her in this embrace of her Son, we too receive in our hearts the wounds of many souls, through Jesus, with Him and in Him. In this way, we live the Holy Sacrifice of the Mass in our ordinary lives.

102. The Arms of Silence Embrace My Crucified Body, Diary of a MOC

Silence allows you to embrace fully the sorrow of your heart. Silence allows you to enter fully the sorrow I am permitting in your heart. As you embrace this pain and suffering, you are embracing Me. You are embracing My pain and suffering and thus entering My Heart, for My Heart is all pain and love. This is My Mercy.

To come to know the love of your Beloved is to come to experience My sorrow. *This is why My Mother is the Queen of Sorrows, for it is she who lived most perfectly consumed in My Heart. My little one, this union of sorrow, must move your heart to love all, by suffering with silence, peace, and abandonment for all your brothers and sisters.*

My sons and daughters, exteriorly smile and tend to the duties of your vocation with detail and love; but interiorly, through the arms of silence, live embracing your sorrows. In this way, you are embracing My crucified Body and soothing My wounds. This is the life of love. This is the life of a Mother of the Cross, for it is the life of My Mother. The Holy Spirit will help you; consecrate yourself to Him this morning. Go in peace, My daughter; I live in you as you live in Me. (8/8/11)

Moved by the Lord's suffering, St. Augustine pleaded with Him to write His wounds on his heart. In this way, he would be able to bear his own suffering in silence for the love of God.

Write, my most loving Savior, write on my heart Thy wounds, in order that I may always behold therein Thy sufferings and Thy love. Yes, because, having before my eyes the great sufferings that Thou, my God, didst endure for me, I may bear in silence all the sufferings that it may fall to my lot to endure.[253]

How do we enter this necessary silence to encounter Jesus? We do so by living the way of life taught in this Path to Union with God. Daily we turn to the Holy Spirit; and with our Mother, we center our lives in the Eucharist, both in Holy Mass and Eucharistic adoration. The risen Lord will show us His wounds as He did to St. Thomas. He will draw us to Himself and make us one with Him in an intimate way.

This is the way of the saints. Mother Theresa of Calcutta's intense life of self-giving was sustained by her daily time of stillness and silence with the Lord in the Eucharist. St. Faustina wrote, "I want to prepare my heart for the coming of the Lord Jesus by silence and recollection of spirit, uniting myself with the most Holy Mother and faithfully imitating her virtue of silence."[254]

Fr. Raniero Cantalamessa explains it this way:

It is by staying *still, in silence,* and possibly for long periods, before Jesus in the Blessed Sacrament, that we perceive what he wants from us, put aside our own plans to make way for His, and let God's light gradually penetrate the heart and heal it.[255]

---

[253] St. Augustine as quoted in St. Alphonsus Maria Liguori, *The Passion and the Death of Jesus Christ* (Benziger Brothers, 1 Jan. 1887), 18, books.google.com.

[254] St. Faustina Kowalska, *Diary, Divine Mercy in My Soul,* n.1398.

[255] Raniero Cantalamessa, *The Eucharist Our Sanctification.* Cf. 2 *Cor* 3:18.

While we may love the concept of silence, we find it very difficult to actually live it. Our minds are distracted by many things. We are constantly talking to ourselves and to others. If we want to enter God's embrace, we must discipline ourselves to have daily periods of silent prayer. This requires that we allow God to guide us and to order our relationships and priorities. **Silence should never be an obstacle to authentic communication**. We should avoid frivolous talk and **discern what to share** based on what is pleasing to the Lord.

103. Mortify Yourself in Silence, Diary of a MOC

> *Mortify yourself in SILENCE… Allow SILENCE to become your most treasured companion… In this way, it is I who will become your closest companion. You will learn to discern My voice immediately.* (8/8/09)

— Letter from a Mother of the Cross to a Beloved Sister in the Community —

I want my love to be heroic… then I see my lack of love… my hardness of heart…

I would have liked to call you tonight to seek consolation… but I know that Our Lord is asking me to mortify myself and enter into my suffering… I embrace it with docility…

Tonight, I abandon myself in my suffering, waiting for it to bear fruit… That this tiny suffering may please the Father—not for its greatness—but because I embrace it and accept it… I do not fight it… I do not rebel.

I offer it for our priest and for you... for our entire spiritual family and for our personal families. I offer it for each lukewarm priest, for each heart that has denied Jesus entrance... Oh, how I desire to suffer for Him!

I enter silently into suffering...

104. Silence Is Not Necessarily Not Talking, Diary of a MOC

Silence is a virtue. Silence is a prayer. Silence is misunderstood by many. There are cloistered souls who practice silence but are not silent because interiorly they are distracted, anxious and chattering. Silence is your soul in communion with God. It is in silence that you come to hear the voice of God. It is in silence that you come to see the face of God. It is in silence that you come to feel the touch of God. **Silence is the embrace of love between a soul and God.**

Learn to enter the prayer of silence. The Holy Spirit and My Mother will teach you. Silence is not necessarily not talking. I spent My days on earth preaching, teaching and conversing with My friends and community. Yes, my daughter, I lived in community. [Jesus immediately responded to my thought when He said "community."] But I entered the prayer of silence daily with my Father. It is the gift and grace of the Holy Spirit that will bring you to live in this communion of silence with Me amidst the exterior noise.

On your part, enter daily the prayer of silence in the Church or in your home. Ask My Mother to guide you and help you in this practice of silence most beneficial for your soul. (7/21/10)

5-C
Tenderness

The God of power and might is also the God who loves us with the tenderness of a mother:

Can a woman forget her sucking child,
that she should have no compassion on the son of her womb?
Even these may forget, yet I will not forget you.
Behold, I have engraved you on the palms of my hands.
– Isaiah 49:15-16

— The Revolution of Tenderness —

"The Son of God, by becoming flesh, summoned us to the revolution of tenderness."[256] These words of Pope Francis refer to a revolution that is completely different from all others, for it is the only one that does not impose itself by force. Instead, it reveals the power of tender love to transform hearts from within.

When we were in darkness and in the shadow of death, the tender mercy of God dawned upon us.[257] The Word came to us in human flesh. His touch and gaze reveal God's tenderness, which He did not hold back because of our sins. Rather, He allowed the nails to engrave us in the palms of His hands; but who believes that

---

[256] *Evangelium Gaudium*, n.88.
[257] Cf. Lk 1:78-79.

this revolution can really change persons and the world? Who continues to show tenderness while treated with offenses and rejection? Pope Francis reminds us that the answer is found in Mary: "She reminds us that the only force capable of conquering the heart of men is the tenderness of God."[258]

Pope Francis explains:

Whenever we look to Mary, we come to believe once again in the revolutionary nature of love and tenderness. In her, we see that humility and tenderness are not virtues of the weak but of the strong who need not treat others poorly in order to feel important themselves. Contemplating Mary, we realize that she who praised God for "bringing down the mighty from their thrones" and "sending the rich away empty" (Lk 1:52-53) is also the one who brings a homely warmth to our pursuit of justice. She is also the one who carefully keeps "all these things, pondering them in her heart" (Lk 2:19). Mary is able to recognize the traces of God's Spirit in events great and small.[259]

---

[258] Pope Francis, to the bishops of Mexico, Cathedral of Mexico, 13 Feb. 2016.
[259] *EG*, 288.

— We Partake of God's Tenderness —

St. Peter writes that Christians have a "tender heart."[260] With Mary, we receive and respond to God's tenderness in our encounters with Him in His Word, in the Eucharist, in confession… and in our brothers and sisters.

When we consecrate ourselves to the Lord, we include our bodies so that they manifest what is in our hearts. St. Francis of Assisi said that serving God means serving our brothers and sisters "more tenderly than a mother cares for her children in the flesh." By **being attentive to how we use our hands or fail to use them; how we gaze at others and what we say,** we will know what is in our hearts and whether the tenderness of God's love is truly flowing from us.

105. Tenderness Manifests Love, Diary of a MOC

> *Tenderness is the virtue in which the love in your heart is manifested through your faculties of touch, sight, and speech. God is love; therefore, here on earth, My love was experienced by many through the touch of My hands, through the gaze of My eyes, and through My words.*
>
> *I am a living torrent of grace, which is the love of God flowing through Me. When you come to possess Me, through the power of the Holy Spirit, My love flows through you. You become My living vessel; you become My hands; you become My gaze; you speak My words. This is what it means to be My living chalices and living hosts. This love is*

---

[260] 1 Pet 3:8.

> *manifested concretely, tangibly, through your tenderness.*
>
> *By being attentive to how you use your hands or fail to use your hands, how you gaze at others, and how the words flow from your lips, you will come to know the sin that remains in your hearts. My Mother is forming each of you to be My living chalices.* (1/2/12)

The woman who publicly washed the feet of Jesus with her tears teaches us a lot about tenderness. She looked at Jesus and was not deterred by fear of being judged by others or by fear of being imprudent. She was moved by love and gratitude. She expected nothing in return. Her heart was pure.

Tenderness has the power to melt the most hardened hearts steeped in pride. As we receive God's love in our hearts, our identity as His beloved sons and daughters is restored. The tenderness of God heals. The caress of God disinfects and cleanses our wounds. The tenderness of God brings peace, serenity, and rest to the afflicted, to the tired and those thirsting for love.

Pope Francis calls us to be tender

Wounds hurt and even more so when not treated tenderly. Looking at baby Jesus, all tenderness, I ask for all, this attitude: That we may know how to treat with care and tenderness all wounds. They are there: It is not possible to hide them or deny them. Just a gentle touch from our heart, with silence and respect, can bring relief. And, since the maximum tenderness is that of God, let us ask Him to bring to each His warm, Fatherly consolation and teach us all not to be alone but to continue to seek the company of brothers.[261]

—How Do We Receive and Give God's Tenderness—

By contemplating Jesus, His touch, His gaze, His words and His gestures of tenderness, we allow Him to reveal His heart, which is pure love. We then become joyful Christians who give and receive the "consolation of the tenderness of Jesus."[262] There are so many in need of our tenderness!

We Can Lose Our Tenderness without Realizing It

When we have been hurt, when we have not received tenderness, we become harsh and controlling. Tenderness then seems like foolishness or weakness. Tenderness separated from Christ becomes a lie used to buy love, manipulate and draw attention to self. True tenderness is not imposed and does not overwhelm.

Once we realize that the love of God is transmitted through our gentle touch, we **re-discover the importance of blessing and showing affection.** This is especially important for parents and priests. Many have difficulty using their hands to bless even their beloved children.

Tania is a woman who took this teaching on tenderness to heart. She was a dedicated mother, providing, teaching and protecting her children as much as she could. However, through the above teaching, she realized that, for years, she had not been tender with them; she had not used her hands to embrace and caress them. She went to the root by asking herself, "Why is it difficult for me to

---

[261] Letter to Bishop Jorge Lozano of Gualeguaychú, Argentina, Dec. 2013, www.romereports.com.

[262] Pope Francis, homily at St. Martha, 9 Dec. 2014, www.news.va.

show tender affection if I love them dearly?" As she dug deep, the light of the Holy Spirit touched upon her relationship with her mother, whom she identified as a dominating, controlling and harsh woman. She was carrying this "mother wound," which was blocking her ability to be tender. As she recognized this, she opened her heart to the Lord and disposed herself to express concrete acts of tenderness. At first, it did not come naturally, but she persevered, pushing herself to do what was difficult. The children were surprised with their mom's new behavior. As she experienced healing in her feminine heart, tenderness began to flow with increasing ease; and the children responded with tenderness towards her.

The feminine heart is most gifted by God to manifest His tenderness. Men learn it mostly from women. Therefore, when mothers have lost their tenderness, it creates deep wounds in their husbands and children. The home becomes cold and sterile.

106. Tenderness Through Our Hands, Diary of a MOC

> *The love of God will stretch your love beyond your physical capacities. The expansion of the tent of your hearts is a most painful process. You have to choose to love those most difficult to love. You must always choose love, patience, and tenderness and never give in to anger and resentment.*
>
> *The tenderness of God was manifested through My hands. The healing grace of God was transmitted through My hands. I need you to be My hands and to transmit the healing grace of God to your spouses, children and many. It is My tenderness that heals the harshness and hardness of hearts. Radiate My tenderness through your hands.*

(3/1/11)

107. Receive My Blood, Be My Hands, Diary of a MOC

> *Each of My wounds is a stream of blood, of grace, that comes from one source. As you can see, My hand is nailed to the Cross. Through this stream of blood, the Cross brings My grace and love. I desire you to receive My blood in your heart so that you can be My hands in the world; My hands that love, heal, unite and bring peace. Do not be afraid to place your hands on others. I will anoint them through you.* (6/30/08)

108. Bless Your Children with Your Hands, Diary of a MOC

> *Bless your children daily. Get up early each morning to bless those that go to school. Bless your husband as he sleeps. Bless your grandchildren each time you see them. It is I, your Heavenly Mother, who will bless them through your hands and provide for each of them greater protection against the principalities of death.* (9/17/10)

Another Way to Express Tenderness Is to Gaze with Love

There is so much that can be said about a loving gaze! Do we look at others with love or with judgment and criticism? Do we focus on the exterior and allow ourselves to gaze with contempt? The gaze of tenderness looks into the heart of others and sees their wounds and brokenness, which moves us to compassion.

— Testimony of a Mother of the Cross —

The Lord took me to the wounds of my relationship with my mother and the tendencies that have come from these wounds. I had dealt with them before, in fact, I speak with her on a daily basis, but the Lord wanted a deeper healing.

Although I lose my patience with her sometimes, anyone would think that our mother-daughter relationship is normal. However, the Lord brought to my attention the many times that I keep a distance from her. We do not touch; we do not hug; there is a huge barrier between us. I am there for her in a time of need, and we even get together as a family often for dinner, but our relationship lacks tenderness and intimacy. Our relationship is purely on the surface.

I also realized that my mother-wounds directly affect my ability to love others, especially those closest to me. I see it in how I love my husband and children. I believe this happens to all of us. The Lord showed me the lack of tenderness and love in the world and how it is directly related to the relationship with our mothers. It is very important to face our mother-wounds and the tendencies that emerge from them.

The Lord called me to be tender towards all, so I called my mother and made an effort to take her out on some errands she had to do. The entire time **I went against my selfish tendencies and was patient with her**; I waited, helped and served her. I also have been trying to do what is most difficult with all those the Lord places in my life, beginning with my husband and with my children. I am being tender, more careful on how I use my hands.

The Lord has called us to love all. He has called us to be His Chalices, pouring out His Precious Blood on all those we encounter. He has called us to be the light in the darkness through the tenderness in our gaze, our touch, and our words. We cannot move forward in this unless we face our wounds and tendencies.

This has been a powerful lesson; however, the Lord was not done teaching me. I began to ponder my relationship with our Blessed Mother, and the Lord showed me again my inability to come close to her. He showed me that although I love our Blessed Mother very much and I go to her quite often, there is still a barrier between us. I realized that I did not have the relationship that she and Our Lord desired. **My relationship with my mother had affected my relationship with our Blessed Mother**. Therefore, as the wounds of my maternal relationship were healed and as I went against the disordered tendencies that emerged from those wounds, I was also able to go to Mother Mary to receive her spiritual milk—her guidance and teachings.

— Men Too Must Be Tender —

Men must also be tender and have the courage to go against the culture. The definition of "tender" is "easily crushed, bruised, fragile," but another definition is: "To be considerate and protective; sensitive to emotions and others' feelings." These are the vital qualities of tenderness men must possess to fulfill their God-given mission, which is to use their strength to love and serve those entrusted to them.

St. Joseph is the perfect example of manly tenderness. He is described in Scripture as a faithful servant of God who shows his love for God in his love for others. In every respect, St. Joseph possessed the heroic love and tenderness needed of the man whom

God entrusted with His two greatest treasures: Jesus and Mary.

In Matthew, we read: "Her husband Joseph, being a just man and unwilling to put her to shame, resolved to send her away quietly" (Mt 1:19). When an angel appeared to St. Joseph in a dream and warned him to take Jesus and his mother to Egypt, his response is immediate and without question: "He rose and took the child and his mother by night, and departed to Egypt and remained there until the death of Herod" (Mt 2:14-15). In every Scripture passage that mentions St. Joseph, we see an exemplar of virtue: he fulfilled his manly mission showing his love for God in his love for others.

As you meditate on these passages, think of St. Joseph's tenderness, honoring and respecting Mary as the spouse of the Holy Spirit. Think of his tenderness towards her son, treating Him as his own, though Jesus was truly the Son of the Most High; think of the tenderness of St. Joseph's hands, the rough hands of a carpenter, which made visible the love and tenderness of God for the Holy Family.

Pope Francis said of St. Joseph:

How does Joseph exercise his role as protector? Discreetly, humbly and silently, but with an unfailing presence and utter fidelity, even when he finds it hard to understand. From the time of his betrothal to Mary until the finding of the twelve-year-old Jesus in the Temple of Jerusalem, he is there at every moment with loving care. As the spouse of Mary, he is at her side in good times and bad, on the journey to Bethlehem for the census and in the anxious and joyful hours when she gave birth; amid the drama of the flight into Egypt and during the frantic search for their child in the Temple; and later in the day-to-day life of the home of

Nazareth, in the workshop where he taught his trade to Jesus.

But to be "protectors," we also have to keep watch over ourselves! Let us not forget that hatred, envy, and pride defile our lives! Being protectors, then, also means keeping watch over our emotions, over our hearts, because they are the seat of good and evil intentions: intentions that build up and tear down! We must not be afraid of goodness or even tenderness!

Here I would add one more thing: caring, protecting, demands goodness, it calls for a certain tenderness. In the Gospels, Saint Joseph appears as a strong and courageous man, a working man; yet in his heart we see great tenderness, which is not the virtue of the weak but rather a sign of strength of spirit and a capacity for concern, for compassion, for genuine openness to others, for love. We must not be afraid of goodness, of tenderness!

How does Joseph respond to his calling to be the protector of Mary, Jesus, and the Church? By being constantly attentive to God, open to the signs of God's presence and receptive to God's plans, and not simply to his own…. Joseph is a "protector" because he is able to hear God's voice and be guided by His will; and for this reason, he is all the more sensitive to the persons entrusted to his safekeeping.[263]

Men are protectors of their wives and families; they defend them if they are attacked physically, but sometimes they fail to realize that God has **entrusted them with the protection of their**

---

[263] Homily celebrating the beginning of his ministry as bishop of Rome, 19 Mar. 2013, w2.vatican.va.

hearts as well. They are called to have the tenderness of God whose love is fully attentive to all that takes place in the interior of each heart. He listens to our cries, knows our desires, fears, sufferings, emotions and temptations.

To accomplish this mission, men must be attentive to their hearts to hear the voice of God, like St. Joseph; and then they must be attentive to the hearts of those entrusted to them, to know how to guide them and protect them. Men tend to overlook this essential aspect of their mission as protectors because they lack tenderness and sensitivity.

One of the deepest sufferings of most wives is that their husbands do not know their hearts. Men think that going deep into the heart is only for women. The result is that few husbands are truly able to love and protect their wives.

A woman in a difficult marriage lamented that, during courtship, she approached her father with specific concerns regarding her future husband. She knew that her father loved her dearly and would do anything for her. She depended on him to protect her and guide her. But the father dismissed her concerns as unwarranted fears that come before the wedding. Because of his lack of attention to the concerns of her heart, he failed to protect her. This resulted in much suffering in her marriage.

St. John is the apostle who **placed his head on the heart of Jesus**. He entered intimacy with Jesus with complete tenderness. This testimony is in the Gospel because God wanted him to be an example to all men. St. John is the beloved disciple, attentive to the heart of Jesus. He is, therefore, the one able to follow Him with Mary to the foot of the Cross. Jesus can then entrust him with the heart of Mary to continue protecting her with the greatest love and tenderness. Mary is the mother of all, yet it is St. John who takes her home and lives with her. Jesus could count on St. John because he was able to enter into the depth of love through intimacy and tenderness. Mary, St. Joseph and St. John are exemplars of the new men and women transformed by the Holy Spirit.

If we persevere in allowing God's tenderness to heal our wounds and forgive our sins, our hearts will gradually be transformed into the tenderness of God. We will be free to allow God to use our faculties to bring His love into the world and pierce the most hardened hearts. We will become His Body; and the mercy of God, acting through us, will save those who are dead in sin.

109. The Lord Says to Us: "I Need You," Diary of a MOC

> *My soul cries without ceasing. My cup overflows with My tears. My beloved children are being lost for all eternity. As a mother laments for her dead child, I weep for My dead children, dead in sin. I need you, My faithful remnant, to save them from Satan's deception. I need you, My holy remnant, to suffer and cry with Me so that the mercy of God, our Father, can save them.*
>
> *You are My Body. My eyes must pierce the darkness through your eyes. My hands must heal the multitudes through your hands. My feet must travel to the ends of the world proclaiming My message of love and mercy through you. My Words of everlasting life must be spoken through your lips.*
>
> *The fire of My Sacred Heart must spread through your hearts that are consumed in the passionate fire of love in Me.*
>
> *Raise up, My little one, My victims of love for the New Evangelization to begin.* (8/28/12)

5-D

Poverty

————————— ❧ —————————

Jesus said: "Blessed are the poor in spirit, for theirs is the kingdom of heaven" (Mt 5:3). These are the hearts that empty themselves for love of God.[264] **It is not enough to give God a portion and then do as we please with "our part."** All we have BELONGS to God; we are His stewards[265] led by the Spirit of love. Love gives all. **Spiritual poverty is the fruit of love**. The more we love, the more we desire to be one with our Beloved who gave Himself totally.

Pope Benedict XVI wrote:

> Jesus is King of the *anawim*, of those whose hearts are free of the lust for power and material riches, free of the will and the search for dominion over others. Jesus is the King of all those who possess that interior freedom that enables them to overcome the greed and egoism of the world, and who know that God is their only wealth.[266]

Spiritual poverty directs our attention away from ourselves and to the needs of others. We need to practice it in our everyday life: in our use of material things, our use of time, talents, interests and attention to others.

Prayer at the fifth station of the Cross:

---

[264] Cf. Mt 13:44.

[265] Cf. *Catechism of the Catholic Church*, n.992.

[266] General Audience, 26 Oct. 2011, w2.vatican.va

Lord Jesus, our affluence is making us less human, our entertainment has become a drug, a source of alienation, and our society's incessant, tedious message is an invitation to die of selfishness.[267]

110. Spirit of Poverty, Diary of a MOC

> *I wish to teach you about poverty, the spirit of poverty. There is physical poverty, but the spirit of poverty is much more beneficial for your soul. It saddens Me greatly when My sons (priests) and religious live physical poverty but remain only there and do not allow the Holy Spirit to bring them to live the spirit of poverty... The spirit of poverty is lived when you allow the Holy Spirit, My Blessed Mother and Myself to strip you of everything interiorly: your desires, expectations, plans, attachments, securities, consolations in friendships, even consolations from Me, so that you are left completely empty. It is a soul that has been stripped of everything, that is empty and can be filled with My life...*
>
> My Lord and my God what can I do to participate in this work?
>
> Jesus answered, *Allow yourself to be perfected through suffering. Suffer with greater trust in Me... Suffer with greater abandonment and love* (7/8/2010).

---

[267] Mons. Angelo Comastri, *Fifth Station of the Cross*, Good Friday, 2006. www.vatican.va

5-E

Purity

"Blessed are the pure in heart, for they shall see God"
–Mathew 5:8

A pure heart is entirely filled with the love of God. We may say, "Jesus is in my heart," but that is not enough because there are many persons and things in our heart. Jesus needs to be on the **throne** of our hearts as He is in the heart of Mary, the Immaculate. We were not conceived in such a state, but by the grace of God, we grow in purity until we reach heaven. With Mary's help, we come in contact with Jesus and experience His touch, the gaze of His eyes, His very self. He makes us clean.

111. Abide in Me, Diary of a MOC

> *Obedience, humility, love, poverty, purity all flow as the living fruit of intimacy with Me, the source of all life. I am The Way, The Truth and The Life. He who abides in Me abides in Love and walks the narrow path of the Cross that leads to eternal life* (1/8/11).

Pope Benedict XVI wrote concerning the words, "you are clean":

In Mark's Gospel, we see the radical transformation that Jesus brought to the concept of purity before God: it is not ritual actions that make us pure. Purity and impurity arise within man's heart and depend on the condition of his heart.[268] ...

How does the heart become pure? Who are the pure in heart, those who can see God?[269] ... Faith cleanses the heart. It is the result of God's initiative toward man. Faith comes about because men are touched deep within by God's Spirit, who opens and purifies their hearts.

Jesus says, "You are already made clean by the word which I have spoken to you." It is His word that penetrates them, transforms their intellect, their will, their "heart," and opens it up in such a way that it becomes a seeing heart.... Jesus' word is more than a word; it is His very self. His word is truth, and it is love...

In place of ritual purity, what we have now is not merely morality, but the gift of encounter with God in Jesus Christ.[270]

"The Precious Blood of Christ, like that of a lamb without blemish or spot,"[271] is His perfect sacrifice, but we must participate in it. Jesus is always pure; we become pure only through union with Him. Peter says, "You have purified yourselves." For this to happen, we must allow the Holy Spirit to reveal and pierce the obstacles in our hearts: our disorders, sins, and wounds. We must enter a painful ongoing process of healing so that we are transformed into Christ. As we are purified we can intercede for the purification of others.

---

[268] Cf. Mk 7:14-23.

[269] Cf. Mt 5:8.

[270] *Jesus of Nazareth, Holy Week: From the Entrance into Jerusalem to the Resurrection,* 58-61.

[271] 1 Pet 1:18-22.

112. Our Blessed Mother, Diary of a MOC

> *The power of your intercession is contained in the purity of your hearts —the purity of your intentions.*
> *Trust and, with patient endurance, allow all your disorders to come to the Light. It is only in this way that you can be made pure in the furnace of God's love. I need you to be my pure intercessors of love before the throne of our Father with me. You are my white army* (8/6/13).

Our Lady spoke about purity in Medjugorje:

I am imploring my Son to give you pure hearts. My dear children, only pure hearts know how to carry a cross and know how to sacrifice for all those sinners who have offended the Heavenly Father and who, even today, offend Him, although they have not come to know Him. I am praying that you may come to know the light of true faith, which comes only from the prayer of pure hearts. It is then that all those who are near you will feel the love of my Son.[272]

---

[272] According to testimony of Mirjana Soldo, 2 Aug., 2012.

113. "I THIRST," Diary of a MOC

My daughter, you will satisfy My thirst for your love...as you lay down your life for the mission I have placed in your heart. This mission is My love for humanity, for each of you. This mission is My thirst, in the depth of My Sacred Heart, for unity in Love. That is, unity in the love of the Most Holy Trinity.

The Holy Spirit consuming My Heart is the thirst of the Father for each of you. This thirst of love moves Me to pour out My Precious Blood for you so that your thirst for love can be quenched. But I continue to thirst and seek souls to quench My thirst for your love.

My Mother brings you to My crucified feet to give Me your kiss of repentance, so that the eyes of your soul can be opened and you can see and taste, through the gaze of My crucified eyes, My love for you.

*My thirst for your love is quenched when I look down from My Glorious Cross and see you, My beloved sons and daughters, **dressed in the white garment of purity**, wearing My crown of thorns, and covered in the radiance of My Blood. Then, My thirst is quenched (6/12/12).*

114. Pure Hands Remove Thorns, Diary of a MOC

> Mother Mary: *I cry tears of blood because my heart profusely bleeds with so many thorns. It is your hands, as you suffer all with Jesus, that removes so many thorns that cause Us to suffer... The hands of purity remove these thorns, but purity in every act, purity in every thought, purity in every desire... It is not busyness, with so much to do, that consoles our Hearts but pure love in every act, thought and desire.* (5/16/11)

5-F
Faith

Pope Benedict XVI gives us a profound insight on how to live by faith:

We will need to keep our gaze fixed upon Jesus Christ, the "pioneer and perfecter of our faith"[273]: in him, all the anguish and all the longing of the human heart finds fulfillment. The joy of love, the answer to the drama of suffering and pain, the power of forgiveness in the face of an offense received and the victory of life over the emptiness of death: all this finds fulfillment in the mystery of his Incarnation, in his becoming man, in his sharing our human weakness so as to transform it by the power of his resurrection. In him who died and rose again for our

---

[273]Heb 12:2.

salvation, the examples of faith that have marked these two thousand years of our salvation history are brought into the fullness of light.

By faith, Mary accepted the Angel's word and believed the message that she was to become the Mother of God in the obedience of her devotion[274] …

By faith, the Apostles left everything to follow their Master.[275] …

By faith, the disciples formed the first community, gathered around the teaching of the Apostles, in prayer, in celebration of the Eucharist, holding their possessions in common so as to meet the needs of the brethren.[276] …

By faith, the martyrs gave their lives, bearing witness to the truth of the Gospel that had transformed them and made them capable of attaining to the greatest gift of love: the forgiveness of their persecutors.

By faith, men and women have consecrated their lives to Christ, leaving all things behind so as to live obedience, poverty, and chastity with Gospel simplicity, concrete signs of waiting for the Lord who comes without delay. By faith, countless Christians have promoted action for justice so as to put into practice the word of the Lord, who came to proclaim deliverance from oppression and a year of favor for all.[277]

By faith, across the centuries, men and women of all ages, whose names are written in the Book of Life (cf. Rev 7:9, 13:8), have confessed the beauty of following the Lord

---

[274]Cf., Lk 1:38.
[275]Cf., Mk 10:28.
[276]Cf., Acts 2:42-47.
[277]Cf., Lk 4:18-19.

Jesus wherever they were called to bear witness to the fact that they were Christian: in the family, in the workplace, in public life, in the exercise of the charisms and ministries to which they were called.

By faith, we too live: by the living recognition of the Lord Jesus, present in our lives and in our history.[278]

115. Faith Perfected, Diary of a MOC

Your faith is perfected in suffering and trials. Perfect faith is complete abandonment to My Father's Will in all things through your union in Me. Therefore, your growth in faith is dependent on the abandonment of your will to Me and also on your knowledge of My perfect love for you.

The shedding of layers of attachments to your will, which is self-love, takes place as you begin to trust in My love for you. This is why suffering all your sorrows with Me is so beneficial for your soul, because in that process you touch the open wounds of My love for you. This perfects a soul quickly in abandonment and trust until you come to experience all, the good and what you perceive as bad, as a gift of My love for you.

The gift of knowing with your mind, heart, and soul that the love of God only desires to make of you the new creation you were created to be from the beginning of time, a creation in the image and likeness of God as holy sons and daughters of the Most High. This is why I came upon the earth: to set

---

[278] Benedict XVI, *Porta Fidei*, apostolic letter for the Year of Faith, Vatican, 2012. w2.vatican.va

> *you free from the bondage of sin, to make of you a new creation and draw you into the ONENESS of the Most Holy Trinity to experience holy bliss for all eternity. What greater love is there than this? (12/14/11)*

Faith brings us into communion with God. He wants to give it to all, but hearts need to be open to the Holy Spirit in humility and simplicity.

Pope Benedict XVI

Let us listen once again to Elizabeth's words fulfilled in Mary's Magnificat: "Blessed is she who believed." **The first and fundamental act in order to become a dwelling place of God and thus find definitive happiness is to believe:** it is faith, faith in God, in that God who showed himself in Jesus Christ and makes himself heard in the divine Word of Holy Scripture.[279]

116. What it Means to Believe, Diary of a MOC

> *What does it mean to believe in the One sent by God to the world? In order to believe in the Word of God, your heart must be pure. It is only through the Spirit that you can believe My Word, not with your mind but with your heart. My Word is My life that must touch the depth of your heart. A hardened heart cannot feel the touch of My living Word. **The intellect can receive My Word and manipulate it, but the Spirit penetrates a heart with My Word and***

---

[279] Benedict XVI, homily, Feast of the Assumption, Vatican, 15 Aug. 2006.

> **transforms it.**
>
> *To believe is to abandon yourself to Me so that I can make you a new creation through My Spirit. What is required to believe? Humility and simplicity. That is why I say you must be like a child to truly come to believe and follow Me. You believe with the heart as you encounter the living God before you, as you hear His voice and gaze into His eyes. That is why it is only the pure of heart who can see, hear and truly know God.*
>
> *Therefore, My daughter, tell My sons to be humble as I am humble, to rely on My Spirit teaching them and not on their own understanding, for their understanding is very limited, but My understanding will bring them to encounter the living God and possess the life of the Most Holy Trinity. (4/25/11)*

— We First Believe and then We Understand —

Many abandoned Christ, even after the miracles He performed in their presence. They expected to understand Him in human terms before believing in Him. But that is impossible because we cannot reach God with our natural intelligence alone. We must believe before we can understand. We believe what He teaches because we have come to know that He is God. We can believe Him without asking for explanations, recognizing with great humility that only later, with His grace, we will begin to understand.

Pope Benedict XVI

Seeing that many of His disciples were leaving, Jesus addressed the Apostles, saying: "Will you also go away?" (Jn 6:67). As in other cases, it is Peter who replied on behalf of the Twelve: "Lord, to whom shall we go? You have the words of eternal life and we have believed and know that You are the Holy One of God" (Jn 6:68-69). On this passage we have a beautiful commentary of St. Augustine, who says in one of his homilies on John 6: "Do you see how Peter, by the grace of God, by the inspiration of the Holy Spirit, has understood? Why did he understand? Because he believed. You have the words of eternal life. You give us eternal life by offering your risen body and your blood, your very self. And we have believed and understood. He does not say we have understood and then we believed, but we believed and then we understood. We have believed in order to be able to understand; if, in fact, we wanted to understand before believing, we would not be able either to understand or to believe. What have we believed and what have we understood? That You are the Christ, the Son of God, that is, that You are that very eternal life, and that You give in Your flesh and blood only that which You are."[280]

Peter had to believe in order to understand, but his faith had a solid base: he had come to know Jesus. He witnessed his miracles; but more importantly, he saw in Jesus, with the eyes of his heart, divine love acting through a human Heart. This too was the experience of Mary Magdalene, St John, and Dismas, the good thief. It is the way of faith.

---

[280]Benedict XVI, *Commentary on the Gospel of John, 27: 9*, Angelus, 29 Aug. 2012. w2.vatican.va.

— A Spiritual Mother Writes to Her Priest-Son Who Is Suffering —

My dearest Father:

I hope all is well with you...

Here I am, one more day in this hospital full of suffering children... and families who suffer through them.

Suffering is still such a mystery to most of us. We don't understand fully its purpose, its value. We don't understand why a loving God permits it but, as I see it, the most important thing is not to understand it. There are a lot of things in our lives we don't fully understand... But if we trust God's goodness, if we don't question our Abba and let Him do with us as He pleases, if we enter His ways that are not our ways, then we start living and experiencing in our hearts His words from the Gospel: "Come to me all who are heavy laden... Because my yoke is easy and my burden is light." (Mt 11:28,30)

My yoke... The definitions of "yoke" speak deeply about our union with our Lord... It binds us to Him... Our burdens, our sufferings, have the purpose of bringing us closer to Him to be so close to Him, so united with Him, that our wounds touch His wounds... Something supernatural happens in the midst of our sufferings IF we yoke ourselves to Him: we become ONE with Him in our sufferings.

If we don't resist Him, if we don't fight Him, if we abandon ourselves to Him, if we accept and welcome His ways of union and communion, then we enter what I would call a supernatural life with Him, in Him—the total abandonment of a true lover to his beloved... The bliss of true love requires our trust.

My dear Father, many times, when I am with you, our Lord grants me the grace to see you as a little child—a little suffering boy that doesn't have the strength anymore to fight the pain and feels overcome by it.

When I see you as a child, I see myself as a child as well, a little girl that has found the way HOME and is coming to hold you by the hand to take you there—to bring you HOME.

It's at HOME that we are touched by Jesus' wounds, renewed, restarted, and healed with His Love.

We have to enter His hospital of love; we have to trust His ways of healing; we have to BELIEVE in His Love for us.

One more day in this hospital room, immersed in His grace, in His love for us—FOR ALL!!!!

One more day with this gift—what appears to be a wasted and useless life… Such a precious time!!!

I ponder all in my heart.

I remain in the stillness of His grace that I share with you today.

ONE with you in the silence of His Heart!

5-G
Joy

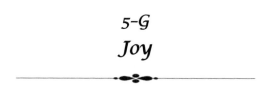

— Joy in Afflictions —

We think that afflictions are contrary to joy. The Bible tells us otherwise:

> I am filled with comfort. With all our affliction, I am overjoyed (2 Cor 7:4).

> Count it all joy, my brethren, when you meet various trials (Jas 1:2).

True joy is knowing God's love, and this knowledge grows when we endure affliction for His sake. Victim souls should be especially joyful to share more closely the sufferings and the love of Christ!

Jesus proclaimed:

> Blessed are you when people insult you, persecute you and falsely say all kinds of evil against you because of me. Rejoice and be glad, because great is your reward in heaven, for in the same way, they persecuted the prophets who were before you (Mat 5:11-13).

St. Paul:

> We also rejoice in our sufferings, because we know
> that suffering produces perseverance (Rom 5:3).[281]

In our sufferings, we might ask, "Where is the joy? I can't even seem to smile." We tend to associate joy with laughter and smiles, but there is also a greater interior joy. The images that come to my mind are the faces of our Mother of Sorrows and of Jesus crucified. We do not see smiles on their faces. Her joy as a mother is to know in faith that she is participating in the bitter chalice of her beloved Son. Her joy is linked to the interior peace of living in the will of God.

The following is a testimony of a Mother of the Cross from our community who found interior joy in her physical sufferings because they united her to the heart of Mary:

I have spent days now suffering a great fatigue. I feel only fatigue and sadness, yet I am in peace and profound interior joy. This fatigue serves to unite me at every moment to my Blessed Mother's pierced heart. I carry this fatigue and sadness as the precious pearl my Lord desires me to have. I am wearing this beautiful pearl with great love and appreciation. My every breath, as I struggle to accomplish the duties of my days, is a prayer for my family, priests and so many souls the Lord places in my heart.

---

[281] Cf. Phil 2:17-18.

— Joy in Knowing the Beloved is with Us —

Christ is our joy! Pope Benedict XVI reflects on how joy is having the beloved near even in suffering:

> If the loved one, the love, the greatest gift of my life, is close to me, if I can be convinced that the one who loves me is close to me, even in situations of suffering, the joy that remains in the depth of my heart is ever greater than all sufferings.[282]

— Faith Gives Joy —

Cardinal Ratzinger

Faith gives joy. **When God is not there, the world becomes desolate, and everything becomes boring, and everything is completely unsatisfactory.** It's easy to see today how a world empty of God is also increasingly consuming itself, how it has become a wholly joyless world. The great joy comes from the fact that there is this great love, and that is the essential message of faith.

To that extent it can be said that **the basic element of Christianity is joy.** Joy not in the sense of cheap fun, which can conceal desperation in the background.... Rather, it is joy in the proper sense, a joy that exists together with a difficult life and also makes this life livable.

The history of Jesus Christ begins, according to the Gospel, with the angel saying to Mary, "Rejoice!" On the night of Nativity, the angels say again: "We proclaim to you

---

[282]Benedict XVI, *Reflection* on 2 Cor 13:11, 3 Oct. 2005, w2.vatican.va.

318

a great joy." And Jesus says, "I proclaim to you the good news." So the heart of the matter is always expressed in these terms: "I proclaim to you a great joy, God is here, you are beloved, and this stands firm forever."[283]

— Joy of Knowing Who We Are —

As a consequence of sin, we don't know who we truly are, so we try to acquire our identity according to the expectations of others. This false identity always leads to unhappiness. Only Jesus can give us our true identity, as He gave it to St. Peter: "I tell you, you are Peter" (Mt 16:18). Knowing Jesus and knowing ourselves we find inner peace and joy. Now we can be free from jealousies and competitions.

117. Know Who You Are, Diary of a MOC

> *Know who you are, as John the Baptist knew who he was and the gift given to him from heaven to accomplish his mission. He was the Bridegroom's best man (prophet) preparing the heart of the bride (the Church) to recognize, know and love the Bridegroom. When the Bridegroom appears, John understands that he must decrease. His joy is made full. You, on the other hand, are My bride, the Church, as one with My Mother, the perfect, pure, holy bride. Your mission, as one with Mary's, is to*

---

[283] Peter Seewald interview with Cardinal Joseph Ratzinger, *Salt of the Earth: The Church at the End of the Millennium*, (San Francisco USA: Ignatius Press, 1997).

bring souls to the foot of the Cross to contemplate the love of their Bridegroom, to look and gaze at the One who has been lifted up and to be healed, restored and made new. (4/28/11)[284]

118. Joy in the Cross, Diary of a MOC

Jesus came to me and said,

Receive the wounds that cost Me My most painful suffering—humiliations, rejection, and ingratitude. My most sensitive Heart continues to suffer these wounds. The greatest gift to mankind, THE CROSS, is rejected by almost all. You are the remnant that has received My gift.

It is only through this gift that they are set free from the chains that bind them. It is only through this gift that they enter perfect union with Me. It is only through this gift that they find JOY... Receive My wounds and give Me rest. (1/5/11)

119. Joy Through Sorrows, Diary of a MOC

Be filled with My joy in believing that God has found favor with you and he delights in you...

I asked, "My Lord, how do I live this joy with so much sorrow?"

Because your sorrows are saving souls... Your tears, united to Mary's, are watering the face of the earth with God's grace. Your sorrows in Me bring forth new life... God the Father showers grace upon the earth through the sorrows of Mary, which are

---

[284] Cf. Jn 3: 22-30.

> *one in My sorrows. Your sorrows united as one to the Mother of Sorrows brings new life upon the earth. Your joy will be found in your perfect faith in this truth. Believe and continue to save souls through your sorrows. (6/3/14)*

120. They Don't Allow Me to Touch Them,

Diary of a MOC

> *As an all-loving Father, I suffer the sickness of My sons' and daughters' hearts, but **My greatest suffering is that they don't allow Me, the Healer of all hearts, to touch them. They seek healing in all forms except in the only One who can bring them to life.***
>
> *I desire for all the Mothers of the Cross to unite as one with My Mother of Sorrows to obtain graces for humanity. The salvation of many is dependent upon your RESPONSE. (6/28/11)*

121. Embrace Your Sorrows with Perfect Joy,
Diary of a MOC

> *Embrace all the sorrows I place in your heart with perfect peace, trust, patience and love.*
>
> *Exteriorly reveal your gentle smile and PERFECT JOY in knowing the love of the Father, Son and Holy Spirit for you,*
>
> *—your PERFECT JOY in knowing that We live in you and you in Us,*
>
> *—the PERFECT JOY in knowing that you have been chosen by God to aid in the salvation of many and that you have responded,*
>
> *—the PERFECT JOY of living in faith, hope and charity,*
>
> *—the PERFECT JOY of possessing the gift of the Cross,*
>
> *—the PERFECT JOY of knowing more intimately LOVE and becoming ONE with LOVE,*
>
> *—the PERFECT JOY of possessing the Holy Spirit as your most treasured Companion,*
>
> *—the PERFECT JOY of seeing yourselves transformed into a new creation in Me,*
>
> *—the PERFECT JOY of knowing Mary and living with her as ONE HEART in My LOVE CRUCIFIED.*
> (06/28/11)

"Rejoice in the Lord always. I will say it again: Rejoice!"
—Phil 4:4

Chapter Six

Victim United to the Victim

——◦❖◦——

6-A
A New Understanding of Victimhood
Based on Love

We are naturally afraid of becoming a "victim": to suffer violence, abuse or injustice, such as the victims of war or the victims of crime. The common definition of "victim soul" is no less frightening. The *Modern Catholic Dictionary* describes a victim soul as "a person specially chosen by God to suffer more than most people during life, and who generously accepts the suffering in union with the Savior and after the example of Christ's own Passion and Death."[285]

Based on this understanding of a victim soul, some consider it imprudent for laypersons to embrace this vocation. They ask, "Is this a wise choice for parents who need to be healthy to care for their children? Is it not enough that they fulfill the duties of their state in life with all its inherent sufferings?" "If God wants victim souls," they reason, "would He not choose priests and religious?"

In this chapter, we seek to present a new understanding of "victim soul" founded on Christ the Victim. What defines Christ's victimhood is not suffering but the love that drives Him to give Himself unconditionally. Christ lived in the will of His Father. When faced with suffering, His flesh wanted to avoid it, but His love moved Him to remain faithful and embrace it: "Not as I will, but as thou wilt."[286]

To be a victim soul is to be ONE with Christ—totally given to the Father's will. A victim soul is not looking for suffering but is not paralyzed by fear of suffering for doing God's will. Such a soul asks for the grace to accompany Jesus in His suffering. This is the vocation of every Christian, whether we are called to the hidden life of a housewife or the foreign missions; whether we are to live our victimhood interiorly or to suffer martyrdom.

> For the love of Christ impels us…, He indeed died for all, **so that those who live might no longer live for themselves but for Him** (2 Cor 5:14-15).

---

[285] Fr. John Hardon, *Modern Catholic Dictionary.*
   http://www.therealpresence.org/dictionary/adict.htm
[286] Mt 26:39.

Pope Benedict XVI

In the end, even the "yes" to love is a source of suffering, because love always requires expropriations of my "I," in which I allow myself to be pruned and wounded. Love simply cannot exist without this painful renunciation of myself, for otherwise it becomes pure selfishness and thereby ceases to be love.[287]

A Christian cannot be just a "good person" who obeys the Commandments. The rich young man of the Gospel kept the Commandments but would not follow Jesus.[288] Christ's disciples no longer have "their own" lives; they have given themselves to Him so that, in their daily lives, He can continue to live for others.

> I appeal to you therefore, brethren, by the mercies of God, to present your bodies **as a living sacrifice**, holy and acceptable to God, which is your spiritual worship. (Rom 12:1)[289]

— The Priesthood of the Baptized —

In baptism, we became both priest and victim as ONE with Christ. With Him, we are called to give ourselves to the Father as a "living sacrifice."

Saint Peter Chrysologus, bishop and Father of the Church, wrote about the priesthood received in baptism:

How marvelous is the priesthood of the Christian, for he

---

[287] Encyclical *Spe Salve*, n.38.
[288] Cf. Mk 10:17-27.
[289] NAbre.

is both the victim that is offered on his own behalf, and the priest who makes the offering. He does not need to go beyond himself to seek what he is to immolate to God: with himself and in himself he brings the sacrifice he is to offer God for himself. The victim remains and the priest remains, always one and the same...

St. Paul says: **I appeal to you by the mercy of God to present your bodies as a sacrifice, living and holy**". The prophet said the same thing: "Sacrifice and offering you did not desire, but you have prepared a body for me.[290]" **Each of us is called to be both a sacrifice to God and his priest.**

Do not forfeit what divine authority confers on you.[291]

Venerable Conchita, wife and mother of nine children, is an example of the fire of love that makes us victims with Christ. Jesus told her: "Offer yourself as a victim for my priests. Unite yourself to My sacrifice for gaining them graces."[292]

God calls all, but due to our fallen nature, we are afraid of what God may do if we truly surrender to Him. We fail to understand that God truly loves us and that He has a unique and perfect plan for each of us.

122. Your "Yes," Diary of a MOC

> *All Christians are called to be victim souls. Only*

---

[290] Heb 10:5.
[291] St. Peter Chrysologus, *Sermon* 108. (Office of Tuesday, 4th Week of Easter).
[292] *Conchita, A Mother's Spiritual Diary*, 85.

> *God is holy; therefore, to be holy means to be transformed into the One you receive in Holy Communion, to become One with Me. Perfect love on earth is expressed by laying down your life for the salvation of your brother and sister.*
>
> ***It is your "yes" to give the oblation of your life that "stirs into flame" the graces of your baptism*** *and you receive the power and fire of the Holy Spirit. It is then, in this way, that your life possesses the "power of God." That is why I desire many victim souls, for it is only the power of pure love that will pierce the darkness that is seeping into the hearts and minds of My people. Bring Me victim souls, My little one. Do not be afraid.* (1/29/11)

— My Testimony —

One early morning in Medjugorje, as I was praying, I heard the Lord's invitation in my heart, "Will you be my victim soul?" My first reaction was fear of suffering. I asked myself, "What do these words mean? Will I be inflicted with some horrible suffering?" Yet, with great peace, I said, "Yes" to the Lord. I realized that He had been preparing me for years to receive this invitation, by drawing me to His Cross. **A new understanding of victim soul was beginning to unfold: the martyrdom of the heart.**

My spiritual director also had concerns. He thought of Blessed **Alexandrina Maria da Costa** of Portugal who, after jumping from a window to escape being raped, was paralyzed until her death 31 years later. The slightest movement caused her agonizing pain. My director admired her very much but was afraid to become a victim soul like her! Later he learned that Alexandrina was not declared blessed because she suffered but because she gave herself completely to God even in suffering. At first, she had asked the Lord to heal her and promised Him to become a missionary if her petition was granted, but as the illness progressed, she embraced the Lord's chosen path for her life and entered a profound union with Him in her suffering. She constantly had on her lips the prayer taught by Our Lady of Fatima: "O Jesus, this is for love of Thee, for the conversion of sinners, and in reparation for the offenses against the Immaculate Heart of Mary."

— Testimony of a Missionary of the Cross —

I was struggling with messages from the Lord asking me to surrender my life as a victim of love and to suffer all with Him, so I asked for a confirmation. A few days later, at a priest retreat, we were all singing before the Blessed Sacrament: "**Come Holy Spirit, set my heart on fire!**" We repeated this line several times, then suddenly, there was a complete silence. Then the Lord spoke to us powerfully through one of the priests. He said, "**You are asking for the fire of the Holy Spirit, but I ask you: 'Where is the victim?'**" I was struck with awe—the Lord was confirming His call to be a victim soul!

For years, in the charismatic renewal, I had prayed for the fire of the Holy Spirit and I had received it, but something was still blocking me: I had not realized that the Spirit's fire comes when He finds a willing victim. **A victim is one who is fully open to be consumed by the fire of love unto the cross!** Jesus, as Victim at the Cross, has given us the Spirit but, for the Spirit to act freely, we must receive Him as victims—ONE with Jesus. I saw that I was afraid of offering my life as a victim soul because I was afraid of what God would do if I abandoned myself completely to Him. This is the fear of fallen humanity that dates back to the garden when Adam and Eve hid from the Lord. We have been hiding ever since. That is why few enter union with God.

I realized that I was ordained to be priest AND victim. I also saw that to be a victim of love is the vocation of every Christian to be fully in the Spirit. In baptism, we were grafted into Christ to become in Him priests and victims of love in the hands of the Father.

In the nine years since I offered my life as a victim of love, I have experienced as never before the love of Christ and the desire to accompany Him in His sorrows. No tragedy has befallen me as a result of being a victim soul, but I trust that when trials and suffering come, as they come to everyone, the Lord will give me the grace to live them joyfully with Him.

— Marriage and Victim Love —

When a couple gets married, they do not secure a guarantee against suffering. They promise to give themselves to each other "in good times and in bad, in sickness and in health." They are not seeking bad times or sickness but, because of love each other, they vow to suffer together any trial.

Should our covenant with Christ be any less? He is the Bridegroom who gave Himself totally for us. Now He pleads to His Bride—to each of us—to respond with all our hearts, to trust and be faithful to Him "in good times and in bad…" If we say "yes," we will no longer be two, but ONE—one Body—one Victim of Love.

123. A Bride Follows Her Spouse, Diary of a MOC

It is My victim souls abandoned to My crucified love that possess the power of God to defeat Satan and usher in the reign of the Immaculate Heart of My Mother.

Do not be afraid to be My voice. Do not be afraid to be crucified with Me. **Be My spouse.** *A bride follows her spouse wherever he goes. Will you follow Me to My Cross where our love will be consummated in the power of God? Suffer all with Me, your Spouse, through the embrace of the silence of the Holy Spirit. This is most pleasing to Me.*

Trust, for there isn't a suffering I permit that will not bring you into the union of love I desire. Trust in the power of suffering all as ONE with Me. It is this power that will set the world on fire with My Spirit. Raise up My victims of love for these decisive times. (7/9/12)

For love of His Bride, Christ took upon Himself the most furious attacks of Satan, endured suffering and defeated him. He gave himself as victim soul—a "victim of love". This love is the power that He now gives to us so that we—the Bride—become ONE with Him at the Cross.

St. Ignatius of Loyola

Few souls understand what God would accomplish in them if they were to abandon themselves unreservedly to Him and if they were to allow His grace to mold them accordingly.

124. Victim Souls Enter the Passage, Diary of a MOC

I pondered St. Paul's words to the Galatians:

"I have been crucified with Christ; and it is no longer I that live, but Christ living in me: and that life which I now live in the flesh I live in faith, the faith which is in the Son of God, who loved me, and gave Himself up for me."[293]

Then I received words from the Lord:

Remain steadfast in your preaching and teaching about victim souls. You will bring many to find the secret passage that leads to transformation into Me, the passage that brings a soul into the life of the most Holy Trinity.

St. Paul entered this passage, as he declares, "I have been crucified with Christ." It is a victim soul's "yes" that "stirs into flame" the power of the Holy Spirit so that the Holy Spirit can lead a docile and willing soul to die with Me. It is this voluntary death that brings the soul to new life. That is why St. Paul can now say, "It is no longer I who live, but Christ who lives in me."

I continue to thirst for love, but it is only the love of My victim souls that satisfies My thirst. It is only the love of My victim souls that has the power to appease the justice of God. Therefore, bring Me many victim souls. (2/1/11)

---

[293] Gal 2:19-21.

— Union with Christ Requires Our Response —

Many say that, since Christ paid the price for our salvation, all we have to do is to believe that He did. They say, "He suffered so that we don't have to." This is a gross misunderstanding of redemption.

Redemption is indeed a gift of God—only by the Holy Spirit can we become one with Christ (cf. Jn 1:32), but we must be active participants in His love and suffering to the measure that He wills it. Remember: we are His Body. Saint Paul writes: **"In my flesh I complete what is lacking in Christ's sufferings for the sake of His body, that is, the church.**"[294] How can Christ's sufferings be "lacking," we may ask? They are lacking in as much as they are lacking in us—His Body. We cannot separate love and suffering, so, in as much as we do not allow Christ to suffer in us "for the sake of His body," we are not allowing Him to love.

We are called to participate in our salvation and the salvation of others. We do so by loving as one with Christ, **gladly embracing suffering for the sake of the beloved.** St. Paul writes: "Jesus also suffered outside the gate in order to sanctify the people through His own blood. **Therefore, let us go forth to Him outside the camp and bear the abuse He endured.**"[295]

St. Benedicta of the Cross wrote, "Voluntary expiatory suffering is what truly and really unites one to the Lord intimately. Only in union with the divine Head does human suffering take on expiatory power."[296]

---

[294]Col 1:24.

[295]Hb 13:12-13.

[296] St. Teresa Benedicta of the Cross, *The Hidden Life: Hagiographic Essays, Meditations, Spiritual Texts*, vol. IV, Collected Works, edited by Dr. L. Gelber and Michael Linssen, O.C.D. Cf. lovecrucified.com/cross/christian_vs_pathological_love_cross.html.

— All Saints Are Victims of Love —

All saints are "victims of love" because all are united to the Victim at the Cross, loving without counting the cost. Every modern saint that I know was conscious of being a victim of love.

Pope Benedict XVI wrote:

The Church's experience shows that every form of holiness, even if it follows different paths, always passes through the Way of the Cross, the way of self-denial…

The more we imitate Jesus and remain united to him, the more we enter into the mystery of his divine holiness. We discover that He loves us infinitely, and this prompts us in turn to love our brethren. Loving always entails an act of self-denial, "losing ourselves," and it is precisely this that makes us happy. [297]

It makes no sense to claim that we have a devotion to a saint if we run away from the radical love that he or she lived. Think of St. Francis, so popular for his love for nature. Who desires to become a victim of love like him? Who is willing to learn from him how to die to self for the sake of Christ? Think of Saint Faustina and the popularity of the message of Divine Mercy. Do we want to love as she did? The following is her offering—ONE with Jesus Victim at the altar—to the Father, during the Holy Mass of her perpetual vows.

Today I place my heart on the paten where Your Heart has been placed, O Jesus, and today I offer myself together with You to God, Your Father and mine, as **a sacrifice of love**

---

[297] Benedict XVI, homily, Solemnity of All Saints, 1 Nov. 2006, www.vatican.va.

and praise. Father of Mercy, look upon the sacrifice of my heart, but through the wound in the Heart of Jesus.[298]

The following experience of Saint Faustina illustrates the Lord's desire for many to become victim souls with Him:

Then I saw the Lord Jesus nailed to the cross. When He had hung on it for a while, I saw a multitude of souls crucified like Him [victim souls]. Then I saw a second multitude of souls, and a third. The second multitude were not nailed to [their] crosses, but were holding them firmly in their hands. The third were neither nailed to [their] crosses nor holding them firmly in their hands, but were dragging [their] crosses behind them and were discontent. Jesus then said to me, **"Do you see these souls? Those who are like Me in the pain and contempt they suffer will be like Me also in glory. And those who resemble Me less in pain and contempt will also bear less resemblance to Me in glory."**[299]

The Lord told St. Margaret Alacoque how much He desired that souls correspond to His Sacred Heart, then He added: **"I wish to give thee My heart, but first, thou must render thyself its victim of immolation."**[300]

_____

[298] Saint Faustina, Diary n239. "Sacrifice of love" is also translated as "victim of love."
[299] Ibid., n446.
[300] History of the Blessed Margaret Mary,. P. O'Shea, publisher, 1867.

— Joyful Victims —

A true victim soul is joyful because he is united with his beloved Jesus. This union of love gives joy even in suffering for Him. St. Paul, as a prisoner, rejoiced in his victimhood:

> Even if I am to be poured as a libation upon the sacrificial offering of your faith, I am glad and **rejoice** with you all. Likewise, you also should be glad and rejoice with me. [301]

I think most of us in our community were afraid when the Lord placed in our hearts the call to be victim souls, but as we trusted in the Lord and persevered, we grew in a joy and a love that we never knew before. God wants us to be joyful saints for, as St. Teresa of Avila said: "An unhappy saint is a pitiful saint."[302] She too was a victim soul, and she knew how to live as such with a great sense of humor even in the little things:

> Pray to the Lord …to give us much in which to suffer, if only from fleas, ghosts and roads.[303]

— St Therese's of Lisieux Victimhood of Love —

Saint Therese of Lisieux saw that Jesus desires to love and to be loved, but that He finds very few who respond. As a result, His love must remain pent up within His Heart. Moved by the Holy

---

[301]Phil 2:17-18.
[302]St. Theresa of Avila, Way of Perfection 18, 5. See Pope Francis, 15 Oct 2014, Vatican.va
[303]Ibid, "Letter to Antonio Gaytan," Segovia, 30 May 1574, our translation.

Spirit, **she offered herself as an "Oblation to Merciful Love."** Her dream was to become a true **"victim holocaust" of Divine Love**, being burned within the flames of Christ's torrent of love. She wanted thus to be "consumed unceasingly," and become "**a martyr to Your Love, O my God!**"[304]

She understood that by her offering she relieved the suffering of the Lord. **She also sought to encourage as many as she could to make the same offering** and begged the Lord to raise up a legion of "little victims." She wrote in her autobiography:

O my God! must Thy Love, which is disdained, lie hidden in Thy Heart? If Thou should find souls offering themselves as victims of holocaust to Thy Love, Thou would consume them rapidly; Thou wouldst be well pleased that the flames of infinite tenderness that are imprisoned in Thy Heart would escape.

If Thy Justice—which is of earth—needs to be satisfied, how much more must Thy Merciful Love desire to inflame souls, since Thy mercy reacheth even to the Heavens? O Jesus! Let me be that happy victim—consume Thy holocaust with the fire of Divine Love!

Dear Mother, you know the love, or rather the oceans of grace which flooded my soul immediately after I made that Act of Oblation on the 9th of June, 1895. From that day I have been penetrated and surrounded with love. Every moment this Merciful Love renews me and purifies me, leaving in my soul no trace of sin. I cannot fear purgatory; I know I do not merit to enter even into that place of expiation with the holy souls, but I also know that the fire

---

[304] See St. Therese *Act of Oblation to God's Merciful Love*: LoveCrucified.com/saints/therese_lisieux/oblation_merciful_love.html.

of Love is more sanctifying than the fire of purgatory. I know that Jesus could not wish useless suffering for us, and He would not inspire me with the desires I feel, were He not willing to fulfill them.[305]

Jesus responded to her three days after she made her oblation. She recounts the experience: "**I was seized by such violent love for God that I cannot explain;** ...I was burning with love and I felt that one minute more, one second more, and I would not have been able to bear this ardor without dying."[306]

Saint Therese answers questions about becoming a victim of love:

Am I worthy of receiving this grace?

In bygone days, only pure and spotless victims were acceptable to Almighty God; to satisfy Divine Justice, they must be perfect. But now the law of fear is superseded by the law of love, and love has chosen me as a victim, frail and imperfect as I am.

Oh Jesus! Why can't I tell all little souls how unspeakable is Your condescension? I feel that if You found a soul weaker and littler than mine, which is impossible, You would be pleased to grant it still greater favors, **provided it**

---

[305] *Story of a Soul: The Autobiography of Saint Therese of Lisieux*, 79, 82. (Aeterna Press). Ch 8. books.google.com

[306] Jean LaFrance. *In prayer with Mary the Mother of Jesus*, (Mediaspaul, 1988), 215. books.google.com

abandoned itself with total confidence to Your Infinite Mercy. …I beg you to do it. I beg You to cast Your divine glance upon a great number of little souls. I beg You to choose a LEGION of little victims worthy of Your love.[307]

Will victims of love be many?

His Holiness Pius XI—in the course of Therese's solemn canonization—repeated her words imploring the Lord "to choose a **legion of little victims** worthy of Your love." Therese also said: "Thus my dreams will be realized."

Will offering ourselves as victims of love bring upon us more suffering?

Therese invited her sister, Marie, to make the offering as a victim of love. Marie at first protested, thinking that to make such an offering would be to invite additional suffering and punishment upon herself. But Therese explained that was not the case:

> I do understand what you are saying, but **to offer oneself to love is an entirely different thing to offering oneself to His Justice. One does not suffer more. It is a matter only of loving God more for those who do not love Him.**

St. Therese found suffering sweet united to the love of Christ, yet she never asked for more suffering:

> I could never ask for greater sufferings—I am too little a

---

[307] *Story of a Soul: The Autobiography of St. Therese of Lisieux.* books.google.com

soul. They would then be of my own choice. I should have to bear them all without Him, and I have never been able to do anything when left to myself.[308]

— Victim Souls Save Souls —

Our concern for the salvation of others is a sign of our union with the heart of Jesus. Jesus—the only one who can save—has willed to make us, like Mary, co-redeemers, and has given us the love to be victims souls for them.

125. A Victim Soul Redeems Souls with Me, Diary of a MOC

> *A victim soul voluntarily chooses to become one with the slaughtered Lamb of God. They choose to wear My wounds of love. In this perfect union of love, they receive the power of God to redeem and save souls with Me. Many are being made clean through the lives of My victim souls. These souls are the ones who truly become My Mystical Body, and because of this, share in the redemption of humanity. The salvation of the multitudes depends on the response of My victim souls (Cf. Jn 6:8,9). These are My saints whose robes have been made clean through the Blood of the Lamb of God and have become pure in the image and likeness of God (Cf. 1Jn 3:3 / Rev 7:14). (11/1/12)*

---

[308] Ibid, *Epilogue: A Victim of Love*, 141. catholicbible101.com

126. A Crusade of Victim Souls, Diary of a MOC

> *Satan is working to bring forth his new world order of destruction, but My crusade of victim souls will possess the power of God to crush the head of Satan. You are the heel of the Queen of Heaven and Earth. Continue giving your life daily for the mission I have entrusted to you... Do not lose hope in all that I have placed in your heart. My crusade of victim souls will have to suffer greatly and be formed to perfection in love to fight this fierce battle but know that My Cross has triumphed. Now, through this crusade, it needs to triumph in the hearts of My people. Persevere in love. Persevere in trust.* (4/10/12)

127. Each Victim Soul Intensifies the Fire of Love, Diary of a MOC

I felt Jesus on the Cross. The flesh on His chest, like a curtain, seemed to open and I could see His Heart as fire. This vision of His Heart as fire in the center of His chest was all in a circle; I felt as the living Eucharist. My Lord had me understand that each of His victim souls is in that fire. Each victim soul intensified the fire of love in Jesus' Heart. Then the fire with all the victim souls consumed the entire Body of Jesus; and the Holy Spirit, as a massive dove, as I saw Him in 2008, flew out from the Cross upon the world. He was covering the earth with a mantle of Jesus' Precious Blood. All of us, His victim souls, were one with the Holy Spirit participating in the fulfillment of the salvation of the world.

Then Jesus said: *My victim souls, united in Me, will bring to fulfillment the salvation of the world. It was not My miracles that saved the world, but My love in suffering revealed on the Cross. My miracles were a gift so that people would know that I am the Son of God. I am the Way, the Truth and the Life... It is the Way of the Cross, the Way of Love in suffering, that is the power of God that saves the world... I desire for My Body, the Church, to complete My love in suffering here on earth.* (7/19/10)

128. My Holy Remnant Will Pierce the Darkness,

Diary of a MOC

I came into the world to suffer and to die. I came into the world for the Cross... See the oppression and darkness in your family as the same darkness in the world and in My Church... This darkness also oppresses My Heart, and I continue to suffer. My daughter, God the Father intended, from the beginning of time, for My Body (the Church) to be united to its Head to pierce this darkness. It will be My holy remnant in My Church that, united in My Cross, will pierce the darkness. My daughter, you must choose to love always. In your family, love through your silence, love through your gentleness, love in kindness, love in patience, persevere in love. Believe, My daughter, all that I have told you. It will all come to pass. (11/29/10)

6-B

We Go to Mass to Become Victims with the Victim

As Catholics, we know that the Mass is the sacrifice of Christ who offers Himself to the Father as a Victim of love, but few realize that the reason we are there is to become **ONE victim with Him.** The Second Vatican Council teaches that **the faithful,** "taking part in the Eucharistic sacrifice, the source and summit of the Christian life, **offer the divine victim to God and themselves along with it.**"[309] During the Canon of the Mass we pray:

> Grant in your loving kindness
> that all who partake of this one Bread and one Chalice…
> may truly become a living sacrifice in Christ.[310]

This victim offering should transform us completely so that we live all things as ONE with Christ, "through Him, and with Him and in Him." This is how saints become saints.

St. Albert Hurtado wrote:

> By participating personally in the victimhood of Jesus Christ, we are transformed in the divine Victim. As the bread is truly transubstantiated into the body of Christ, all the faithful are transubstantiated spiritually with Jesus Victim. Then personal immolations are elevated to become Eucharistic immolations of Jesus Christ, who, as Head,

---

[309] *LG*, n.11, www.vatican.va.
[310] Eucharistic Prayer IV.

assumes and makes His own the immolations of His members. … A soul remains superficial as long as it has not suffered. **In the mystery of Christ, there are divine depths where only crucified souls penetrate, and they do so by affinity**.[311]

Frequent reception of the Eucharist will not bring us to intimacy with Christ unless we allow Him to make us ONE with Him who is the Victim of Love. Jesus said: "He who eats my flesh and drinks my blood abides in me, and I in him" (Jn 6:56). As we previously stated, Christ is the Bridegroom who gives Himself totally to His bride at the Cross. His Body is "given up" for us and His Blood is "shed" for us. Now He waits for the bride to correspond and give herself to Him.

Thomas a Kempis

Jesus: Behold I offered Myself without reserve to the Father for you! I have also given you My whole Body and Blood for your food, that I might be wholly yours, and you might be Mine to the end. But if you stand on self and do not freely offer yourself to my will, the oblation is not complete, neither will there be entire union between us.[312]

Becoming ONE Victim of love is a way of life and not just a one-time offering.

Pope Francis

Nourishing ourselves on that "Bread of Life" means entering into harmony with the heart of Christ, assimilating

---

[311] Fr. Alberto Hurtado, "Text n.33," our translation. www.padrehurtado.com.

[312] Thomas a Kempis, *Of the Oblation of the Cross*, Ch. VIII. books.google.com

his choices, his thoughts, his behavior. It means entering into a dynamism of love and becoming people of peace, people of forgiveness, of reconciliation, of sharing in solidarity. The very things that Jesus did.[313]

One Host, One Victim, Jesus' longing revealed to Conchita

All the victims united with the great Victim. …One Host, one Victim, one priest that immolates himself and immolates Me in your heart on behalf of the world. The Father will receive with pleasure this offering presented by the Holy Spirit and the graces of heaven will descend as rain on the earth.

This is the nucleus, the global, the concrete ensemble and essence of perfection in my Works of the Cross. Clearly, my immolation suffices and more than suffices to appease the divine justice of God. But true Christianity, the flower of the Gospel, is it anything else or does it aim at anything other than uniting all victims into ONE, all sufferings, virtues and merits into the ONE that I am, so that all these may be of worth and obtain graces?

What does the Holy Spirit intend in My Church save to form in Me the unity of wills, of sufferings and of hearts in My Heart? What was the desire of My Heart throughout My life, but to bring about that ONENESS with Me by charity, by love? Why did the Word descend into this world save to form with His immaculate flesh and His most pure Blood, one blood to expiate and to win souls? Has the Eucharist any other purpose than to unite bodies and souls with Me, transforming them and divinizing them?

---

[313] Pope Francis, Angelus, 16 Aug. 2015, w2.vatican.va.

And not only on altars of stone, but in hearts, living temples of the Holy Spirit, is the Victim to be offered to heaven. In doing so the souls become with Him hosts and victims ... God will be thereby profoundly touched.[314]

The Catechism of the Catholic Church, after teaching in No. 1367 that Christ is the Eucharistic Victim, goes on to state:

The Eucharist is also the sacrifice of the Church. The Church, which is the Body of Christ, participates in the offering of her Head. With Him, she herself is offered whole and entire. She unites herself to His intercession with the Father for all men. In the Eucharist, the sacrifice of Christ becomes also the sacrifice of the members of His Body. The lives of the faithful, their praise, sufferings, prayer, and work, are united with those of Christ and with his total offering, and so acquire a new value. Christ's sacrifice present on the altar makes it possible for all generations of Christians to be united with his offering.

In the catacombs, the Church is often represented as a woman in prayer, arms outstretched in the praying position. Like Christ who stretched out His arms on the Cross, through Him, with Him, and in Him, she offers herself and intercedes for all men.[315]

All the faithful silently join the offering as Christ speaks through the priest the words of consecration: "For this is My Body, which will be given for you"; "For this is the chalice of My Blood, the Blood of the new and eternal covenant, which will be poured

---

[314] Ven. Concepcion Cabrera de Armida, 6 June, 1916.
[315] *Catechism*, n.1368.

out for you and for many for the forgiveness of sins. Do this in memory of me." Ven. Conchita, at the moment of the consecration of the Precious Blood, united her own blood with that of Jesus, sacrificing it for love of the Father.[316]

The Catechism teaches that the laity at Mass can offer as a **sacrifice all aspects of their lives united to Christ's offering:**

For all their works, prayers, and apostolic undertakings, family and married life, daily work, relaxation of mind and body, if they are accomplished in the Spirit—indeed even the hardships of life if patiently born—all these become spiritual sacrifices acceptable to God through Jesus Christ. In the celebration of the Eucharist, these may most fittingly be offered to the Father along with the body of the Lord. And so, worshipping everywhere by their holy actions, the laity consecrate the world itself to God, everywhere offering worship by the holiness of their lives.[317]

129. Chain of Pierced Hearts, Diary of a MOC

The flow of My Blood intensifies through My Body, the Church. The triumph of My sacrifice of love will be fulfilled through My Body, the Church.

My Mother is Bride and Church, imitate her. She, as ONE with My Body, united her tears to My Precious Blood and in this way redeemed souls with Me. You are called to do the same. The saving grace of My Precious Blood will enter all hearts that are open through you, My Body. Therefore, My little ones, suffer all with Me so that many can enter the

---

[316] See her prayer, p 446.
[317] *Catechism,* n.901-902; cf. *LG* n.10; 1 Pet 2:5.

fold of My Sacred Heart. You must become the chain of pierced hearts that will unbind the chain of darkness and bondage. Bring Me many victim souls. (12/19/11)

The Need to be Bound in Love to Christ
Pope Benedict XVI

"Bound" is first a word of the theology of the Cross, of the necessary communion of every evangelizer, of every pastor with the supreme Pastor, who redeemed us by "giving himself," suffering for our sake. Love is suffering, it is giving oneself, it is losing oneself and in this very way is fruitful. Yet, another aspect appears and shines through the external element of the chains, of freedom no longer present: namely, that the true chain which binds Paul to Christ is the bond of love. "A prisoner for love": a love that gives freedom, a love that enables him to make Christ's Message and Christ himself present. And **for all of us too, this must be the ultimate chain that sets us free, bound to Christ by the chain of love**. Thus, we find freedom and the true path of life and, with Christ's love, we can also guide to this love which is joy and freedom, the people entrusted to our care.[318]

---

[318] Pope Benedict XVI, Meeting with the parish priests of the Rome diocese, 23 Feb. 2012, www.vatican.va.

6-C
Mary Is the Perfect Victim of Love

Jesus Christ is the perfect, pure Victim of Love and Mary is the perfect, pure victim united to the Victim. Mary is not only the Mother of Jesus, but also the Bride of the Lamb, who with the Holy Spirit, say to Him, "Come!" As His bride, she became one with Jesus' interior crucifixion and the crucifixion on Calvary. The Co-Redemptrix, filled with the Holy Spirit, cries out to the Father, "Abba, Father, save them!"

Therefore, to come into the most perfect intimate relationship of love with Jesus Christ here on earth, which is the relationship of victim united to the Victim, we need to consecrate ourselves to Mary, Mother and Bride, with the understanding and abandonment that she will bring us to the foot of the Cross. It is at the place of encounter—at the foot of the Cross—where we gaze at Jesus crucified, where we can touch His wounds, and where Mary is able to form us most perfectly in all her virtues which are the virtues of Jesus.

Therefore, becoming a victim of love is a spiritual process of growing and entering a deep intimate personal relationship with Jesus Christ Himself, a relationship that moves us with Mary into spiritual marriage with the Bridegroom. It is this passionate love affair that moves us to desire to love Him as He has loved us; the love of the unblemished Lamb that lays down His life for His Bride—for us, the Church.

To be a victim soul is not understood by most people because Love is not known nor understood. To love is to suffer. To love is to lay down your life for another. To understand victimhood, we must contemplate Jesus' victimhood and Mary's victimhood united to His.

130. Mary Is the Bearer of the Messiah, Diary of a MOC

Mary is the bearer of the Messiah, Who comes through her virginal womb. My daughter, you are preparing the passage for the Second Coming of Christ. He will come in all His splendor to be recognized by all. The preparation of this passage is being laid out by the blood of His victim souls. Mary, as Spouse of the Holy Spirit, will walk through this passage first led by the holy sons of God (priests). This will be the reign of the Holy Spirit. Within a short time, I will come in all My glory to be seen by all. You must extend the carpet of victim souls, which creates the holy passage for God. (12/15/11)

131. Jesus, Mary and Joseph Were Victim Souls,
Diary of a MOC

St. Joseph and Mary were perfect, holy victim souls. They were united as one to the Victim of Love. St. Joseph never uttered a complaint during his many trials, struggles, and sufferings.

The human existence here on earth is full of struggles, challenges, difficulties, sufferings, trials and tears because of the fall. I came to transform human suffering through My death and resurrection. The Holy Family lived the human condition through Me, with Me and in Me; thus their lives were transformed into Love, the love of the Most Holy Trinity.

> *The world is foundering into the abyss of evil and darkness because My Spirit is not sought and loved. It is through Mary, the Spouse of the Holy Spirit, that you obtain most perfectly the power of the Holy Spirit. It is the Holy Spirit that will unite you as One Body to My crucified Love to participate in the salvation of the world. It is only My victim souls who participate in the work of redemption and who will conquer the principalities of death with Me. Therefore, My little one, bring Me victim souls!* (1/31/11)

— Like a Carpet —

Important persons get the "red carpet treatment." The Lord used that image to call us to become, ourselves, the "red carpet" for our Queen, the Blessed Virgin Mary, who comes to reign. The Mothers of the Cross and lay Missionaries of the Cross are part of the red carpet that represents the blood of the hidden martyrs of love, the passage which Mary will walk through, as the Queen bringing forth the New Pentecost. She will be ushered in by the priests who offer themselves as victim souls. The red carpet represents the passage composed of victim souls to prepare the way for the reign of the Holy Spirit. The carpet serves to bring the priests forward in the path through victimhood and to sustain them.

St. Faustina

I will immolate myself for the benefit of souls. I will not count the cost of any sacrifice. I will cast myself beneath the feet of the sisters like a carpet on which they cannot only tread, but also wipe their feet. My place is under the feet of the sisters. I will make every effort to obtain that place unnoticed by others. It is enough that God sees this.[319]

Saint John Paul II, remembering how he was prostrated on the floor the day of his ordination, wrote the following poem:

Peter, you are the floor, that others may walk over you ... not knowing where they go. You guide their steps. ...
    You want to serve their feet to pass
    as rock serves the hooves of sheep.
    The rock is a gigantic temple floor,
    The cross a pasture.[320]

St. Andrew of Crete expressed the same desire to prostrate before the Lord:

Let us run to accompany Him as He hastens toward His passion, and imitate those who met Him then, not by covering His path with garments, olive branches or palms, but by doing all we can to prostrate ourselves before Him by being humble and by trying to live as He would wish. Then we shall be able to receive the Word at His coming, and God, whom no limits can contain, will be within us. ...
    So let us spread before His feet, not garments or soulless olive branches, which delight the eye for a few hours and then wither, but ourselves, clothed in His grace, or rather,

---

[319] Faustina Kowalsda, Saint, *Diary: Divine Mercy in My Soul*, n.243.
[320] John Paul II, *Gift and Mystery*, 45.

clothed completely in Him. We who have been baptized into Christ must ourselves be the garments that we spread before Him.[321]

132. Participate in My Interior Crucifixion, Diary of a MOC

My daughter, I desire souls to participate in My interior crucifixion as ONE with My Mother. It is in this way that you will obtain the greatest amount of graces for the world.

A time of great destruction is coming to the world; it is My hidden martyrs of love that the Father will use to aid many to the Light. It is My hidden martyrs of love that possess the power to raise up My army of holy priests needed for the decisive battle that is at hand. My little ones, you are called to help form My hidden martyrs of love to perfection in Me. Accept My chalice of love and suffering and suffer with Me, as ONE with Me, the sorrows of My Sacred Heart. As an all-loving Father, I suffer the sickness of My sons' and daughters' hearts; but My greatest suffering is that they don't allow Me, the Healer of all hearts, to touch them. They seek healing in all forms except in the only One that can bring them to life. I desire for all the Mothers of the Cross to unite as one with My Mother of Sorrows to obtain graces for humanity. The salvation of many is dependent upon your RESPONSE. (6/28/11)

---

[321] As cited in the Office of Readings of Passion Sunday.

The Holy Spirit is raising up victim souls by forming them in the hidden martyrdom of the heart. They are warriors of love for these decisive times who, with Mary, will conquer the dragon and bring forth the reign of her Immaculate Heart and the New Pentecost.

6-D
Victim Souls Hold the Power of God

Jesus is victor through His victim sacrifice. So it is with Christians. Fr. Raniero Cantalamessa writes:

In almost all ancient myths the victim is the defeated and the executioner the victor. Jesus changed the sign of victory. He inaugurated a new kind of victory that does not consist of making victims, but in making himself victim. *"Victor quia victima*!" (Victor because victim); thus Augustine describes the Jesus of the cross. The modern value of the defense of victims, of the weak and of threatened life, is born on the terrain of Christianity; it is a later fruit of the revolution carried out by Christ.

We have the counter-proof. As soon as the Christian vision is abandoned (as Nietzsche did) to bring the pagan back to life, this conquest is lost and one turns to exalt "the strong, the powerful, to its most exalted point, the superman," and the Christian is described as "a morality of slaves," fruit of the mean resentment of the weak against the strong. [322]

133. Victims of Love Will Set the World on Fire,
Diary of a MOC

> *It is My victims of love that the Father will use to set the world on fire. My victims of love possess the fire of My Spirit. Enter the furnace of My love through the passage of choosing to suffer all with Me in the hiddenness of your lives. My Heart thirsts for such love.* (7/1/11)

134. My Victim Souls Have the Power to Bring Back to Life Dead Hearts, Diary of a MOC, Feast of the Sacred Heart Jesus.

This morning in Mass I saw Jesus interiorly in my heart, in radiant Light, holding His Heart in his left hand. His entire being was Light, not just His Heart. A Light moving out, expanding, penetrating... A Light that also drew you into Himself.

Then tonight I began to see Jesus again in the same way; but there was no light coming forth from Him, and the heart I was now seeing in His hand was small, shriveled and black. It seemed like a dead heart to me. I could not understand what the Lord was revealing to me. After the Mass, before the Blessed Sacrament, our Lord explained:

The Light of God will not shine forth for a time. It is you (meaning plural) that must keep My Light shining in the world. This heart dead in sin, which I

[322] Raniero Cantalamessa, St. Peter's Basilica on Good Friday, 2010. http://www.ewtn.com/library/PRIESTS/zcant10gdfri.htm

reveal to you tonight, (this one dead heart represented many), will come back to life through the blood of My martyrs of love. Receive tonight on the Feast of My Sacred Heart these hearts.

How, My Lord, do I receive them?

Water these hearts with your tears of sorrow, pray for them through the prayer of your pure suffering, bless them with your kiss of love and anoint them with the graces of My Eucharist. It is the life of My victim souls that has the power to bring back to life the dead. My daughter, raise up many victims of love, for many will be lost during the time of great darkness. (6/15/12)

135. Jesus' Wounds and the Power of Our Prayers as Victim Souls, Diary of a MOC

Last night as we prayed the rosary during our cenacle I first saw interiorly Jesus' wounds as very large passages. Then Jesus raised up my body into His crucified embrace. The family of LC was interceding with great love for many souls. I then saw a long line of men, women and children entering Jesus' wounds. He allowed me to see most clearly the faces of the children. Their eyes were the blank gaze of hopelessness. At the same time, through the gaze of their eyes, I felt the immense pain and suffering in their hearts. I couldn't contain my tears to see and feel such woundedness and pain in the Body of Christ, my brothers and sisters. My tears continue to come this morning as I continue to see into the eyes of our Lord's children. I shed tears for them and cry with my Lord and Mother, suffering as ONE heart with them for all humanity. What pain, what suffering, what love! Come Holy Spirit, come to renew the face of the earth!!

My wounds are the passage to enter the infinity of God. I allowed My Body to become one wound (meaning His entire Body was pierced and wounded) so that ALL humanity could enter. Each victim soul has the power from God, because of My Victimhood, to draw souls into My wounds.[323]

Your "fiat" in your desire to be My victim souls has allowed the Holy Spirit to unite you into My crucified love. I first revealed to you the infinite depth and width of each of My wounds. Then I raised you, My little victims of love, into My crucified embrace. As you (LC) prayed as ONE heart and mind through Me, with Me and in Me, your prayer received the power of the Holy Spirit to draw souls into My wounds. Believe in the power of your prayers as ONE with the perfect Victim of Love. Continue praying and living as God's hidden force. (2/1/11)

---

[323] Cf. Jn 12:20-33; Message of 14 Dec. 2011.

136. No Salvation Outside the Cross, Diary of a MOC

> *There is no salvation outside of the Cross... All My sons and daughters have been called to enter the Cross, unite themselves to Love Crucified and participate in the salvation of the world... Bring Me victim souls! Proclaim My glorious Cross to the world with the power of the Holy Spirit given to you. Give your lives for this mission. (8/11/10)*

We conclude this chapter with an observation from a beloved priest who lives this Path:

It is clear to me that a victim soul is a precious pearl: unique, rare, infrequent. Yes, we are all called, but how many constraints prevent us from approaching, even a little, this fullness! How many Christians, even consecrated by vows or by the priesthood, do not even suspect that they could live this relationship with the Lord! Maybe that's why I felt so called to support you with my prayers, so that the miracle of "raising victim souls" and bringing them to the Lord may be realized.

Chapter Seven

Spiritual Motherhood for Priests

This chapter is written by two Mothers of the Cross with a Missionary of the Cross whose desire and hope is to humbly share with you what we have learned and are personally living as spiritual mothers and father, through our intimate union with the Hearts of Jesus and Mary. This is our prayer:

We consecrate this chapter to the Immaculate Heart of Mary, Universal Mother, and Dispenser of all Graces. With her, at the foot of the Cross, we implore the Holy Trinity to give us the grace to be His instruments of light and love that will reveal the hidden treasure of Spiritual Motherhood to those souls chosen by the Lord, our Love Crucified, and to sow in them the seeds of New Life that, in due time, will blossom and bear abundant fruit in the heart of a renewed and faithful Church. Come Holy Spirit! Come!

We cannot begin to share about this vocation without first making an emphatic clarification:

SPIRITUAL MOTHERHOOD CAN BE LIVED
ONLY IN MARY

If lived without her, it is not spiritual motherhood. The Blessed Virgin Mary is the source of spiritual motherhood instituted by Christ from the Cross. We need to imitate her qualities, virtues, and characteristics. We are to carry in us the essence of Mary, her spiritual DNA.

7-A
What then Is Spiritual Motherhood?

In the document of the Congregation for the Clergy, "Eucharistic Adoration for the Sanctification of Priests and Spiritual Maternity," the Church tells us:

The VOCATION to be a spiritual mother for priests is LARGELY UNKNOWN, SCARCELY UNDERSTOOD and, consequently, RARELY LIVED, notwithstanding its FUNDAMENTAL IMPORTANCE. It is a vocation that is FREQUENTLY HIDDEN, INVISIBLE TO THE NAKED

EYE, but MEANT TO TRANSMIT SPIRITUAL LIFE. [324]

This short paragraph broadly defines what Spiritual Motherhood is:

1. A VOCATION: It's a call from God.
2. LARGELY UNKNOWN: Despite being a vocation which is specifically lived for love of the priesthood, the vast majority of priests are unaware of it; it is consequently feared, distrusted and misjudged.
3. SCARCELY UNDERSTOOD: Very few have understood the width, depth, length and height—the full dimension of the mystery of love that is held in Spiritual Motherhood.
4. RARELY LIVED, NOTWITHSTANDING ITS FUNDAMENTAL IMPORTANCE: Even though the Lord is calling many to live this spiritual union, very few do, and few have come to understand and assimilate its importance and value.
5. It's a FREQUENTLY HIDDEN VOCATION.... INVISIBLE TO THE NAKED EYE: Just as the vocation of motherhood is so often unnoticed and unappreciated, so is spiritual motherhood. It is lived in the hidden daily sufferings of the feminine heart.
6. MEANT TO TRANSMIT SPIRITUAL LIFE: We can transmit to our spiritual sons only what we have in us; therefore, the women who respond must be, as Mary, Eucharistic adorers. The food and nourishment, the source of life of a Spiritual Mother, must be the Eucharist. Mary and the

---

[324] Congregation for the Clergy, *Adoration, Reparation, Spiritual Motherhood for Priests*, (8 Dec. 2007), 10. This and other documents on Spiritual Motherhood: www.LoveCrucified.com/spiritual_motherhood/_spiritual_motherhood.html.

Eucharist are the life of the priesthood.

The document lays the foundations of spiritual motherhood:
- To pray for priests with or without their knowledge.
- To offer sacrifices and penances for them.

This understanding calls for deeper reflection on the gift of spiritual motherhood—a mystery that encompasses the totality of the human person and can be approached only with the grace of the Holy Spirit. Let us begin by contemplating the natural characteristics of motherhood:

1. The fruit of the union between a man and a woman brings life in her womb. A woman becomes a mother when she conceives.
2. From the moment of conception begins a communion of body and soul between mother and child. It is the gestation.
3. Especially during pregnancy, mother and child live in DEEP INTIMACY. What affects the mother affects the child—health or illness, joy or suffering.
4. It is the mother who nourishes him in the womb with her own blood.
5. It is the mother who, through her own pain, brings him into the world: "Lo da a luz," which means that she brings him into the light.
6. It is the mother who nurses him with her milk until the child reaches maturity for solid food.

God has willed for the bond between mother and child to be a profound, intimate and solid union. This communion is essential for the healthy formation and development of the child. Without this natural bonding, motherhood would enter a DISORDER, and the child wouldn't thrive. This has been scientifically proven, revealing how essential motherhood is for the wellbeing of humanity.

Through our contemplation of the lives of Jesus and Mary, we have received understanding of how essential spiritual motherhood also is for the wellbeing of humanity. We must go to them and drink from the source.

First, through Mary's spousal union with the Holy Spirit, Jesus is conceived. From the moment of His conception begins a total union with Mary, which we can call the gestation of their love. This deep intimacy continues and grows throughout their entire life on earth. Mary is prepared for over thirty-three years in her union with Jesus to become the Spiritual Mother of humanity at the foot of the Cross. She was prepared as she lived the interior crucifixion with Jesus during those years. Their love is consummated on the Cross as their hearts are pierced as ONE. This perfect union of love brings to life a new creation—the "new Adams" and the "new Eves."

7-B
The Birth of the "New Adams and Eves" at the Foot of the Cross

———————•❖•———————

The first fruit of Jesus and Mary's love at the Cross is St. John, the chosen of the Lord, His beloved disciple. Of all the apostles, he is the one who knew the heart of Jesus intimately. From this intimacy is born his openness to intimacy with Mary at the Cross. His union with her is the fruit of the deep and painful piercing for love of the Two Hearts. In this new union of St. John and Mary, established by Jesus at the foot of the Cross, we find the purest essence of spiritual motherhood.

Jesus waited until He could share His Passion with them, until He was agonizing, to call them forth to become mother and son/disciple. **They could not be mother and son to each other without first being victims of love, one with Christ's Passion**. Union with Christ at the Cross is at the center of Mary's motherhood and at the center of St. John's son/discipleship. At the Cross, they come together, and their relationship acquires a new meaning and a new fecundity because it has the fire of pure and perfect love. When it reaches maturity, it blossoms as Spiritual Motherhood.

Mary's motherhood for John far surpasses the models we have for a mother's relationship with an adult son. **She becomes God's instrument to continue the work of redemption in him,** especially through the healing and formation of his heart. This includes the healing of his emotions, feelings, desires and his self-image. Jesus, the man, formed him; then Mary, the woman, completed the formation of his heart as only a woman can.

She is also his companion. The Lord said, "It is not good that the man should be alone; I will make him a helper fit for him" (Gen 2:18)[325]. No one is more apt to accompany and help man than the woman Mary. The relationship of Mary and St. John shows that Jesus meant the complementarity between man and woman to find expression, not only in marital relationships oriented towards having children but also in spiritual relationships that bring spiritual life to many.

"Woman, behold, your son!" (Jn 19:26). "Woman" is an allusion to Genesis, for Mary is the new Eve, the Immaculate, the one who unties the knots of sin, the one victorious over the Serpent. This is the Mother and companion Jesus gives us. But Jesus also spoke to St. John, "Then He said to the disciple, 'Behold, your mother!'" (Jn 19:27). **He can be blessed with the gift of Mary only if he responds with all his heart.** He must "behold" her. John understood that, to behold Mary, meant to receive her; therefore, "from that hour the disciple took her to his own home" (Jn 19:27). She is not a mother whom we visit while keeping her at a distance. He took Mary into his own home, into his heart—a heart that belongs to Jesus—and allowed her to enter the intimacy of his priesthood.

St. John receives from Christ: the pierced heart of the Mother of the God-Man, the Immaculate Heart of the Daughter of the Father, and the fecund Heart of the Spouse of the Holy Spirit. He inherits the creature full of the Holy Trinity. By living in intimacy with Mary, he receives the graces of her Spiritual Motherhood and lives his priesthood fulfilling the Will of God. Without Mary as his spiritual mother, the disciple could not have risen to the heights of mystical union that allowed him to write the Book of Revelation, which reveals the depths of the heart of God. St. John with Mary,

---

[325] *Revised Standard Version*, Cath. edition

in their union of hearts that love each other in Christ Crucified, are filled with the Holy Spirit and help each other fulfill their mission.

In this drama at the Cross, in the midst of the most excruciating pain, there is another beloved of the Two Hearts, a witness of honor: Mary Magdalene. She is the inseparable companion of our Heavenly Mother and Jesus. What unites them, what has made them ONE heart, is the infinite love that these two women have for Him. Yet, they are two very different women in their origin: The Blessed Mary is full of grace, the Immaculate, redeemed by Christ as well, but never stained by sin. Mary Magdalene is the woman from whom seven demons had gone out (Lk. 8:2). Her response to Christ's redeeming love saves her, purifies her, restores her, and dignifies her.

Through her piercing of love at the foot of the Cross in union with Mary, she receives her full identity as a spiritual mother. For the one that is dying is her Beloved as well, the Lord and Master of her heart. She is also experiencing the helplessness of Christ on the Cross. Her Master is dying—her "Rabbouni" (Jn 20:16) is fading away, her Jesus, her Life, her ALL. She suffers WITH Jesus no longer two but one in His sacrifice of love. As one with Mary, her spiritual maternity is born.

Mary, now the Mother of the Church, remains to form St. John and Mary Magdalene in the school of her heart, as she does with each of us. She is Mary Magdalene's greatest and closest friend, her teacher and sister in the Lord, and now, above all, her Mother! We, like them, must be formed in the School of Love: The Immaculate Heart of Mary.

In the new Adam and new Eve, Jesus and Mary, we find the perfect harmonious relationship. They are the model and source of grace for all renewed men and women.

Having united Mary and the beloved disciple, Jesus, "knowing that all was now finished," said, "I thirst" (Jn. 19:28). His earthly mission was fulfilled. With Saint John and Mary Magdalene begins a new lineage of renewed men and women, cleansed in the Blood of the Lamb; new Adams and new Eves formed in the heart of the New Adam and the New Eve. It is the beginning of a covenant of love with Christ through Mary.

7-C
Spiritual Motherhood Lived in the Martyrdom of Mary

Spiritual Motherhood is not a program nor a new apostolate nor something that you do following a set of rules. We become spiritual mothers as we come to know intimately the passionate love of our Bridegroom, Jesus Christ, through the power of the Cross and choose to respond passionately. Spiritual motherhood is a GIFT of the Holy Spirit that grows as the Spirit heals our feminine hearts through the precious Blood of Jesus and transforms us to become a new creation.

On the occasion of the closing of the Second Vatican Council, Pope Paul VI spoke prophetically about women:

The hour is coming, in fact has come, when the vocation of woman is being achieved in its fullness, the hour in which woman acquires in the world an influence, an effect and a power never hitherto achieved.

That is why, at this moment when the human race is undergoing so deep a transformation, women impregnated with the spirit of the Gospel, can do so much to aid mankind in not falling.[326]

What the Pope foresaw is realized when women embrace their God-given identity as brides of Jesus and spiritual mothers. The Bridegroom is pleased to share everything with His bride, hence her powerful influence upon the world.

St. John Paul II said that "holiness is measured according to the 'great mystery' in which the Bride responds with the gift of love to the gift of the Bridegroom."[327] A holy bride of Jesus is one who responds with her whole heart, abandoning herself completely. Then the Bridegroom shares His power with her to fulfill her maternal mission towards the spiritual sons that He entrusts to her.

The Church is discovering the urgent need for priests to have such spiritual mothers. As Christ purifies hearts in the fire of His Sacred Heart, He restores men and women's ability to truly love and complement each other in the service of the Kingdom. In our brokenness, we may find it hard to believe that a mother-son relationship between women and priests is possible or even desirable. We tend to think only of the dangers that stem from our fallen nature, but we also need to believe that Christ at Calvary poured out His Spirit to make all things new. He established spiritual motherhood when he joined the Blessed Virgin Mary and St. John as mother and son. The Lord continues to raise up relationships between spiritual mothers and priests, but this is possible only to the extent that they are truly victim souls, one with The Victim!

The mission of a spiritual mother is to help her priest sons live fully the call to be a victim and not to forget the importance

---

[326] Message to women, 8 Dec. 1965, www.vatican.va.
[327] *Mulieris Dignitatem*, n.27.

of it. Mary went to Calvary with St. John and wants to take every priest to her Crucified Son. The mother of the Maccabees encouraged each of her sons to become a martyr: "Although she saw her seven sons perish within a single day, she bore it with good courage because of her hope in the Lord." [328] It is a relationship that has to be lived with the same purity, with the same passion and the same dedication with which the first Mother of the Cross lived it with the Beloved Disciple. And this, in our humble opinion, is essential for these decisive times we have entered.

137. Mothers Are the Strength of Priests, Diary of a MOC, (IV Station of the Cross: Mary Meets Jesus)

Walk with Me in My passion. Through Mary, My Mother, I received the strength and zeal I needed to continue to the Cross... She was not only My consolation but also My strength. My Mother knew and accepted My mission... In Her great and pure love of God, she encouraged Me and brought Me to the Cross. It was she that encouraged Me to begin My mission at the Wedding at Cana... Do you see the importance of holy mothers for My priests, who are living images of My Mother? My priests need these holy mothers to help strengthen and encourage them. (2/20/09)

---

[328] 2 Macc 7:20.

138. Will Bring Each of Them to the Cross, Diary of a MOC

I, the Mother of all in heaven and on earth, the Mother of all priests, desire for their holiness. As I embraced St. John at the foot of the Cross, enveloped in the precious blood of my most adorable Son, I also want to embrace each priest. Through my Son, they are each my sons. I love them with my motherly pure heart. I want to lead them to be holy as Jesus is holy. I want to lead them into the abode of His pierced Heart. I will bring each of them to the Cross as I accompanied my Son. I will form them to be perfect victims as I formed my Son. I will place in their hearts the love of the Cross as the Father placed this love in the Heart of my Son and in mine.

My daughter, I want you to help each priest come to the Cross. Share with them your experience of the Cross. My little one, share with them your life. It is living testimonies of my Son's grace that touches and awakens hearts. Tell them to allow me to reveal to them the love of Jesus Crucified. It is only this love that has the power to transform. It is when each of my consecrated priests unite themselves, through my heart, to Love Crucified that the hearts of the faithful will be opened. (8/5/09)

Mary's fecundity as a Spiritual Mother is the fruit of her hidden martyrdom of heart. Jesus explained it to Venerable Conchita in this way:

At the foot of the Cross, all her children were born. My

death gave them life in the heart of My Mother. But before her death she had to manifest this MATERNITY ON EARTH, gaining, by the sufferings of my absence, an infinitude of graces present and future for her children. Her title, Mother of Mankind, Mary won by the martyrdom of her solitude after my death.[329]

Therefore, a spiritual mother must be a mother of the Cross, a victim soul who lays down her life for love of her spiritual children. The Ven. Archbishop Luis Martinez understood the power of spiritual mothers and encouraged Conchita to persevere in love:

You, too, like Jesus, must love the Father on behalf of all your children and for all the souls that God has linked with you through the outstanding grace of spiritual maternity…. Some of your children will love the Father with many limitations. You must supply for them. Perhaps some of them—may the Lord not permit it!—will never love. You must love for them. With what desire you must try to love for all in order that the Father may not lack even a spark of love from your spiritual family.[330]

---

[329] Conchita Cabrera de Armida, (*Diary*, 131, June 30, 1917).
[330] *To Be Jesus Crucified*, (Alba House, 2013), 12-13. Notes of retreat conducted by Archbishop Luis M. Martinez.

139. These words concerning the Mothers of the Cross were given by our Lord to our Love Crucified Community:

As Mothers of the Cross, pray for My beloved priests as you pray for your sons. Give your lives for them as you give your lives for your children. Your voices (MOC) are united as one with My Mother before the throne of God. Your lives united in Mary are bringing down graces upon My priests. (11/9/08)

The Mothers of the Cross unite their fiat to My Mother of the Cross as victim intercessors. They live a life of prayer, penance, and sacrifice, united in My crucified love, for the expiation of sins and the sanctification of My priests. Their ordinary lives lived in simplicity, humility, interior silence and prayer are a sweet fragrance that reaches the heart of My Father. The prayers, sacrifices, sufferings and tears of mothers, united to the Cross through Mary, is a hidden force that will sanctify, purify and aid in the salvation of many souls!

140. Words from our Blessed Mother to the Mothers of the Cross:

> *The mothers of the cross are my maidens that, united to me, will renew the priesthood. Your "fiat" to be victim souls will be perfected in my "Fiat." Your lives will be a holy cloth that soaks up the precious Blood of Jesus. In this way, you will become pure living chalices filled with the Blood of Jesus. You will live your hidden lives like me in prayer, sacrifice and suffering. Your hidden lives lived in your domestic monasteries will be a source of grace for the sanctification of priests.*
>
> *You will imitate to great perfection my virtues of humility, simplicity, gentleness, silence and charity. You will be women of an intense prayer life centered in the Eucharist. Your lives will be a continuous prayer offering as you offer up your daily sacrifices and duties on the altar of your homes. As you love in suffering, imitating Jesus and me, you will be our joy and consolation.* (6/13/09)

A spiritual mother is a victim soul who first and foremost loves the Lord and lives in total docility to Him. He is the one who has loved her, who has drawn her to fall in love with Him. She gives Him a blank check, having full confidence in Abba, and we say *Abba* because we see ourselves as the apple of His eye, like a little girl under the pleased gaze of her father who loves her passionately! Through God's love for her, a spiritual mother loves all those He places in her heart.

St. Therese of Lisieux lived her spiritual maternity as a victim of love through her passionate, feminine heart as one with Jesus crucified:

> I felt a great pang of sorrow when thinking this blood was falling to the ground without anyone's hastening to gather it up. I was resolved to remain in spirit at the foot of the Cross and to receive the divine dew. I understood that I was then to POUR IT OUT UPON SOULS. The cry of Jesus on the cross sounded continually in my heart: "I thirst." These souls ignited within me an unknown and very living fire. I wanted to give my Beloved to drink, and I felt myself consumed with a thirst for souls. As yet, it was not the souls of priests that attracted me, but those of great sinners; I burned with the desire to snatch them from the eternal flames.[331]

Jesus especially inflamed her maternal heart with the fire of His love for priests. She wrote to her sister:

> O Celine, let us live for souls, let us be apostles, let us save especially the souls of priests; these souls should be more transparent than crystal… Alas, how many bad priests, priests who are not holy enough… let us pray, let us suffer for them, and in the last day Jesus will be grateful. We will give Him souls…! Do you understand, Celine, the cry of my heart…?[332]

> Celine, I feel that Jesus is asking both of us to quench His thirst by giving Him souls, the souls of priests especially.
> Let us convert souls; this year we must form many priests who love Jesus and handle Him with the same tenderness with which Mary handled Him in the cradle.[333]

---

[331] St. Therese of Lisieux, *Story of a Soul* Cp 5.

[332] St. Therese of Lisieux Letter 94, 14 July, 1889.

[333] Frederick L. Miller, *The Trial of Faith of St. Therese of Lisieux*, (Alba House, 1998), 33-34.

Jesus taught **Venerable Conchita** that, as a spiritual mother for priests, she was first called to become a victim of love with Him in her ordinary life as wife and mother:

> I want souls who are dedicated with fervor, with determination and without looking for rest, to plead day and night for My priests[334].

> Offer yourself as a victim for My priests. Unite yourself to My sacrifice to gain them graces... It is Christ, ever crucified in the members of His Mystical Body, who saves the world[335].

Jesus wants Conchita to give Him holy priests. United to Him, she will belong to priests in the sense that her life will be an oblation for them. Jesus tells her:

> This will truly be a solace to My heart, giving Me holy priests. Tell Me you accept, that you will belong with Me to priests always since your mission on behalf of them will continue in heaven.
>
> Yet here you have another Martyrdom. **What priests will do against Me, you will feel, since it is in this that basically associating yourselves to My priesthood consists,** in that you feel and you suffer because of their unfaithfulness and wretchedness. In this way, you glorify the Trinity. We will have the same reasons for suffering.[336]

Pope Benedict XVI wrote about **St. Veronica Giuliani's** intercession as a spiritual mother:

---

[334] http://www.apcross.org/priests.htm.

[335] *Conchita: A Mother's Spiritual Diary*, M.M. Philipon, ed., A.J. Owen, trans. (New York, Alba, 1978), 103. Conchita diary 24 Sept. 1927.

[336]Ibid, 246.

She offered her prayers and sacrifices for the Pope, her bishop, priests and for all needy persons, including the souls in Purgatory. She summarized her contemplative mission in these words: "We cannot go preaching around the world to convert souls, but we are obliged to pray continually for all those souls who are offending God… particularly with our sufferings, that is with a principle of crucified life." Our saint conceived this mission as a "being in the middle" between men and God, between sinners and Christ Crucified.[337]

Pope Benedict XVI said that **St. Catherine of Siena**, "though aware of the human failings of the clergy, always had the greatest reverence for them because through the Sacraments and the Word they dispense the salvific power of the Blood of Christ." The Pope added:

They called her "mother" because, as her spiritual children, they drew spiritual nourishment from her. **Today too the Church receives great benefit from the exercise of spiritual motherhood by so many women, lay and consecrated,** who nourish souls with thoughts of God, who strengthen the people's faith and direct Christian life towards ever loftier peaks. "Son, I say to you and call you", Catherine wrote to one of her spiritual sons, Giovanni Sabbatini, a Carthusian, "inasmuch as I give birth to you in continuous prayers and desire in the presence of God, just as a mother gives birth to a son"…

The Sienese Saint always invited the sacred ministers, including the Pope… to be faithful to their responsibilities,

---

[337] General audience, 15 Dec. 2010, www.zenit.org/en/articles/on-st-veronica-giuliani.

motivated always and only by her profound and constant love of the Church.[338]

Jesus told St. Faustina

I place in your care two pearls very precious to My Heart: these are the souls of priests and religious. You will pray particularly for them; their power will come from your diminishment. You will join prayers, fasts, mortifications, labors and all sufferings to My prayer, fasting, mortifications, labors and sufferings and then they will have power before My Father.[339]

United with all the holy women of God we pray this prayer written by a Mother of the Cross, inspired by Venerable Conchita:

My Lord and my God, give me a loving and humble heart, a courageous heart full of zeal and boldness, a tender heart, a meek and docile heart that will be willing to take, one by one, the thorns that pierce Your most tender Heart, and pierce with them my heart with no other desire but to be Your consolation in every moment of my life.

My heart is wounded for love of you, My Lord; and moved with profound compassion, together with Mary, Venerable Conchita, and all the Holy Women that have walked on the path of Spiritual Motherhood from the beginning of time, I offer myself completely as a victim united with the Victim, for the sanctification of every priest and the salvation of every man in every walk of life! Jesus, my Savior and my God! Save them! Save them!

---

[338] Pope Benedict XVI, General audience, 24 Nov. 2010, w2.vatican.va.
[339] St. Faustina, *Diary, Divine Mercy in My Soul*, n.531.

7-D
Priests Need to Receive the Gift of Spiritual Motherhood

Priests should yearn as well for the gift of a spiritual mother as it is the Lord's way to unite them with Him. If God himself established this type of union, how can we ignore it? Why would we reject it or deny it? He, who knows what we need, our weaknesses… He, who knows our longings, our loneliness, and our deserts… He, being God, wanted her with Him. And since it is God's Will, those who live spiritual motherhood will enjoy these fruits: a clear sense of identity, the force and power of the Holy Spirit in our individual vocations, strength in temptations and difficulties, support, consolation, harmony in our lives, spiritual maturity, spiritual stability, total purification, joy…

It's a relationship that, if lived correctly, is called to bear much fruit! What unites Mary and the Beloved Disciple is the extreme and unconditional love both feel for Jesus. The total and complete love she feels for Jesus, she can express now, by Divine Will, in this beloved disciple. How? Giving her life for him. And John becomes Christ to love her as well, with the same love of his Lord! He grows in holiness in full compliance with the Will of God that asks him from the Cross to love her, to receive her, to make her his mother.

Since the beginning of the Church, women and men have served together. Women were among the disciples of Jesus and St. Paul. Cardinal Ratzinger told bishops: "The women were never in fact bishops or priests, but they were among those who carried forward the apostolic life and its universal task." Jesus' relationship with women, as described by St. John Paul II, is the perfect model for spiritual sons: "Transcending the established norms of His own culture, Jesus treated women with openness, respect, acceptance and tenderness. In this way, he honored the dignity which women have always possessed according to God's plan and in His love." Priests today also need to face the challenging prospect of transcending established norms.

In light of the urgent need for renewal of the priesthood and of knowing that spiritual mothers for priest are "meant to transmit spiritual life" to them, we can see why Cardinal Hummes, as prefect of the Congregation for the Clergy, wrote:

> We cannot do without a spiritual motherhood for our priestly life… It has always silently accompanied the chosen ranks of priests in the course of the Church's history. It is the concrete entrustment of our ministry to a specific face, to a consecrated soul who has been called by Christ and therefore chooses to offer herself, with the necessary suffering and the inevitable struggles of life, to intercede for our priestly existence, thereby dwelling in Christ's sweet presence…
>
> This motherhood, which embodies Mary's loving face, should be prayed for because God alone can bring it into being and sustain it.[340]

Jesus told St. Catherine of Siena that men "who image themselves learned and wise" have become proud and that He will send women to instruct them:

---

[340] Letter - World Day of Prayer for the sanctification of priests, 22 Apr. 2008, http://www.vatican.va/roman_curia/congregations/cclergy/documents/rc_con_cclerg y_doc_20080530_santificazione-sacerdotale_en.html

I will raise up women, ignorant and frail by nature, but endowed with strength and divine wisdom. Then, if they (proud men) will come to their senses and humble themselves, I will behave with the utmost mercy towards them, that is to say, towards those who, according to the grace given them, receive my doctrine, offered them in fragile but specially chosen vessels, and follow it reverently. Those who will not accept the salutary lesson, I shall with perfect justice reduce to such confusion that the world will look upon them as objects of contempt and derision.[341]

Who would have thought that God's way of renewing the priesthood would be through spiritual mothers! But for priests to benefit from this grace they have to humbly receive it and recognize when the Lord works through spiritual mothers.

7-E
All Women Are Called to Share Mary's Spiritual Motherhood

According to Pope Francis, motherhood "is not merely a biological fact; it entails a wealth of implications." He said that "woman has a particular sensitivity to the 'things of God', above all in helping us understand the mercy, tenderness and love that God has for us."[342] Spiritual maternity is in the soul of all women.

St. Benedicta of the Cross wrote:

---

[341] Bl. Raymond of Capua, *The Life of St. Catherine of Siena: The Classic on Her Life and Accomplishments as Recorded by Her Spiritual Director* (Tan Books, 2001).
[342] Pope Francis - 25th anniv. of *Mulieris Dignitatem*, 12 Oct. 2013, w2.vatican.va

For an understanding of our unique feminine nature, let us look to the pure love and spiritual maternity of Mary. Spiritual maternity is the core of a woman's soul. This holds true whether the woman is married or single, professional or domestic or both, a Religious in the world or in the convent. Through this love, a woman is God's special weapon in His fight against evil.[343]

Some object saying that only Mary can be a spiritual mother. But if we recognize, as St. Benedicta did, that spiritual motherhood is the core of the feminine soul, then all women are called by God to be spiritual mothers with Mary.

When Elizabeth said to Mary: "Blessed are you" (Lk1:42), she was recognizing her as the chosen one of God; when she added "among women," she was prophesying that all women are called to partake in Mary's blessedness and mission. God chose Mary "among women," not to separate her from her sisters but to become the channel of grace for all of them to share in her vocation.

Fr. Raniero Cantalamessa, the preacher to the papal household, wrote:

Only men can be priests, but the wisdom of God has kept for women, an even higher task in a certain sense, which the world does not understand and thus rejects with disdain: that of forming priests and of contributing to raising the quality, not the quantity, of Catholic priesthood.[344]

---

[343] Saint Benedicta of the Cross, as cited by Freda Mary Oben in *The Life and Thought of St. Edith Stein* (New York: Alba House, 2001), 82.

[344] Fr. Raniero Cantalamessa O.F.M. Cap., *Sober Intoxication of the Spirit*, Part II: Born Again of Water and the Spirit (Cincinnati: Servant Books, 2005), 61.

Fr. Cantalamessa believes that the spread of spiritual motherhood worldwide is the work of the Holy Spirit in the Church for these times:

> The Lord today is calling the faithful in ever-growing numbers to pray, to offer sacrifice, in order to have holy priests. A concern, a passion, for holy priests has spread as a sign of the times throughout today's Church.
>
> The royal and universal priesthood of believers has found a new way of expressing itself: contributing to the sanctification of the ministerial priesthood. Such vocations are extending out more and more beyond the walls of the cloistered monasteries, where they have been hidden, and are reaching the faithful. This vocation is becoming widespread, a call that God addresses to many.[345]

Following is a testimony of the power of spiritual motherhood as a Mother of the Cross opens her heart to another MOC regarding her suffering for a priest in crisis:

> My dearest, dearest little Sis:
>
> So much sorrow and pain in our hearts... How can I express the feelings of my heart when I hear a priest tell me that priesthood was not really his vocation and that he's ready to start a new life, look for a good wife and have a family... And in my heart, my dear Sis, I feel this is the same as if you or I would say: "Marriage and motherhood are not really my vocation. I don't feel that I am fulfilling my life this way, so I am going to start a religious life as a consecrated woman. I was too young, or I was misled, or

---

[345] Ibid., 60.

my marriage was arranged!"

The truth of this matter is that people are walking away from the cross. Nobody wants to lose his or her life anymore! Nobody wants to offer his life to save souls or to suffer with the Beloved because in reality there is no Beloved for them… Their first love is self-love, self-preservation, self-realization… It is puzzling to hear a priest tell you this kind of thing and then see him at peace, happy and relaxed, accepting this as an option before God, and then justifying his position because he went through depression and anxiety—and why should he!! We could tell him a bunch about our anxieties, our depressions, and sorrows of our hearts—all that we carry day in day out… Apparently, now a Christ follower, a disciple of our Lord is supposed to come to this world to enjoy it, to be happy, to have a pleasant and fulfilling life!! Yes, our joy and fulfillment should be and should come from consoling the Beloved, to suffer with Him, to accompany Him in His passion of love for all humanity—that's what a follower of Christ should be!!! But the world, the flesh, and Satan are changing humanity very, very fast!

Who will remain, my dearest Sis? I believe very few will remain at the foot of the Cross, very few will accept to be, with Christ, an oblation to Abba, in reparation for the sins of the world, to save souls! So, ONE with Christ, we can only suffer and cry the loss of another disciple that walks away from true LOVE, leaving that eternal TRUE LOVE for a lesser and ephemeral love. Have mercy on us, my Lord!

I can only love and suffer for this spiritual son where he is… And I hope and pray that a miracle will change his way of thinking and perceiving life. So, let's unite our prayers, sacrifices, and oblations of love to our Crucified Love, with real trust and believe in Abba's promise to us! Let us be the ones that REMAIN, the ones that love our Lord and Savior passionately!

7-F
Urgency for Spiritual Motherhood

The Church recognizes that it is more urgent than ever to raise an army of spiritual mothers for priests and seminarians. Cardinal Piacenza wrote:

> This work of true support, which has always been essential to the life of the Church, today seems more urgent than ever, especially in the secularized West, which awaits and stands in need of a new and radical proclamation of Christ. Mothers of priests and seminarians thus represent a true and veritable "army," which from earth offers prayers and sacrifice to heaven, and from heaven intercedes in even greater number so that every grace and blessing may be poured out upon the lives of the Church's sacred ministers.[346]

The mission of the Love Crucified Community is to help raise up God's army of victim souls, spiritual mothers, to bring forth His

---

[346] Cardinal Piacenza, Prefect of the Congregation for the Clergy, 2 Jan. 2013, http://lovecrucified.com.

"Apostles of Light" for the decisive battle at hand:

141. Bring Life to My Priests, Diary of a MOC

You, My little ones, are the consolation of My suffering Heart because you each have united yourselves to Mary, the Mother of God and the Mother of all. As I gaze at each of you, I see her beauty radiating from you. Allow her to form each of you to perfection.

*I need you, My faithful ones, to bring life to My Missionaries of the Cross. It is My hidden martyrs of love, in perfect union with the Queen of Martyrs, that will raise up My Apostles of Light. Know that I have taken My abode in each of your hearts; therefore, **radiate the humility and purity of My Mother**.*

Do not grow weary in your hidden lives of suffering all with Me, for you are My holy remnant that God the Father will use to purify My Church and pierce the darkness penetrating Her. Therefore, go forth, My daughters, as My holy warriors with Mary to seize the dragon and cast him into hell.

I bless you with My Precious Blood and seal you with the power of My Cross. (4/1/11)

142. Renew the Church, Diary of a MOC

Mary: *We will use your hidden lives, lived in Jesus crucified, to aid in the renewal of the Church, the sanctification of priests, and the salvation of many souls. You will be the hidden force that raises up my army of holy priests. These are the priests who will usher in the reign of my Immaculate Heart, a new Pentecost for the Church. The ways of God are not the ways of the world. He will use the vocation of motherhood, united in me, to bring new life to the Church. Know that the most ordinary tasks of motherhood, lived in sacrificial love, please greatly the Father. He will use these simple and generous mothers, united to me, to renew the Church. This is the power of the Cross: souls united to Love Crucified solely to love Jesus as He has loved you. This is the love that will transform the world.* (6/13/09)

143. Raise up Fallen Priests, Diary of a MOC

Mary draws my heart to the Stations of the Cross. She asks me to contemplate fallen priests and a fallen humanity in each fall of Jesus.

Believe, my daughter, that the Mothers of the Cross will help raise up many of my fallen priests. Your hidden lives, lived in deep contemplation with me, will be a hidden force raising up my priests. (2/3/09)

144. Allow My Mother to Form each of You, Diary of a MOC

It is through the hidden life of the Mothers of the Cross that My army of holy priests will be raised up. These spiritual mothers will live the tears and sorrows of their hearts united as one with My Mother of Sorrows. It is My Mother's sorrows that continue to shower grace upon the world, and as My MOC unite as one with My Mother, the shower will become a living torrent of grace. Therefore, each MOC must be perfected in living her hidden ordinary life with all its trials, sorrows, exhaustion.... with pure love; and in this way, she will find her joy: the joy of knowing that she is participating in the hidden sorrows of My Mother for the salvation of many souls.

Allow My Mother to form each of you, My daughters. It is Rosa Mystica who wants to form your gentle hearts. Mary reveals the sorrows of her pierced heart that continue to remain hidden and the roses of prayer, sacrifice, and penance. You must imitate Mary. In this way, your lives will become the sweet fragrance of prayer, and your sacrifices and penances will be lived in the most ordinary of your duties as women.

Your lives as My victims of love will go unnoticed by the world but will be seen by the eyes of the Father. He will use your hidden lives of love to humble the proud. Know that you are My consolation. (5/31/11)

145. Bring to Life the Dead Bones of My Sons,
Diary of a MOC

> *It is the hidden force of the Mothers of the Cross that will help to bring to life the dead bones of My sons (priests).* (8/10/11)

7-G
Correspondence between Priests and their Spiritual Mothers

A spiritual son's letter #1:

Dearest in Christ,

I think it's providential that I increasingly feel my incapacities and my human and Christian smallness. It's hard to recognize them. But they are everywhere. Incapacities to love, to communicate the Gospel, to be a father to the people with whom I interact pastorally. And that brings with it a temptation of distrust and inner sadness.

I try to see and feel the presence of God in my life, but it does not come. Or rather, it does not come as I would like. I must continue to be in purification. Walk in faith, even when the heart is lonely and overwhelmed, seeing the endless needs of the people. And in this inner path of trials, your messages are a balm and a light that God gives me. I thank you very much. God will say how long I will be in this phase and what is it that I should really learn and understand.

Your son asks your prayers and humbly blesses you,

A spiritual son's letter #2:

Beloved in the Lord,

This setback put me to the test. I could have rebelled inwardly and taken a victim attitude, looking for subtle revenge or simply fallen into bitterness, thinking that "the other prevailed." It was not easy, but I rejected these attitudes, moved especially by faith. I see in this trial a sign of Abba, who puts in my hands a difficult sacrifice to offer… for many people.

With this interior struggle and asking the Lord for strength, I celebrated Mass. Immediately I felt the presence of the Spirit around me, accompanying me. It was like an invitation to renew, during Mass, my offer as a victim to the Lord with this new situation. I did so and, as a result, I obtained an almost total inner peace.

I saw that the grace of God comes to us, but, in order to bear fruit, it is necessary that we not only ask for it but that we be willing to receive it, even when it is painful.

I only ask you to help me with your prayer. I see that the enemy realized this inner struggle in me and often suggests thoughts of revenge, rebellion, etc. He must be defeated through prayer.

With my filial affection in St. John and my blessing,

A spiritual son's letter #3:

Beloved in the Lord:

Today, day of St. John, I was able to pray with tranquility. What fortune, what happiness that of St. John, to be able to welcome his home the Virgin Mary! She was a living reminder of all that Christ did, said and asked. And she would warm up the heart of John to all this heritage for him to live it fully and transmit it to the world.

What the Lord has given me to live with you is something similar. I found myself, almost unwillingly, to be your St. John. I certainly must learn a lot, but what we have lived is something great. It is born neither from you or me, and it faces a future that we cannot imagine.

With the intercession of St. John, I bless you, and ask your motherly and Marian blessing,…

A spiritual mother's letter #1:

THANK YOU for allowing me the honor of being the custodian, as one with Mary the Mother of the Cross, of your priestly vocation as your spiritual mother. This is something that I treasure and take so seriously. THANK YOU for blessing me and my family through who you are as Christ's ordained priest/victim!!!!

My dear father/son, through the words you write me, I see the beauty of what God is doing in your heart! I see the power of the Holy Spirit working the transformation of your heart! I have been thanking and praising God for His mercy and love being lavished upon you!

Yes, the Cross is the place of our deep purification, of our dying to self, of our letting go of our control, of our titles, of our limited way of thinking… And it is also the place where we enter the most profound intimacy with God!

Father, persevere in SUFFERING ALL WITH JESUS, and you will enter the fire of the Holy Spirit in the Sacred Heart of Jesus. Continue to PERSEVERE as I read that you are doing. Yes, you are not walking alone, I am with you, and you are with me. We are helping each other, as Mary and St John, to die as ONE with Christ, so that we can become the SAINTS He created us to be!!!!!! The new men and women of the Kingdom of Christ!!

My heart is filled with EXCITEMENT and ANTICIPATION knowing how powerfully the Spirit is working in you. TRUST! TRUST! TRUST! You are becoming a new man, the new Adam!!!

May you always be consoled in remembering that I am sustaining you as God's "hidden force." I pray for you daily before the Blessed Sacrament, and it is a great honor offering my life as a living sacrifice with Jesus and Mary for you! I am greatly consoled and also sustained through your prayers and priesthood!! THANK YOU AGAIN!!

I humbly receive your priestly blessing and I send you my maternal love through our Mother of Sorrows!

A spiritual mother's letter #2:

My dear Father:

My father and my son in Christ.

And you are telling me that you have not learned how to be a FATHER?? You're a Father to the core!!! You overflow it… You're deep, tender, sensitive, humble… very important qualities in a true man of God, because that's how Christ is, and that's how He wants His priests to be. And on top of it, you're observant. You don't miss anything! In fact, because you listen and you pay attention you know the human heart. You have a great sense of humor—one that does not offend! Blessed be God!!!

You're brave. You only needed a little love from the heart of your mother-daughter to come out of your anonymity. Behind the timidity, behind those fears, was hiding the WONDERFUL PRIEST you are and that I am so proud to call Father, to call son… The Priest of Christ for whom I thank God every day, for whom I gladly offer my life, that gives meaning and brings great joy to my spiritual motherhood. Do you realize how much of a FATHER you are??

You're right: We have lived a precious spiritual adventure together, and together we will live many more!! And the thing is that, as did the Blessed Virgin Mary with Her Jesus, so will I accompany you in your priesthood. You always have my motherly blessing with all the love of my heart!

Your mother-daughter in Christ,

Response from spiritual son:

Beloved in Christ,

Once again, thank you very much for everything. Thank you for your selfless interest. Your messages accompany me and will sustain me and all my priestly life…

I do not have much more to say right now. I'm simply impressed at how much you've helped me, to know that I can always count on your help and the other victim souls. With your answers, I have enough material to meditate for a while and to appreciate more the vocation to which the Lord has called me.

A spiritual's mother letter #3:

My dear Father:

Four years as a priest this Christmas time! Now I come to understand why your priesthood is such a great gift for me… Your priesthood is a PRECIOUS gift to God!!!!

He knows that certain things that are involved in your priestly life are very hard for you; He gives you the option and encourages you to lose the fear of flying! To lose the fear to love!! And to let others love you because that's also something that frightens us… And the Lord tells you through me: "You move us!!" There is such a precious simplicity in you—that moves me! There is a purity in you so beautiful—that moves me! There is a truth that lives in you—that moves me! There is so much love in you, although still shy to express it, it's there… Yes, still afraid to give it, But it's there!!! And I know that the more you open yourself to love (which is to have no fear to love and to give yourself to others), the more you will be free and the more you will experience the true joy, the happiness of seeing with the eyes of God, to carry within you His same feelings, to carry in you the tenderness of a dad who loves us with tender love, with motherly love, as Pope Francis tells us.

Listen when you can to the homilies in Santa Marta. The one from the 11th of Dec. is a treasure!! God Himself affirms us and confirms us through our Holy Father.

How much I love you, My beloved Father!! You are a precious gift to my heart! Forever, Merry Christmas!! Be born in my spiritual motherhood to a new life in the Spirit… as did the Child Jesus in the Blessed Virgin Mary!!!

Receive all my love that overflows for you in this Holy Christmas! May you be blessed, my beloved father!!!

We are ONE with Jesus and Mary!

Chapter Eight

Readiness
for the Decisive Battle

8-A
Signs of the Times and Prophecy

— Be Prepared for Battle—

Christ defeated Satan at the Cross, but the battle rages fiercely until His Second Coming. Scripture warns us: "But woe to you, O earth and sea, for the devil has come down to you in great wrath because he knows that his time is short!"[347]

This chapter is not about apocalyptic speculation. It seeks to raise awareness about what is happening in the world and how we must prepare and fulfill our mission in light of what the Lord has taught us.

---

[347] Rev 12:12.

Our tendency, when faced with danger, is to try to save our skin, but, as we have been learning in this book, Christ's salvation is a much bigger reality. This Path to Union is the formation for the spiritual battle that has already begun. You can see how the dragon is causing havoc everywhere. Many will despair, but the faithful remnant will be able to witness Christ with the certainty of His victory.

We are living in times of persecution. 10% of the Christians of the world suffer some sort of persecution for their faith, some are suffering a true genocide: 82% of the Christian population of Iraq has been either killed or exiled; two-thirds of Syria's Christians have been slaughtered or displaced; Asia Bibi, a wife and mother, is languishing in a Pakistani dungeon because of her Christian faith; in Nigeria, Christians many churches have been set ablaze and with the parishioners inside of them; in some countries, Christian women are kidnapped and sold as slaves with impunity… These are just examples.

In the West, a great apostasy is underway. According to a Pew Research study of Sept. 2, 2015, the majority (52%) of American adults raised as Catholics left the Church at some point in their lives and 41% have stayed away. Baptisms and marriages in the Church have drastically decreased. The situation in Europe is even worse. In 2016, 4% of Catholic Germans attended Sunday Mass regularly and, according to a study by the Allensbach Institute, 60% of the "faithful" say they don't believe in life after death and only one third believe in the resurrection of Christ. In France, a poll published by *Le Monde* (2007) found that 51% of the French population described themselves as Catholics, but only half of the Catholics believed in God![348]

A Christianity that no longer has the light of Christ is unable to witness to unbelievers. Instead, it becomes a scandal and an obstacle to evangelization. But the Church will survive the storm with those who remain faithful to Christ. They will be increasingly ostracized and perceived as obstructing progress. Christians are increasingly expelled from their jobs, penalized or jailed for their faith… But **none of these are reasons for pessimism** because we know that Christ has already won. We are presented with the opportunity to accompany Christ to the Cross and be His instruments in these decisive times.

— The Maximilian Kolbe Preparation —

Governments will not be able to stop the breakdown of civilization. Terrorism and social upheaval will not be resolved merely by relying on human efforts because the root of the problem is that the Lord of life has been rejected. **What happens when the light is turned off? We are in darkness. We can only be in the light if we return to Christ.**

Christians have the mission of being the light of the world. As in the past, **the battle will be won by a faithful remnant** of men and women that the Lord is raising to be His warriors in these decisive times. To be among them, we must be willing to be stripped of our sin and pride and learn to be guided by the Spirit. We must discern the signs of the times and enter the battle fully engaged, well armored and willing to lay down our lives.

---

[348] The Telegraph, 10 Jan, 2007.
http://www.telegraph.co.uk/news/worldnews/1539093/France-no-longer-a-Catholic-country.html

This preparation is what this Path has been teaching us. **We call this the St. Maximilian Kolbe preparation.** He saw the signs of the times and prepared. He founded the Militia of the Immaculate whose members became spiritual warriors through a total consecration to Mary. By the time the Nazis invaded Poland, his country, in 1939, there were 1,000,000 Knights worldwide and St. Maximilian had founded the largest Franciscan friary in the world with over 900 friars. They were publishing 1,000,000 magazines monthly as well as 125,000 copies of a daily paper to form and prepare all who would listen.

St Maximilian was not afraid to speak the truth about his times even if it got him into conflicts because he knew the nature of the battle and his mission. He wrote:

Modern times are dominated by Satan and will be more so in the future. The conflict with hell cannot be engaged by men, even the most clever. The Immaculata alone has from God the promise of victory over Satan.

However, assumed into heaven, the Mother of God now requires our cooperation. She seeks souls who will consecrate themselves entirely to her, who will become instruments in her hands for the defeat of Satan and the spreading of God's kingdom upon earth.[349]

The Nazis destroyed everything but they could not destroy the souls who were ready. St. Maximilian's preparation was not to avoid suffering but rather to be able to carry out fully the mission which the Lord entrusted to him in the midst of enormous trials: to be faithful and to be a beacon of light for

---

[349] The Original Charter of the Militia of the Immaculate, cited by Fr. Jeremiah J. Smith in *The Knight of the Immaculate: Father Maximilian Kolbe* (Pickle Partners Publishing, Nov 11, 2016) books.google.com.

others. The fear of suffering and death could not stop him. While many Christians collaborated with evil or fell into despair during the Second World War, St. Maximilian was ready to give his life as a martyr in Auschwitz.

We do not know if we will be called to be martyrs by shedding our blood, but we all must live the white martyrdom of suffering faithfully with Jesus in these trying times. We do not know when the end of the world will come, what we do know is that each one of us has a mission in this battle and a short time to accomplish it. There is no time to waste.

> Watch therefore, for you do not know on what day your Lord is coming. But know this, that if the householder had known in what part of the night the thief was coming, he would have watched and would not have let his house be broken into. Therefore, you also must be ready; for the Son of man is coming at an hour you do not expect. (Mt 24:42-44)

— The Purpose of Prophecy —

Jesus inaugurated a period of time called the "Last Days," so called because He is the full and definitive revelation. There is nothing any prophet can add to Christ, and no sign can point to a different direction.[350] St. Augustine writes: "Though God is all powerful, He is unable to give more; though supremely wise, He

---

[350]Cf. *Catechism of the Catholic Church*, n.66: "The Christian economy, therefore, since it is the new and definitive Covenant, will never pass away; and no new public revelation is to be expected before the glorious manifestation of our Lord Jesus Christ."

knows not how to give more; though vastly rich, He has nothing more to give." This does not mean that prophecy has ceased—Christ continues sending us prophets—but now **their role is to bring us to a deeper understanding of what Christ has already revealed.** This is the work of the Holy Spirit: "to teach you all things, and bring to your remembrance all that I have said to you."[351]

Through prophecy, the Holy Spirit rekindles in us the fire of Christ's Word, teaches us to read the signs of the times and gives us understanding so that we can cooperate in His work and abide in Him through trials. Prophets admonish us and call us to repentance. Cardinal Ratzinger, commenting on the Fatima prophecies, said: "Prophecy in the biblical sense does not mean to predict the future but to explain the will of God for the present, and therefore show the right path to take for the future."[352]

Many ignore signs and prophecy, arguing that Jesus told us that we know neither the day nor the hour. However, precisely because we don't know, we need to be watchful as St Paul teaches:

> For you yourselves know very well that the day of the Lord will come like a thief at night. When people are saying, "Peace and security," then sudden disaster comes upon them, like labor pains upon a pregnant woman, and they will not escape.
>
> But you, brothers, are not in darkness, for that day to overtake you like a thief. For all of you are children of the light and children of the day. We are not of the night or of darkness. Therefore, let us not

---

[351]Jn14:26.
[352] Cardinal Ratzinger, "The Message of Fatima," Theological Commentary", 26, june, 2000.

sleep as the rest do, but let us stay alert and sober (1 Thes 5:2-6).

St. Paul's analogy of a pregnant woman is significant. She has to be attentive to the signs and symptoms of her body throughout her pregnancy, not just on the day of birth. She does not know her "hour" beforehand, but she would be foolish to delay preparations until the birth pains begin. In the same way, Christians must be attentive as the signs of the times unfold—signs of the "pregnancy" of our times in which we must labor in Christ. "The whole creation has been groaning in travail together until now; and not only the creation, but we ourselves."[353]

The battle is more dangerous when we think that all is peaceful and safe. Complacency blinds us. Why are we so good at reading the signs we care about, those that affect our business or our personal interests? Are we attentive to the signs of the Lord in the same way? Are His plans our priority? Do we realize that He expects us to read the signs of the times and to respond?

> When you see a cloud rising in the west, you immediately say, "It is going to rain"; and so it happens. And when you see the south wind blowing, you say, "There will be scorching heat"; and it happens. You hypocrites! You know how to interpret the appearance of earth and sky, but why do you not know how to interpret the present time? (Lk 12:55-56).

True prophecy is counter-cultural. Culture is like a very powerful current that drags with it everything along its path which

---

[353] Rom 8:22-23.

is not firmly anchored. Many Christians are being swept; they are accommodating their understanding of the Gospel to the prevailing "new normal." They are thus unable to discern prophecy or the signs of the times. Prophets are also often dismissed because they are simple and ordinary persons; God chooses the humble to confound the proud.

Pope Francis

Many times we find, among our faithful, simple old women who perhaps didn't finish elementary school, but who speak to you about things better than a theologian, because they have the Spirit of Christ....

The authority of Jesus — and the authority of the Christian — comes from this very capacity to understand the gifts of the Spirit, to speak the language of the Spirit; it comes from this anointing of the Holy Spirit[354].

False Prophecy is another reason why many ignore the true ones. Lack of mature faith and discernment coupled with curiosity and fascination with knowing the future lead to useless speculation and to the proliferation of false prophecies. **But we should beware of an opposite reaction that closes our hearts to God's authentic messengers.** Rejection of the prophets resulted in the fall of Israel into many calamities, and rejection of Christ's signs led to the destruction of Jerusalem and the end of the world as the Jews knew it. Jesus lamented: "If you, even you, had only recognized on this day the things that make for peace! But now they are hidden from your eyes. For the days shall come upon you... they will not leave one stone upon another in you; because you did not know the time of your visitation." (Lk 19:42)

---

[354]Homily, St. Martha, 2 Sept. 2014, w2.vatican.va

— Discernment Is Essential —

It is easy to accept or reject prophecy without discernment, but to do so is to block the guidance of the Lord. St. Paul writes: "Do not quench the Spirit. Do not despise the words of prophets, but test everything; hold fast to what is good" (1Thess 5:19-21).

Prophecy and the signs of the times must be discerned in the context of the Catholic Faith, for the same Spirit speaks to the entire Church. This requires hard work and humility. Cardinal Ratzinger, as Prefect of the Congregation for the Faith, wrote when the secret of Fatima was made public:

> To interpret the signs of the times in the light of faith means to recognize the presence of Christ in every age. In the private revelations approved by the Church—and therefore also in Fatima—this is the point: **they help us to understand the signs of the times and to respond to them rightly in faith...**
>
> To understand the signs of the times means to accept the urgency of penance—of conversion—of faith. This is the correct response to this moment in history, characterized by the grave perils outlined in the images that follow...
>
> The angel with the flaming sword on the left of the Mother of God recalls similar images in the Book of Revelation. This represents the threat of judgment, which looms over the world. Today the prospect that the world might be reduced to ashes by a sea of fire no longer seems pure fantasy: man himself, with his inventions, has forged the flaming sword.[355]

---

[355] Ibid.

The Church teaches us to value private revelation: "to help live more fully [public revelation] in a certain period of history."[356]

Pope Francis tells how to discern:

We must open ourselves to the power of the Holy Spirit and clearly understand what is happening within and around us through discernment. …How can we do this, which the Church calls "recognizing the signs of the times?" Times are changing. And it's precisely Christian wisdom that recognizes these changes…

First of all, in order to understand the signs of the times we need silence: to be silent and observe. And afterward we need to reflect within ourselves. One example: why are there so many wars nowadays? Why did something happen? And pray… silence, reflection, and prayer. It's only in this way that we can understand the signs of the times, what Jesus wants to tell us.[357]

— Embrace the Cross and Be Courageous —

Why did John Paul II repeat so often "Be not afraid" if not because we are to face storms that require great courage? Why did he speak of a coming springtime if not to raise our hopes to look forward as we go through trials? Why did he consecrate the Church to Mary and presented her to us with such insistence if not so that we listen to her and walk with her to the Cross?

We need courage to see the truth about our times and take our place in the battle. We need to know who we are and the mission

---

[356]*Catechism of the Catholic Church,* n.67.
[357]Daily Meditations, 23 Oct. 2015, w2.vatican.va

that God has given each of us. We need to strengthen our family relationships. It is also important to belong to a community where brothers and sisters minister God's love, truth, and healing so that we can embrace the Cross and persevere in Christ.

8-B
Learning from Prophecies

The saints took to heart God's directions and warnings and thus were able to endure many trials while many unprepared Christians were swept by the tide of the world. The prophecies of the past are timeless. St Cyprian wrote in the third century:

> We are now threatened by a fight, harder and more fierce, to which the soldiers of Christ must prepare with an incorrupt faith and robust virtue, considering that this is why they drink daily the chalice of the Blood of Christ, to be themselves able to pour the Blood of Christ.[358]

There are also many prophecies directed to our times. The Prophet Amos wrote: "Surely the Lord God does nothing, without revealing his secret to his servants the prophets"[359]

The Lord is now preparing us **through the popes, Marian visitations, recent saints as well as ordinary humble persons including words to our community. He is calling us to repentance and conversion and teaches us the way to union with Him. He also warns us of the consequences if we**

---

[358]Saint Cyprian (III Century Martyr), Letter 58, n.1.
[359]Am 3:7.

obstinately ignore Him.

"The Church's Ultimate Trial"
Catechism of the Catholic Church[360]

Before Christ's second coming the Church must pass through a final trial that will shake the faith of many believers.[361] The persecution that accompanies her pilgrimage on earth[362] will unveil the "mystery of iniquity" in the form of a religious deception offering men an apparent solution to their problems at the price of apostasy from the truth. The supreme religious deception is that of the Antichrist, a pseudo-messianism by which man glorifies himself in place of God and of his Messiah come in the flesh.[363]

The Antichrist's deception already begins to take shape in the world every time the claim is made to realize within history that messianic hope which can only be realized beyond history through the eschatological judgment. The Church has rejected even modified forms of this falsification of the kingdom to come under the name of millenarianism,[364] especially the "intrinsically perverse" political form of a secular messianism.[365]

The Church will enter the glory of the kingdom only through this final Passover, when she will follow her Lord in his death and Resurrection (cf. Rev 19:1-9). The kingdom

---

[360] *Catechism of the Catholic Church,* n.675-677.

[361] Cf. Lk 18:8; *Mt* 24:12.

[362] Cf. Lk 21:12; *Jn* 15:19-20.

[363] Cf. 2 Thess 2:4-12; 1 Thess 5:2-3; 2 Jn 7; 1 Jn 2:18,22.

[364] Cf. *DS* 3839.

[365] Pius XI, *Divini Redemptoris,* condemning the "false mysticism" of this "counterfeit of the redemption of the lowly"; cf. *GS* 20-21.

will be fulfilled, then, not by a historic triumph of the Church (cf. Rev 13:8) through a progressive ascendancy, but only by God's victory over the final unleashing of evil (cf Rev 20:7-10, which will cause his Bride to come down from heaven (cf. Rev 21:2-4). God's triumph over the revolt of evil will take the form of the Last Judgment (cf. Rev 20:12) after the final cosmic upheaval of this passing world (cf. 2 P 3:12-13).

Like the wise virgins of the Gospel, the Lord expects us to be watchful for His coming. **We are responsible for preparing the world through our witness and evangelization**. Cardinal Piacenza, Prefect of the Congregation for the Clergy, said at a meeting with priests in Los Angeles:

> The Church is able to resist every attack, all the assaults that political, economic and cultural powers can unleash against her, but she cannot resist the danger that comes from forgetting this word of Jesus: "You are the salt of the earth, you are the light of the world." Jesus himself indicates the consequence of this forgetfulness: "But if the salt has lost its taste, how shall its saltiness be restored?"[366]

In times of trial, God raises exemplars to remind us that Christ is more powerful than the world. Such was Titus Brandsma, a frail and peaceful Dutch priest. The Nazis called him "that dangerous little friar." They feared the power of his witness and words. By holding fast to love and truth he came into conflict with the forces of evil. He wrote: **"He who wants to win the world**

---

[366] Cardinal Piacenza, "The priesthood in the XXI century", 4 Oct. 2011, zenit.org ; cf. Mt 5:13-14.

for Christ must have the courage to come in conflict with it."
He died a martyr, executed at Dachau on the 26th of July, 1942.
Cardinal Ratzinger challenged the bishops with the same message:

> There must not be a concept of "communion" in which the
> avoidance of conflict becomes the prime pastoral value.
> Faith is always also a sword and may indeed promote
> conflict for the sake of truth and love.[367]

8-B-1
— The Modern Popes Face the Battle at Hand —

The spiritual battle was dramatically fueled in the 1960's by
secularism and relativism. The sexual revolution was spreading like
wildfire. Pope John XXIII saw that the Church urgently needed a
renewed reliance on the power of God and in 1959 he surprised
everyone by announcing the Second Vatican Council.[368] To prepare
for it, the Pope implored the whole Church to pray to God: "Renew
Your wonders in this our day, as by a new Pentecost."

The Council opened the doors for a new appreciation of the
dynamic action of the Holy Spirit both in the Church and in each
believer, the awareness that all the baptized are called to holiness
(universal call to holiness) and the importance of living and taking
the faith into the world. But a battle ensued as many tried to use the
teachings of the Council to accommodate the Church to the secular
culture. There was widespread dissent when Pope Paul VI, in his
encyclical, *Humanae Vitae*,[369] warned that the contraceptive

---

[367] Cardinal Ratzinger, address to bishops, May 1998, as cited in: *New Outpourings of
the Holy Spirit,* (Ignatius Press, Oct., 2007), 59). (Cf. *Mt* 10:34).

[368] John XXIII announced the Council on 25 Jan, 1959 and convoked on 25 Dec, 1961.

[369] 25 July 1968.

mentality would lead to a breakdown of marriage and family. Time proved that his words were prophetic.

— St. John Paul II —

No one was more aware of the crisis in the Church and in the world than St. John Paul II. Two years before ascending to the papacy he said on a visit to the USA:

> We are now standing in the face of the greatest historical confrontation humanity has gone through. I do not think that wide circles of American society or wide circles of the Christian community realize this fully. We are now facing the final confrontation between the Church and the anti-Church, of the Gospel versus the anti-Gospel.
>
> We must be prepared to undergo great trials in the not-too-distant future; trials that will require us to be ready to give up even our lives, and a total gift of self to Christ and for Christ. Through your prayers and mine, it is possible to alleviate this tribulation, but it is no longer possible to avert it… How many times has the renewal of the Church been brought about in blood! It will not be different this time.[370]

The importance of the above message for our times is underlined by the fact that, in November 11 of 2013, the papal nuncio read it to the bishops of the USA as a reminder.[371]

Pope John Paul II had experienced firsthand the murderous power of evil during World War II and the subsequent long

---

[370] Cardinal Karol Wojtyla, address to USA bishops, 1976. Reprinted Wall Street Journal, 9 Nov. 1978.

[371] Nuncio Archbishop Vigano address to the USCCB General Assembly, 11 Nov, 22013, http://www.usccb.org/about/leadership/usccb-general-assembly/2013-november-meeting/nuncio-address-2013.cfm

Communist occupation of his beloved Poland. He understood the root of the problem: Western civilization was rapidly losing its Christian faith and moral principles and therefore was heading towards self-destruction. When the light of Christ is rejected, demons take advantage of the ensuing darkness, and nihilism paves the way to radical ideologies. One fruit of such darkness was the legalization of the "right" to kill the unborn. This new holocaust soon claimed more lives than the two world wars combined.

The Pope realized that God had assigned him a "special task in the present situation of man, the Church and the world."[372] He believed that the key to winning the battle was to "open wide the doors to Christ" and to proclaim with urgency the need to understand and receive God's mercy, as the Lord told St Faustina.[373]

Visiting the USA, this time as pope, John Paul II said:

This marvelous world... is the theater of a never–ending battle being waged for our dignity and identity as free, spiritual beings. This struggle parallels the apocalyptic combat described in Rev 11:19; 12:1-6...

In our own century, as in no other time in history, the culture of death has assumed a social and institutional form of legality to justify the most horrible crimes against humanity: genocide. "final solutions," "ethnic cleansings" and the massive taking of lives of human beings even before they are born, or before they reach the natural point of death...

Vast sectors of society are confused about what is right and what is wrong, and are at the mercy of those with the

---

[372] JPII, Sanctuary of Merciful Love in Collevalenza, Italy, 22 Nov. 1981.
[373] JPII canonized her —the first of the XXI century.

power to "create" opinion and impose it on others. The family especially is under attack…

The "dragon" (Rev 12:3), the "ruler of this world" (Jn 12:31) and the "father of lies" (Jn 8:44), relentlessly tries to eradicate from human hearts the sense of gratitude and respect for the original, extraordinary, and fundamental gift of God: human life itself. Today that struggle has become increasingly direct.[374]

— Pope Benedict XVI —

Many years before becoming pope, he foresaw that "**the Church will become small**"

The church will become small and will have to start afresh more or less from the beginning. She will no longer be able to inhabit many of the edifices she built in prosperity. As the number of her adherents diminishes, she will lose many of her social privileges. … As a small society, [the Church] will make much bigger demands on the initiative of her individual members. …

It will be hard-going for the Church, for the process of crystallization and clarification will cost her much valuable energy. It will make her poor and cause her to become the Church of the meek. … The process will be long and wearisome as was the road from the false progressivism on the eve of the French Revolution—when a bishop might be thought smart if he made fun of dogmas and even insinuated that the existence of God was by no means certain… But

---

[374] Homily, Solemnity of the Assumption, 8th World Youth Day, Cherry Creek State Park, Denver, Colorado, USA, 15 Aug. 1993), w2.vatican.va

when the trial of this sifting is past, a great power will flow from a more spiritualized and simplified Church. Men in a totally planned world will find themselves unspeakably lonely. If they have completely lost sight of God, they will feel the whole horror of their poverty. Then they will discover the little flock of believers as something wholly new. They will discover it as a hope that is meant for them, an answer for which they have always been searching in secret.

Consequently, it seems certain to me that the Church is facing very hard times. The real crisis has scarcely begun. We will have to count on terrific upheavals. But I am equally certain about what will remain at the end: not the Church of the political cult, which is dead already, but the Church of faith. She may well no longer be the dominant social power to the extent that she was until recently; but she will enjoy a fresh blossoming and be seen as man's home, where he will find life and hope beyond death.[375]

Pope Benedict clearly saw that Christians will face great trials in the near future, but he also saw that, with faith, those trials become opportunities to give glory to God. He said to the youth:

Dear friends, may no adversity paralyze you. Be afraid neither of the world, nor of the future, nor of your weakness. The Lord has allowed you to live in this moment of history so that, by your faith, his name will continue to resound throughout the world.[376]

---

[375] Joseph Ratzinger, *Faith and the Future,* 1969 (San Francisco: Ignatius Press, 2009), p114.

[376] Benedict XVI, homily, Madrid, Spain, 20, Aug. 2011 w2.vatican.va

The future depends on allowing God to be the center.
The pope spoke of a crisis due to loss of faith:

> Truly the world is dark wherever men and women no longer acknowledge their bond with the Creator and thereby endanger their relation to other creatures and to creation itself. The present moment is sadly marked by a profound disquiet and the various crises—economic, political and social—are a dramatic expression of this.[377]

Our many problems will only increase until we turn to God and give Him authority over our lives so that we become His presence in the world. This is what we face according to Pope Benedict XVI:

> I believe that the future of the world in this dramatic situation is decided today: whether God—the God of Jesus Christ—exists and is recognized as such, or whether He disappears.[378]

> It is imperative that the entire Catholic community in the United States come to realize the grave threats to the Church's public moral witness presented by a radical secularism which finds increasing expression in the political and cultural spheres. The seriousness of these threats needs to be clearly appreciated at every level of ecclesial life.[379]

---

[377] Ibid, address to the Vatican Diplomatic Corps, 9 Jan. 2012. w2.vatican.va.

[378] Ibid, Homily to the Bishop of Switzerland, 7 Nov. 2006), www.vatican.va.

[379] Ibid, address to the bishops of USA during *Ad Limina* visit, 19 Jan., 2012.

The preparation of committed lay leaders and the presentation of a convincing articulation of the Christian vision of man and society remain a primary task of the Church in your country.[380]

We see how evil wishes to dominate the world and that it is necessary to enter into battle with evil. We see how it does so in so many ways, bloody, with the different forms of violence, but also masked with goodness and precisely this way destroying the moral foundations of society.[381]

Pope Benedict XVI commented on the Gospel of the Tenants who are put to death because they killed the son:

These tenants are also a mirror of ourselves… We want unlimited possession of the world and of our own lives. God is in our way. Either he is reduced merely to a few devout words, or he is denied in everything and banned from public life so as to lose all meaning. The tolerance that admits God as it were as a private opinion but refuses him the public domain, the reality of the world and of our lives, is not tolerance but hypocrisy… But nowhere that the human being makes himself the one lord of the world and owner of himself can justice exist. The threat of judgment also concerns us, the Church… With this Gospel, the Lord is also crying out to our ears the words that in the Book of Revelation he addresses to the Church of Ephesus: "If you

---

[380] Ibid.
[381] Ibid, Address to the College of Cardinals, 22 May, 2012.

do not repent I will come to you and remove your lampstand from its place" (2: 5). Light can also be taken away from us and we do well to let this warning ring out with its full seriousness in our hearts.[382]

Pope Benedict has given us a vision of the sign of our times and the consequences if we do not respond.

— Pope Francis —

Pope Francis continues to alert us about the signs of the times in line with his predecessors: "I tell you that today there are more martyrs than during the early times of the Church";[383] "Humanity is experiencing a turning-point in its history";[384] "We have entered into the Third World War, only that it is being fought in pieces, in the chapters."[385]

In November of 2013, Pope Francis said:

Christians that suffer through times of persecution, through times when worship is prohibited, are a prophetic sign of what will happen to everyone. However, precisely in moments such as these, when the times of the pagans are being fulfilled, "raise your heads, because your redemption is drawing near."[386]

Only a few months later, in July 2014, radical militias expelled all

---

[382] Ibid., homily, 2 October, 2005 w2.vatican.va

[383] Pope Francis, homily, 4 Mar. 2014, w2.vatican.va.

[384] Ibid., *Evangelii Gaudium*, n.52, w2.vatican.va.

[385] Ibid., Comment to journalist, 18 Aug. 2014, flight from South Korea, www.repubblica.it. After the terrorist attack in Paris, 13 Nov. 2015, the pope reiterated that we are living "piecemeal World War III." www.catholicnewsagency.com.

[386] Ibid., homily, 28 Nov. 2013, w2.vatican.va.

Christians from Mosul, Iraq. For the first time in 1600 years, no Mass is celebrated there. Do we have to wait until it happens to us in order to wake up? Do we suffer their pain as one Body in Christ? Do we see what is happening to families all around us? Pope Francis observes:

> We have to remember that the majority of our contemporaries are barely living from day to day, with dire consequences. A number of diseases are spreading. The hearts of many people are gripped by fear and desperation, even in the so-called rich countries. The joy of living frequently fades, lack of respect for others and violence are on the rise, and inequality is increasingly evident. It is a struggle to live and, often, to live with precious little dignity.[387]

---

[387] Ibid., *Evangelii Gaudium,* n.52, w2.vatican.va.

8-B-2
— *Mary Prepares Us* —

Her messages have a common thread: she draws us to the love of God; she alerts us great dangers due to evil in the world and she exhorts us to strive to be faithful to her Son. Here are a few of the most well known:

— Our Lady of Guadalupe —

At the dawn of Christendom in America, between the 9th and 12th of December of 1531, Our Lady visited St. Juan Diego at Tepeyac, Mexico. Evangelization was not advancing due to the bad example of many Spaniards. Tensions were mounting and war seemed imminent.

Our Lady's appearance was such that both natives and Spaniards could identify her as the Mother of God and their mother. "Guadalupe" in Aztec language sounds like the word, *coatlaxopeuh*, which means "The one who crushes the serpent." But Our Lady of Guadalupe was also the name of the patroness of Caceres, a Spanish province which was home to many conquistadors.[388]

The Mother of all brought reconciliation and an unprecedented wave of evangelization. In the seven years after the apparitions, an average of 3000 natives daily were baptized. Considering that this is the same number that joined the Apostles on the day of Pentecost, we can see that Mary propitiated a Pentecost in Mexico that lasted seven years and brought eight million to the Church!

Our Lady of Guadalupe also came to the rescue of Europe at a decisive moment for its survival. As the Ottoman Empire was poised to submit Europe to Islam, Pope S. Pius V tried to unite the

---

[388] http://www.lovecrucified.com/catolico/maria/guadalupe_espana.htm

Christians to muster a defense but, as often happens, few responded. Yet he managed to form a Catholic League, **a faithful remnant.** On October 7 of 1571, only forty years after Our Lady came to Mexico, the two fleets met at the battle of Lepanto. The Christians, with 101 galleons, were at a great disadvantage against a Muslim fleet of 300. They knew that only God's hand could save them. The Pope asked that Christians pray the rosary. A large crucifix displayed on the main galleon presided the Christian fleet, and a replica of Our Lady of Guadalupe that had come from Mexico was enthroned on the ship of Admiral Juan Andrea Doria. The soldiers entered the battle in prayer and achieved a miraculous victory. In gratitude, Pope S. Pius V established October 7 as the Feast of Our Lady of the Rosary.

Today Christendom is again in great danger. Saint John Bosco saw in a prophetic dream another decisive naval battle to be waged by the Church. The Blessed Mother is preparing her faithful remnant.

— Our Lady of Good Success[389] —

In Quito, Ecuador, during the XVII century, Our Lady announced to Ven. Mother Mariana de Jesus Torres that during the 20th Century, "Corruption of customs will be almost universal, and the light of the first faith will be almost extinct." She warned of attacks against marriage and the innocence of children... But a **faithful remnant of victim souls will remain**: "The small number of souls who will preserve faith and morals, will undergo cruel... and long martyrdom." She added: "Those whom the merciful love of my Most Holy Son has destined for such restoration will require great strength of will, constancy, courage and great trust in God" Mary announced her final victory: "I, in an amazing way will

---

[389] http://www.lovecrucified.com/catolico/maria/buen_suceso_english.htm

dethrone the proud and cursed Satan, putting him under my feet and chaining him in the infernal abyss."

— An Age of Unprecedented Marian Presence —

Our Blessed Mother has visited us throughout the centuries, but her presence has become increasingly frequent since her apparition in Paris in 1830, known as the Miraculous Medal. While the French Revolution spawned an age of disbelief, the Mother of God came to rescue her children and raise them up as a faithful remnant to do battle against the serpent.

St. Louis Marie de Montfort wrote in "True Devotion":

It was through Mary that the salvation of the world was begun and it is through Mary that it must be consummated. Mary hardly appeared at all in the first coming of Jesus Christ... But in the second coming of Christ, Mary has to be made known and revealed by the Holy Ghost, in order that through Her, Jesus Christ may be known, loved and served.[390]

— Our Lady of the Miraculous Medal —

18th of July, 1830. Visionary: Sister St. Catherine Labouré at the Convent on Rue du Bac, Paris, France.

The faithful had just suffered the terrors of the French Revolution, and the "Enlightenment" was threatening to rob their faith. Mary came to offer her protection and gave us the Miraculous Medal and the prayer, "O Mary, conceived without sin, pray for us

---

[390] St. Louis de Montfort, True Devotion to Mary (Rockford, Ill.: Tan Publishers, 1985), 28

who have recourse to thee." The battle was on…

— Our Lady of La Salette —

On the 19th of September of 1846, Our Lady appeared to the children, Melanie Calvat and Maximin Giraud, at La Salette, France. Our Lady was weeping because the faith was waning. She lamented that few went to Mass on Sunday and that there was much blasphemy and contempt for God. Our Lady had on her chest a large crucifix with a hammer and pincers on either side of it. In this way she showed us that we have a choice: we either nail Jesus to the Cross or we pull out the nails. She asked the children to propagate her message, for which they suffered much.

— Our Lady of Lourdes —

On the 11th of February, 1858, Mary appeared to St. Bernadette Soubirous at Lourdes. The Immaculate Conception came to rescue her children from a tide of filth. France was being swept by atheist rationalism. Faith was considered to be ignorance. St. Bernadette was harassed and ridiculed, even by many in the Church, first for her reports about the apparitions and later for miraculous healings. She became a witness that the battle against Satan is won by the pure and humble of heart when they remain firm in the faith.

— Our Lady of Pontmain —

It was January of 1871. Again, Our Lady came to French children at a time of crisis, this time as Mother of Hope. Hope was much needed because the invading Prussian army had conquered most of France and was approaching the little town of Pontmain. The young men of the town were drafted to the front lines. Also, an epidemic broke out, and on Jan. 17, there was an earthquake. Everyone was terrified. Some said, "Why pray? God does not listen." But that same day the parish priest asked the children to pray. In the evening, Our Lady appeared to the children in the sky, but the adults could not see her so they reproached the children. A message appeared in the sky in golden letters: "Pray, my children… God will soon grant what you ask… My Son allows himself to be moved to compassion." Our Lady gazed at a blood colored crucifix that appeared in front of her. During the precise time of the apparition, the Prussian general who was about to advance in the direction of Pontmain, received orders to stop. Eleven days later, an armistice was signed. Even then, the children were victims or harassment at the hands of some clergy and the military, but they remained faithful. The apparitions were approved by the Church the following year.

— Our Lady of Fatima —
An Urgent Call from Heaven

Our Mother Mary plays a crucial role in God's plan to wake us up, prepare us for the battle and lead us to heaven. In 1917, towards the end of the First World War, she appeared to the children, Lucia, Jacinta and Francisco at Fatima, Portugal. Our Lady asked with urgency to **pray the rosary for peace and the conversion of sinners.** "Pray, pray much, and make sacrifices for sinners, for many souls go to hell because they have no one who sacrifices and prays for them." **She told us the importance of adoring the Blessed Sacrament and the power of the hidden, ordinary life of prayer.**

When Cardinal Ratzinger was asked why the third secret of Fatima had not been revealed, he responded:

A stern warning has been launched from that place that is directed against the prevailing frivolity, a summons to the seriousness of life, of history, to the perils that threaten humanity. It is that which Jesus himself recalls very frequently: "Unless you repent you will all perish" (Lk13:3). Conversion—and Fatima fully recalls it to mind—is a constant demand of Christian life. We should already know that from the whole of sacred Scripture.[391]

Revelation terminated with Jesus Christ. He Himself is the full revelation of God. But we certainly cannot prevent God from speaking to our time through simple persons and also through extraordinary signs that point to the insufficiency of the cultures stamped by rationalism and positivism that dominate us. The apparitions that the Church has officially approved—especially Lourdes and Fatima—have their precise place in the development of the life of the Church in the last century. They show us, among other things, that Revelation—still unique, concluded and therefore unsurpassable—is not yet a dead thing but something alive and vital.[392]

Years later, Ratzinger, as Pope Benedict XVI, visited Fatima and warned us:

We would be mistaken to think that Fatima's prophetic mission is complete. Here there takes on new life the plan of God which asks humanity from the beginning: "Where is your brother Abel [...] Your brother's blood is crying out to me from the ground!" (Gen 4:9). Mankind has succeeded in

---

[391] Cardinal Ratzinger with Vittorio Messori. Transl. by Salvator Attanasio and Graham Harrison. *The Ratzinger Report: An Exclusive Interview on the State of the Church.* (San Francisco: Ignatius Press, 1987), p.110. books.google.com

[392] *Ibid.,* p.111.

unleashing a cycle of death and terror, but failed in bringing it to an end… In sacred Scripture we often find that God seeks righteous men and women in order to save the city of man; and he does the same here, in Fatima, when Our Lady asks: "Do you want to offer yourselves to God, to endure all the sufferings which he will send you, in an act of reparation for the sins by which he is offended and of supplication for the conversion of sinners?" (Memoirs of Sister Lucia, I, 162).[393]

— Our Lady of All Nations —

The Blessed Mother prophesied (1949-1952) a decline of faith as never before and a time of great trials ahead. She also gave us the remedy: To turn with her to the Cross which is our victory and that we ask for the Holy Spirit. These are a few excerpts:[394]

I see a long, beautiful road. I have to start along that road, but it is as if I have no mind for it. I represent humanity... I feel so tired; yet I must plod on, very slowly.

My Son is being persecuted again. Take the Cross and plant it in the center! Only then will there be peace.

Pray then before the Cross: "Lord Jesus Christ, Son of the Father, send now your Spirit over the earth. Let the Holy Spirit live in the hearts of all nations, that they may be preserved from degeneration, disaster, and war..."

In this modern world, which knows so well how to act promptly and quickly in material affairs, it is equally

---

[393] Homily at the Shrine of Our Lady of Fátima, 13 May 2010, vatican.va.

[394] Messages 5th (7 Oct.1945), 17th (1 Oct.1949), 27th (11 Feb 1951), 29th (28 Mar. 1951), www.de-vrouwe.info/en/messages.

necessary for spiritual matters to act quickly, promptly and in a modern way.

— Our Lady of Akita, Japan —

The Second World War brought incredible devastation upon Japan. Everyone suffered without distinction of their involvement in the war. Atomic bombs annihilated two of its cities. It is, therefore, remarkable that Our Lady warned the world at Akita that if we do not turn to God, "Fire will fall from the sky and will wipe out a great part of humanity, the good as well as the bad." Akita is not an apparition, rather, Mary shows the continuity of her presence through tears shed by a statue of Our Lady of All Nations. Akita was approved by the Vatican. These are excerpts: [395]

August 3, 1973

Many men in this world afflict the Lord. I desire souls to console Him, to soften the anger of the Heavenly Father. **I wish, with my Son, for souls who will repair by their suffering and their poverty for the sinners and ingrates**... I have prevented the coming of calamities by offering Him [The Father] the sufferings of the Son on the Cross, His Precious Blood, and **beloved souls who console Him forming a cohort of victim souls. Prayer, penance and courageous sacrifices can soften the Father's anger. I desire also this from your community...** Already souls who wish to pray are on the way to being gathered together.

October 13, 1973

If men do not repent and better themselves, the Father will inflict a terrible punishment on all humanity. It will be a

---

[395] http://www.ewtn.com/library/Mary/Akita.htm

punishment greater than the deluge, such as one will never have seen before. Fire will fall from the sky and will wipe out a great part of humanity, the good as well as the bad, sparing neither priests nor faithful. The survivors will find themselves so desolate that they will envy the dead. The only arms which will remain for you will be the Rosary and the Sign left by My Son. Each day recite the prayers of the Rosary. With the Rosary, pray for the Pope, the bishops, and priests.

The work of the devil will infiltrate even into the Church in such a way that one will see cardinals opposing cardinals, bishops against bishops. The priests who venerate me will be scorned and opposed by their confreres…churches and altars sacked; the Church will be full of those who accept compromises, and the demon will press many priests and consecrated souls to leave the service of the Lord.

The demon will be especially implacable against souls consecrated to God. The thought of the loss of so many souls is the cause of my sadness…

— Our Lady of Kibeho (Our Lady of Sorrows)[396] —

Rwanda, Africa, 1981-1989. As tensions increased among tribes and the path of faith was rejected, Mother Mary appeared to Alphonsine, Anathalie, and Marie Claire to warn and prepare them. She showed them rivers of blood and called all to repentance. No one imagined what was coming. Then, in 1994, a tribal war broke out which resulted in a genocide. Neighbors killed neighbors, husbands killed their wives... While the world remained silent, more than 800,000 people were murdered, among the dead were many who were present at the apparitions.

---

[396] kibeho-sanctuary.com/index.php/en/apparitions/message.

425

The messages in essence

1. An urgent appeal to the repentance and conversion of hearts: "Repent, repent, repent!" "Convert while there is still time."

2. An assessment of the moral state of the world: "The world hastens to its ruin; it will fall into the abyss." "If you do not repent and do not convert your hearts, you will fall into the abyss."

3. The deep sorrow of the Mother of God: Mary because of people's unbelief and lack of repentance.

4. "Faith and unbelief will come unseen." These mysterious words were repeatedly spoken by Mary to Alfonsine at the beginning of the revelations. Indeed, both faith and unbelief are growing in unexpected ways. The Lord is preparing His remnant while the enemy is sowing rebellion.

5. The suffering that saves: "No one will reach heaven without suffering." "A child of Mary does not reject suffering." The visionaries were invited to live accepting suffering through faith in love, mortifying themselves and denying themselves pleasures for the conversion of the world.

6. "Pray always and single-heartedly." Mary begs us to pray with greater zeal and purity of heart. Pray in abundance for the whole world, teach others to pray, and pray for those who do not pray themselves.

7. Marian devotion expressed through sincere and regular praying of the rosary.

8. Pray always for the Church, when many troubles are upon her in the times to come.

These Church approved messages are an urgent warning from our Mother to the entire world. What occurred in Rwanda is brewing globally with the loss of faith, violence and threats of nuclear war. Mary does not come to cause fear but to make us aware of what we face, so that we let ourselves be carried by her to Jesus crucified.

8-B-3
— A Prophetic Age —

There is an extraordinary amount of prophecy that pertains to our times. We have sampled some approved messages from Our Blessed Mother and the popes. Let us now look at the saints canonized in recent times. St. Therese of Lisieux, Saint Faustina, Saint Maximilian Kolbe, Padre Pío and Saint Benedicta of the Cross stand out for their prophetic mission and words, but there are many others. The unprecedented number of canonizations after the Second Vatican Council is itself a prophetic sign of our times.[397] Many of them received prophetic messages.

— St Therese of Lisieux: A Remnant of Victim Souls —
Saint Therese, whom St. John Paul II named Doctor of the Church in 1997, wrote:

> The **legion of little souls, victims of merciful Love**, will become as numerous "as the stars of heaven and the sands of the seashore." It will be terrible for Satan; it will help the Blessed Virgin to crush his proud head completely.[398]

---

[397] St. John Paul II alone beatified and canonized more people than his predecessors of the previous five centuries.

[398] St. Thérése of Lisieux, *The Legion of Mary Handbook*, 256-257.

Mary will to form these little souls into great saints,[399] Christ's hidden force able to see the truth and fight the battle as His courageous witnesses for our salvation and the salvation of many. His little victim souls will be a powerful army who will conquer the forces of Satan and will propitiate a new Pentecost and the triumph of the Immaculate Heart.

— St. Faustina: Divine Mercy and the Second Coming —

The doctrine of Divine Mercy has always been at the heart of the Gospel, yet the Lord willed for our age to receive, through St. Faustina, a deeper appreciation and an unprecedented propagation of the message of God's mercy. She warned her sisters that a great war was coming and asked them to pray for Poland. She died at the age of 33, on October 5th, 1938. The Second World War began with the Nazi invasion of Poland on September 1st, 1939.

Devotion to Divine Mercy spread quickly at first but, on March 6th, 1959, the Holy Office forbade the use of "images and writings that promote devotion to Divine Mercy in the forms proposed by Sister Faustina." It seemed to be the end of the devotion.

After almost twenty years, on April of 1978, the Vatican reversed the ban, thanks to the prayers of many and the work of another Polish saint: Cardinal Wojtyła of Krakow. A few months later he became Pope John Paul II and the 30th of April of 2000, canonized St. Faustina, the first saint of the XXI century!

Do we appreciate the urgency of turning to God's mercy? Jesus told St. Faustina that the message of mercy was a preparation for His final coming.

---

[399] See: L.M.G.de Montfort, *True Devotion to Mary*, ch. 2 n35.

- "You will prepare the world for My final coming."[400]
- "Speak to the world about My mercy ... It is a sign for the end times. After it will come the Day of Justice. While there is still time, let them have recourse to the fountain of My mercy."[401]
- "Tell souls about this great mercy of Mine, because the awful day, the day of My justice, is near."[402]
- "I am prolonging the time of mercy for the sake of sinners. But woe to them if they do not recognize this time of My visitation."[403]
- "Before the Day of Justice, I am sending the Day of Mercy."[404]
- "He who refuses to pass through the door of My mercy must pass through the door of My justice."[405]

The Blessed Mother also spoke to St. Faustina:

You have to speak to the world about His great mercy and prepare the world for the Second Coming of Him who will come, not as a merciful Savior, but as a just Judge. Oh, how terrible is that day! Determined is the day of justice, the day of divine wrath. The angels tremble before it. Speak to souls about this great mercy while it is still the time for granting mercy.[406]

We encourage you to take to heart the Lord's words found in

---

[400] St. Faustina Kowalska, *Diary, Divine Mercy in My Soul,* n.429.

[401] Ibid., n.848.

[402] Ibid., n.965.

[403] Ibid., n.1160.

[404] Ibid., n.1588.

[405] Ibid., n.1146.

[406] Ibid., n.635.

St. Faustina's Diary. They are more relevant and urgent than ever. Remember that the Lord desires that we receive Him so that He can make us saints as He did with St. Faustina.

— Blessed Elena Aiello —

By beatifying Sister Elena Aiello on the Feast of the Holy Cross, 2011, Benedict XVI drew our attention to her many prophecies. They have much in common with those of Fatima, Akita, Padre Pio, St. John Bosco and others: an urgent call to turn to the Lord and be prepared for trials. Here is a sample:[407]

> Jesus: "Oh! How sad is My Heart to see that men do not convert (or respond) to so many calls of love and grief, manifested by My Beloved Mother to errant men. Roaming in darkness, they continue to live in sin, and further away from God! But the scourge of fire is near, to purify the earth of the iniquities of the wicked. The justice of God requires reparation for the many offenses and misdeeds that cover the earth, and which can no longer be compromised. Men are obstinate in their guilt, and do not return to God.
>
> The Church is opposed, and the priests are despised because of the bad ones who give scandal. Help Me, by suffering, to repair for so many offenses, and thus save at least in part, humanity precipitated in a slough of corruption and death.
>
> Make it known to all men that, repentant, they must return to God, and, in doing so, may hope for pardon, and be saved from the just vengeance of a scorned God".

---

[407] Blessed Elena Aiello, Good Friday, 16 Apr. 1954. See http://www.mysticsofthechurch.com/2011/09/blessed-elena-aiello-mystic-stigmatic.html

In so saying Our Lord God disappeared. Then the Madonna appeared to me. She was dressed in black, with seven swords piercing Her Immaculate Heart. Coming closer, with an expression of profound sorrow, and with tears on her cheeks, she spoke to me, saying:

"Listen attentively, and reveal to all: My Heart is sad for so many sufferings in an impending world in ruin. The justice of Our Father is most offended. Men live in their obstinacy of sin. The wrath of God is near. Soon the world will be afflicted with great calamities, bloody revolutions, frightful hurricanes, and the overflowing of streams and the seas.

Cry out until the priests of God lend their ears to my voice, to advise men that the time is near at hand, and if men do not return to God with prayers and penances, the world will be overturned in a new and more terrible war. Arms most deadly will destroy peoples and nations! The dictators of the earth, specimens infernal, will demolish the churches and desecrate the Holy Eucharist, and will destroy things most dear. In this impious war, much will be destroyed of that which has been built by the hands of man.

Clouds with lightning flashes of fire in the sky and a tempest of fire shall fall upon the world. This terrible scourge, never before seen in the history of humanity, will last seventy hours. Godless persons will be crushed and wiped out. Many will be lost because they remain in their obstinacy of sin. Then shall be seen the power of light over the power of darkness.

Be not silent, my daughter, because the hours of darkness, of abandonment, are near. I am bending over the world, holding in suspension the justice of God. Otherwise, these things would already have now come to pass. Prayers and penances are necessary because men MUST RETURN TO GOD and to My Immaculate Heart—the Mediatrix of men to God, and thus the world will be at least in part saved.

Cry out these things to all, like the very echo of my voice. Let this be known to all because it will help save many souls, and prevent much destruction in the Church and in the world."

— A New Combat
Will Require New Power and Understanding—
Prophecy of Ralph Martin at St. Peter's Basilica.[408]

Because I love you, I want to show you what I am doing in the world today. I want to prepare you for what is to come. Days of darkness are coming on the world, days of tribulation… Buildings that are now standing will not be standing. Supports that are there for My people will not be there. I want you to be prepared, My people, to know only Me and to cleave to Me and to have Me in a way deeper than ever before. I will lead you into the desert… I will strip you of everything that you are depending on now, so you depend just on Me.

A time of darkness is coming on the world, but a time of glory is coming for my church, a time of glory is coming for My people. I will pour out on you all the gifts of My Spirit. I will prepare you for spiritual combat; I will prepare

---

[408] Ralph Martin is consultor for the Pontifical Council for the Promotion of the New Evangelization. Prophecy received during the closing Eucharist of the International Conference of the Catholic Charismatic Renewal, Pentecost Monday, 19 May 1975, Vatican.

you for a time of evangelism that the world has never seen. And when you have nothing but Me, you will have everything: land, fields, homes and brothers and sisters and love and joy and peace more than ever before. Be ready, My people, I want to prepare you…

I speak to you of the dawn of a "new age" for My church. I speak to you of a day that has not been seen before. Prepare yourselves for the action that I begin now because things that you see around you will change; the combat that you must enter now is different; it is new. You need wisdom from Me that you do not yet have; you need the power of My Holy Spirit in a way that you have not possessed it; you need an understanding of My will and of the ways that I work that you do not yet have. Open your eyes, open your hearts to prepare yourselves for Me and for the day that I have now begun. My church will be different; My people will be different; difficulties and trials will come upon you. The comfort that you know now will be far from you, but the comfort that you will have is the comfort of My Holy Spirit. They will send for you to take your life, but I will support you. Come to Me. Band yourselves together around Me. Prepare, for I proclaim a new day, a day of victory and of triumph for your God. Behold, it is begun.

I will renew My Church. I will renew My people. I will make My people one. I am calling you to turn away from the pleasures of the world. I am calling you to turn away from seeking the approval of the world in your lives. I want to transform your lives. …I have a word for My church. I am sounding My call. I am forming a mighty army. …My power is upon them. They will follow My chosen shepherd(s). …

Be the shepherds I have called you to be. ...I am renewing My church. I will free the world.

Know that I, your God, brought Peter and Paul to Rome to witness to My glory. I have chosen you also and have brought you to Rome to bear witness to My glory, confirmed now by your shepherd. Go forth to the healing of the nations. Know that I am with you; and though you may pass through tribulation and trial, I will be with you even to the end. I am preparing a place for you in glory. Look to Me and I will deliver you from the power of the evil one. Behold I am with you now, all days, even till the end of time...

You have known the truth these days. You have experienced the truth these days. It is clear to you at this moment what the truth is. It is the truth of My Kingdom, My kingdom that will prevail... I want you to take that truth, to rest in that truth, to believe in that truth, not to compromise it, not to lose it in confusions, not to be timid about it, but to stand simply, in love, firmly rooted in the truth as foundation stones upon which My church can have new life and new power.

8-B-4
— Prophecies Received by Our Community —

We are also impelled to transmit to you the Lord's messages to our Love Crucified Community. They are an urgent call to enter the *Path*, to be ONE with Him as victims of love in the heart of the Church. In this way, we are called to be the light in times of darkness to prepare for a New Pentecost.

146. The Justice of God, Diary of a MOC

> *The justice of God is upon My people. It is My holy remnant of victim souls whose prayers and sacrifices will cover the earth as heavenly dew (Cf. Mic 5:7-9). The justice of God will come upon the world. My daughter, the great and terrible day is approaching upon the earth. The majority will be caught in total dismay. Life as you know it will cease to exist. It is My holy remnant of victim souls that will defeat Satan and all his principalities. Persevere in suffering all with Me. Persevere as ONE with the Word of the Cross, for then and only then, do you hold the power of God.*
>
> *Your lives in My crucified love become the sword of righteousness. Bring Me many victim souls for the battle at hand. My little ones, I need you. (9/26/11).*

147. Prepare to Encounter Justice, Diary of a MOC

> *Prepare the way. Prepare for what? Prepare to encounter Justice (God). Love (God) is Justice. You have been encountering Mercy, but each soul must*

435

prepare to encounter Justice. On that day, will you remain standing or will you be swept away in His justice? My little one, very few are prepared to encounter Justice. The gaze of Justice will condemn you or embrace you in an instant. Few are prepared to encounter Justice, the gaze of Truth. You are called to help many prepare the way through the Simple Path to Union I have entrusted to you.

My hidden martyrs of love are a gift of Divine Mercy to help many be prepared to encounter the gaze of Justice. My hidden victims of love are preparing the way through the power of their blood united to My Precious Blood being poured upon many by the mercy of Abba.

Be pure and holy as I am Holy. Live who you are as MY martyrs of Divine Love preparing the multitudes for the great and terrible day. Prepare the way as the new men and women clothed in the white gown made clean in the Blood of the Lamb. You are My white army being sent out into the world to prepare the way for the encounter with Justice (of God). 12/11/13

148. David and Goliath, Diary of a MOC, (Cf. *Sam* 17: 32-51).

My little one, the time draws near. You hold the sword of the Spirit in the mission given to you. My family of LC are My warriors of love that will defeat the dragon in the decisive battle that draws near. Be ready to approach this evil in the same way that David approached Goliath. You will conquer the dragon in your littleness and purity because it is

*God who is with you. You must not fear and believe with the innocence and zeal of David. My daughter, form My family well in the teachings I give to you. You each must also approach the battle with **five stones**. **First**, the stone of **humility**, possessing the perfect knowledge of your nothingness and of My power and majesty. **Second**, the stone of **purity**, purity of mind, heart, intention, word, desire… **Third**, **simplicity**, detached from all, most especially from your ego. **Fourth**, **trust** perfectly abandoned to My will. **Fifth**, **courage**, courage rooted in love of Me to be perfectly obedient to My commands.*

These stones are your weapons for battle, for the dragon will not be defeated according to the standards of the world but in the Light of Love. Therefore, My family, prepare for battle. Be attentive to Me. (1/18/12)

149. "I'm Forming You as My Warriors of Love,"

Diary of a MOC

Become the Sword of the Spirit to conquer the dragon.

The armor you put on is to protect you from being overcome and conquered by the enemy, but your sword is what has the power to pierce the enemy and conquer it. "To put on the armor of light… to put on your Lord Jesus Christ" (Rom 13:12;14) is to become the Sword of the Spirit. I have been leading you through the passage of union with your Crucified Lord—union with the Word of the Cross. It is in this union that you enter your

Crucified Lord and, beginning at the foot of the Cross with Mary, your lives become the Sword of the Spirit. These are the warriors that will fight the decisive battle and have the power of God to conquer the dragon. I desire each of you to become ONE with the Sword of the Spirit through My Cross. (11/2/11)

150. The Time Is at Hand, Diary of MOC

The time is at hand when all will be called to suffer persecution for My sake. This time of persecution will divide My followers into two camps: those with Me and those against Me. Few will remain with Me in the time of the great tribulation. You, My little ones, are being prepared for this time. Your lives lived in humility and purity of heart, united to Me, will be the light in this darkness. Your lives, hidden and transformed in My crucified love, will usher in the New Pentecost for the world.

My hidden force of spiritual mothers, as one with My Mother of Sorrows, will raise up God's army of holy priests for the decisive battle to be waged against the principalities of darkness...

My hidden martyrs of love are the power of God to wage this war against the principalities of death. Do not be afraid to speak from the housetops what I speak to you in the hiddenness of your heart. I am making all things new through My hidden victims of purified love... Trust and suffer all with patient endurance. (2-25-2014)

151. Be My Prophets of Light to Warn and Awaken,
Diary of a MOC

> *I have formed you, trained you, dressed you to be My prophets of light to warn and awaken My people before the horrible day of judgment comes down upon you. There will be wailing, groaning and grinding of teeth in your streets. The darkness of evil will cover you. Be prepared when these things happen that I speak to you about. Do not let the thief catch you unprepared. Believe, you are My people, My little ones, held in the Father's palm. Believe that I am one with you, the Light in the world, My living hosts. Believe, so that My Light can shine through you to penetrate the darkness consuming the world. Believe in the Power of God working through His hidden force. Love and continue to suffer ALL, as one with Me in My sacrifice of love, to enter prepared with God's armor the fiercest battle that is at hand. Do not be ashamed of My words (cf. Mk 8:38) and share the treasure of heaven that has been entrusted to you (The Simple Path to Union) with many. Complete My Path and, as My Heralds of Hope, teach it from the housetops. This is your mission. Respond with great zeal and courage of heart, as My warriors of love, for these decisive times.* (10/20/2012) [409]

---

[409] Cf *Mt* 24:42-51.

152. Be Little to Conquer with the Cross, Diary of a MOC

Believe that the sword of this mission will conquer the dragon.

(The Holy Spirit then brought to my mind David and Goliath.) How could it be that the little one who could not wear the armor of the mighty warriors defeats the giant? The ways of God are never the ways of the world. He was wearing the armor of God, and he possessed the power of God. He trusted in God with the innocence of a child. God defeated the enemy through His humble vessel so that all glory is given to God, not man.

The enemy will be conquered and all things will be made new but never in the ways of the world. God has chosen to give the sword of righteousness to His little mustard seed. The sword of the mission is the power of God that will pierce and conquer the dragon.

You must remain little, *insignificant and innocent, drinking the pure milk of the words I bring to you (cf. 1 Pet 2). Believe, My little ones, believe that the God of heaven and earth has chosen you for the decisive battle. Live with the innocence of a child the mission given to you. Be little, pure and humble, be nothing; and it is I Who will do the impossible. Trust with the innocence of a child... for you are nothing; but I am God, and I will use My little ones to confound the mighty ones of the world. Believe in the power of My Cross and the power of My Precious Blood, for it is only through the Triumph of My Cross that all darkness will be conquered.*

Live, love and suffer as ONE with Me; and you will become the sword that will pierce this darkness. (11/12/11)

153. New Pentecost, Diary of a MOC

The time is near, quickly approaching. Are you responding fully, My little ones? Are you ready, for the great and terrible day [that] is upon you? You are My people. I have been forming you for the battle that draws near. Are you ready, My family? Heaven watches with anticipation, for soon the eyes of many will contemplate My glorious Cross upon the sky. Raise up My hidden martyrs of love for the decisive battle that draws near. Call forth My victims of love, for it is they that are the passage for the Queen of Heaven to usher in the new Pentecost for the world. (1/26/12)

154. "New Combat," Diary of a MOC

The world depends on swords, missiles, and guns to win battles, but this decisive battle will be won by the Cross. My victim souls, uniting themselves to My love crucified, will free the world from the bondage and darkness of Satan. (1/29/2010)

155. Only Purified Love Can Win this Battle, Diary of a MOC

My dearest ones, the time is short, and the battle is fierce. You are waging war against the principalities of darkness that have overcome the earth. The time of My triumphant Cross is also near. I am forming My holy remnant to fight the fiercest battle in the history of salvation... You must be willing to fight according to My will and plan. It is only purified love that can win this battle and bring forth My peace. It is only the love of My victim souls that can fight this battle and win. Bring Me, and form with Me, many holy victim souls. Know that it is the laity that will respond first, and My sons will be the last; for their hearts have grown cold and hardened.

You must be willing to be My prophets for these times. Satan will try to silence your voice because it is My voice, but you must persevere with zeal and humility. Do not fear to speak the truth of the sin in the hearts of My people with courage and love and call them to repentance at My crucified feet.

My daughter, I promise you that those that come and kneel, and kiss My feet, will receive the graces of the gold of precious repentance. You must be the voice in the wilderness preparing the path for My Mother. You must extend the carpet of victim souls. (7/15/1)

— **Christ Is Victorious!** —
— **Evil Will Not Prevail!** —

Christ has conquered the forces of the enemy with His crucified love. Now He calls us to partake in the battle and in the victory. Pope Benedict XVI reminded us of Jesus' promise: "Evil will not prevail."

"The gates of the underworld," that is, the forces of evil, will not prevail, "non praevalebunt." One is reminded of the account of the call of the prophet Jeremiah, to whom the Lord said, when entrusting him with his mission: "**Behold, I make you this day a fortified city, an iron pillar, and bronze walls,** against the whole land, against the kings of Judah, its princes, its priests, and the people of the land. They will fight against you; but they shall not prevail against you—non praevalebunt—for I am with you, says the Lord, to deliver you!" (Jer 1:18-19)… **God's power is love, the love that shines forth from Calvary.**[410]

Victory is assured but we have to respond.
Will you join Christ in His Path to the end?

---

[410] Homily, Solemnity of St. Peter and Paul, 29 June 2012, w2.vatican.va.

443

The Return of the Prodigal Son
Rembrandt

When we suffer with Christ and journey with Him on the way to Calvary, He takes us into the heart of the Father.

Prayers

Consecration to the Holy Spirit

Venerable Felix of Jesus Rougier, M.Sp.S.J.

O Holy Spirit,
receive the absolute and complete consecration of
my whole being.
In every instant of my life and in all my actions,
be my Director, my Light, my Guide, my Strength,
and the Love of my heart.
I surrender myself without reservations
to the loving action of your grace.
I desire to always be docile to your inspirations.
Transform me through Mary
in Christ, Priest and Victim,
that I may console His Sacred Heart
and extend your kingdom of holiness
for the glory of the Father
and the salvation of mankind.
Jesus, Savior of mankind,
Save them!

Consecration of Oneself to Jesus Christ, Wisdom Incarnate, through the Hands of Mary
St. Louis-Marie Grignion de Montfort—Short Form.

I, ….. an unfaithful sinner, renew and ratify today, through you, my baptismal promises. I renounce forever Satan, his empty promises, and his evil designs, and I give myself completely to Jesus Christ, the incarnate Wisdom, to carry my cross after him for the rest of my life, and to be more faithful to him than I have been till now. This day, with the whole court of heaven as witness, I choose you, Mary, as my Mother and Queen.

I surrender and consecrate myself to you, body and soul, with all that I possess, both spiritual and material, even including the spiritual value of all my actions, past, present, and to come. I give you the full right to dispose of me, and all that belongs to me, without any reservations, in whatever way you please, for the greater glory of God in time and throughout eternity. AMEN.

At the Consecration of the Precious Blood
Ven. Concepcion Cabrera De Armida

Beloved Father! Through the immaculate hands of Mary, receive my blood, which I place in that chalice in union with the blood of Jesus, sacrificing it for love of you, for your priests and for the salvation and regeneration of the world through the cross.

Accept it, Father, and sprinkle with it the good and the bad, the living and the dead, making fruitful the field of the

Church through this sacrifice. Amen.

Jesus, savior of mankind, save them!

Abrogated version used by Love Crucified

Beloved Father! Through the immaculate hands of Mary, receive the blood of Jesus and ours as one sacrifice of love, for your priests and for all.

Offering as Living Hosts
Ven. Concepcion Cabrera De Armida

Heavenly Father, through the hands of Mary, we offer You Jesus, the Incarnate Word, the Victim in whom You are well pleased. Moved by the love of the Holy Spirit in our hearts, we offer ourselves completely with Him as living hosts. May we be a living sacrifice out of love for You, in all the events of our lives, obtaining graces for the world, the Church and especially Your priests. Jesus, savior of mankind, save them!

Fatima Angel Prayer

My God, I believe, I adore, I hope, and I love You. I beg pardon of You for those who do not believe, do not adore, do not hope, and do not love You.

Most Holy Trinity, Father, Son, and Holy Spirit, I offer You the most precious Body, Blood, Soul, and Divinity of Jesus Christ, present in all the tabernacles of the world, in reparation for the outrages, sacrileges and indifference with which He Himself is offended. And through the infinite merits of His Most Sacred Heart, and the Immaculate Heart of Mary, I beg of You the conversion of poor sinners.

Fiat to Mary
Venerable Concepcion Cabrera De Armida

O holiest Mother, dry your tears, for I promise what you ask. But grant me what I am going to ask you in order to be able to give you joy. I believe, but fortify my faith; I hope, but strengthen my hope; I love, but increase my love; my sins weigh upon me, but stir up my repentances; I desire to weep for your sorrows, but make these echo in the heart of your child. Direct me, Mother; guide, lead, and protect me. I offer you in your solitude, my intelligence to think of you, my words to speak of you; my works and my labors to be suffered for you. I desire what you desire, Mary, but enlighten my understanding, set my will afire, purify my body and sanctify my poor soul that my pride will not entangle me, nor praise alter me, nor the world deceive me, nor Satan seize me.

Purify my memory, holy Virgin, restrain my language, recollect my vision, correct my evil inclinations, cultivate my virtues, and above all, my Mother, cast into my freezing heart one spark of the fire of your charity, so that it will thaw my heart to tenderness for your sorrows. Amen.

Love Crucified Community Covenant

Heavenly Father, moved by Your love and Your grace,
in union with the Blessed Virgin Mary, my Mother,
and the family of Love Crucified,
I (name) resolve to deny myself, to take up my cross daily,
and to follow Jesus, Love Crucified.

Through the immaculate hands of Mary, receive my blood,
united to the Precious Blood of Jesus,
as a sacrifice of love for You, for Your priests, families,
for the most hardened hearts, and for the salvation of the world.
Transform my heart into Your living chalice
so that I become Your companion of love.

Inspired by Venerable Conchita and our patron saints,
I offer myself as a victim united to Jesus, the Victim of love.
I surrender my entire heart, will, plans, desires, sacrifices,
sufferings, joys, prayers, works, every thought and action,
uniting all to Christ's sacrificial love on the Cross,
so that no longer I live but Christ, Love Crucified, lives in me.

I surrender myself to the Holy Spirit
and vow to be attentive to His promptings and movements in my soul,
that I may come to a deeper knowledge of Christ and of myself,
to learn from Him love, tenderness, mercy, humility, docility,
obedience, purity, silence, service and all the virtues.

I promise full assent and obedience
to all the Catholic Church teaches
and to treasure the Eucharist, the Word, reconciliation
and all the Lord provides for our sanctification.

I enter into a covenant of love
with my brothers and sisters of the Love Crucified Community

and commit to its way of life.
My words and actions shall reflect my love for all,
so that we can help each other live the Path to Union
and be witnesses to the world.

All for the glory of God and the renewal of the Church through a new Pentecost.

Every movement of my soul shall say with Christ:
"Suffer all with Me, no longer two but ONE, in My sacrifice of love."
—Amen.

Litany of Humility
Rafael Cardinal Merry del Val (1865-1930)

O Jesus! Meek and humble of heart, Hear me.
From the desire of being esteemed,
Deliver me, Jesus.
From the desire of being loved…
From the desire of being extolled…
From the desire of being honored…
From the desire of being praised…
From the desire of being preferred to others…
From the desire of being consulted…
From the desire of being approved…
From the fear of being humiliated…
From the fear of being despised…
From the fear of suffering rebukes…
From the fear of being calumniated…
From the fear of being forgotten…
From the fear of being ridiculed…
From the fear of being wrong…

From the fear of being suspected…

That others may be loved more than I,
Jesus, grant me the grace to desire it.

That others may be esteemed more than I…
That, in the opinion of the world,
others may increase and I may decrease…
That others may be chosen and I set aside…
That others may be praised and I unnoticed…
That others may be preferred to me in everything…
That others may become holier than I, provided
that I may become as holy as I should…

Chaplet of Unity
in the Blood of Jesus and the tears of Mary
Love Crucified

Using the rosary, begin as usual:
Creed, Our Father, Hail Mary

In the "Our Father" beads say:
Jesus, Victim of Love, Love Crucified /
for the sake of Your Precious Blood and Your mother's
tears, make us one.

In the "Hail Mary" beads say:
With Your Precious Blood and Your Mother's tears /
purify our hearts and make us one.

End with:

-3x:

"Suffer all with ME, no longer two but ONE, in my sacrifice of love"

-1X:

Hail Holy Queen.

Jesus Thirsts for You

He said:
"When I am lifted up from the earth,
I will draw everyone to Myself" (Jn 12:32)

Gaze upon Our Lord on the Cross and allow Him to draw you!

The members of the Love Crucified Community are praying that
The Simple Path to Union with God
helps you to enter and be consumed in the fire of His love.

For more information about the Love Crucified Community, to
order or to download this book, please visit our website:

WWW.LOVECRUCIFIED.COM
Español: www.amorcrucificado.com